The Mirage of Oil Protection

A Cato Institute book

The Mirage of Oil Protection

Robert L. Bradley, Jr.

University Press of America
Lanham • New York • London

University Press of America,® Inc.

4720 Boston Way
Lanham, MD 20706

3 Henrietta Street
London WC2E 8LU England

Printed in the United States of America

British Cataloging in Publication Information Available

Co-published by arrangement with the Cato Institute

Library of Congress Cataloging-in-Publication Data

Bradley, Robert L., 1955–

The Mirage of Oil Protection.
Includes bibliographical references.
1. Tariff on petroleum products—United States.
2. Free trade and protection—Free trade. 3. Tariff—
United States. I. Title.
HF1718.P44B7   1988   382'.42282'0973   88–26125
ISBN 0–8191–7202–2 (alk. paper)
ISBN 0–8191–7203–0 (pbk. : alk. paper)

All University Press of America books are produced on acid-free paper.
The paper used in this publication meets the minimum requirements of
American National Standard for Information Sciences—Permanence of Paper
for Printed Library Materials, ANSI Z39.48–1984.

To Nancy and Catherine

Contents

Preface

The debate over oil tariffs revolves around the question, Should consumers pay higher prices now and in the future to prevent an oil supply calamity? A number of economists and industry experts, in addition to many individuals within the industry, have answered this question affirmatively. They have called for a tariff on crude oil and oil products to protect the domestic industry—and, in turn, consumers and the economic and military interests of the nation as a whole—from low-cost and reserve-rich foreign suppliers who do not have our best interests in mind. To justify this position, the tariff lobby has replaced special-interest arguments with utilitarian ones. Some of the latter are quite sophisticated; others offer little more than superficial appeal.

This book attempts to show that even the most sophisticated arguments for oil protectionism are not convincing. The case for tariffs rests on faulty historical, institutional, and theoretical pillars. The *historical* fallacy attributes past oil crises to exogenous events that only precautionary government intervention can prevent. It will be argued here that oil (and gas) shortages throughout this century have been inextricably linked to major government intervention rather than to the exogenous events that protectionism promises to neutralize. The *institutional* fallacy posits either the debilitating effect of nation-to-nation embargoes on the present and foreseeable world oil market or the likelihood of concerted OPEC production cuts or disruptions, and ineffective entrepreneurial responses to both. This book will show that (1) the complexity and interdependence of the world petroleum market, in addition to the promoted role of interfuel substitution, limit the ability of oil embargoes and cutoffs to disrupt consumption effectively, and (2) any concerted production cut faces many internal and external obstacles—especially the factor of anticipatory entrepreneurship—that limit its negative effects on the domestic economy.

The *theoretical* fallacy is the postulated "market failure" of the price system—the alleged gap between the market price and the "true" price of imported oil. Some economists believe that the "negative externalities" of imported oil make its "true" price higher than its purchase price and that a tariff is needed to close the gap and induce efficiency. On the contrary, economic theory does not support the notion that the price of oil imports fails to reflect relative scarcity and expectations of future market conditions. Nor can theoretical investigation conclude that the national security cost of uncertain imports is greater than the national security cost of artificially accelerated domestic reserve depletion.

Stripped of its rationale, protectionism is subject to many telling criticisms. A major tariff represents a multibillion-dollar annual wealth transfer from energy consumers (individuals, firms, and the U.S. government itself) to energy producers and the U.S. Treasury. Nonpetroleum industries left with higher energy costs face international competitors with lower energy costs. The domestic petroleum industry as well as the international industry are disadvantaged, in both direct and subtle ways, by the intervention. As a major regulatory program, a tariff inflicts "dead-weight" losses on the economy from the industry and government side. The tax spawns energy-user inequities that hit many poorer citizens the hardest. With these considerations controlling, the conclusion is reached that tariffs (or similar interventions such as quotas) cannot be justified on utilitarian grounds. The case for oil protectionism thus collapses into a special-interest argument—aid for its own sake—that is incompatible with the broader considerations of consumer sovereignty and the national well-being.

The promises of protectionism are thus a mirage. For consumers, the illusion is that higher prices now will be more than offset by lower prices tomorrow. For producers, the illusion is that tariffs or quotas will usher in stability and prosperity. For energy planners— whether in government, industry, or academia—the illusion is that protectionism will lead to "energy security."

To deflate the intellectual case for oil tariffs is not to conclude that the petroleum industry does not deserve relief from its present state. In the interest of consumer and national welfare, the industry can and should be helped. What is required is a market-oriented, not government-oriented, means of relief that does not injure consumers of oil and oil substitutes and does not hold uncertainties for, and offer false promise to, the industry. The free-market alternative, composed of deregulation, tax reduction, and privatization, has the unique attraction of significantly increasing industry profitability within an environment of lower, volatile oil prices. It also best positions the industry not only for the known but unknown challenges that lie ahead.

Acknowledgments

This book culminates several years' involvement with the oil tariff question. In my two-volume history of oil and gas regulation for the Cato Institute *(Oil, Gas, and Government: The U.S. Experience,* forthcoming), I examined the history of oil protectionism from the time of Standard Oil in the last century through the Mandatory Oil Import Program (1959–73) and subsequent license fees. When protectionism again became a live issue, first with independent refiners in 1984–85 and then with independent producers beginning in early 1986, I wrote several articles and testified on oil tariff proposals before a congressional subcommittee.

As the oil tariff debate escalated with deteriorating industry conditions, the need for a systematic analysis of the case against oil protectionism became obvious. With leading figures on both sides of the debate conceding that there was a national security problem with rising oil imports—thus trivializing the argument into whether a tariff to reverse this trend was affordable—a different perspective was called for. This book is the end result of that inspiration.

In a sense this book is not original. Its primary purpose is to bring together many arguments and insights provided by industry and outside experts on the national security question in order to sift the good from the unsatisfactory. A historical perspective is added by revisiting previous protectionist and open-trade periods, and theoretical insights from the market-process and public choice schools of economics are incorporated at crucial junctures of the argument. The book also attempts to combine both an academic and industry perspective on the subject.

I have many persons to thank for this book. First of all, my gratitude goes to my wife, Nancy, who had the patience to allow the author to "moonlight" nights and weekends over the last year to prepare the manuscript. Helpful comments were provided by Emma Brossard, Tyler Cowen, Jack High, William Johnson, and Anne Roland on particular sections of the manuscript. David Boaz as project editor and Ruth Schein as copy editor improved the manuscript with corrections and suggestions. My primary thanks goes to the Cato Institute for their continued support of my research and writing in the energy field. Needless to say, any remaining errors of fact or analysis are my responsibility alone.

Part I

Present and Past Protectionism

1. The Current Industry Crisis and Debate

A. From Boom to Bust

The prosperity enjoyed by U.S. oil companies in the 1973–81 period was unparalleled in the history of the industry, rivaled only by the flurry of activity that accompanied its birth in the 1859–65 period. Never before in this century had the price of oil increased as much, absolutely or relatively, and never had so many segments of the business participated in the prosperity. Until then, industry prosperity had been confined to significant new oil-field discoveries such as Spindletop in 1901, Cushing in 1915, Seminole in 1926, Oklahoma City in 1928, and East Texas in 1930–31. But while these discoveries were a boon to the oil companies and communities involved, the resulting price pressure from increased supply took a toll on traditional investments. Thus, oil "booms" were a localized, firm-specific phenomenon. For the industry as a whole, a buyer's market for crude oil persisted from the mid-1920s to the early 1970s, interrupted only by World War II and its aftermath. The experience that began in 1973, in short, was a sharp break from over four decades of peacetime experience.[1]

Two major factors worked together to create the anomaly of the oil boom of 1973–81. One was international; the other, domestic. Government intervention was crucial to both.

The Arabian-American Oil Company (ARAMCO) nationalization of 1973 and 1974, which shifted production decisions from Exxon, Gulf, Texaco, and Chevron to Saudi Arabia, had a decided influence on events to follow. Not only did it simplify the Organization of Petroleum Exporting Countries (OPEC) cartel, which since its founding in 1960, had longed to increase oil export prices, but it also replaced present-oriented owners who favored higher output at lower prices with future-oriented owners who favored lower

---

[1]For a table comparing the real and inflation-adjusted wellhead prices from 1900 to 1986, see appendix A, pp. 245–47.

production at higher prices. The high time preference of the majors was amplified by a soon-to-be-confirmed fear that their property rights in the foreign reserves were insecure. This uncertainty depreciated the tradeoff of maintaining the capital value of the reserves by slower depletion relative to current profits through maximum depletion; thus, present production replaced future production to this extent. Accelerated production by the U.S. majors was particularly prevalent from 1970 to 1973. With nationalization, property rights became secure (for Saudi Arabia), and the previous bias toward maximum production was replaced with a longer-run view toward cautious depletion. Politically inspired production decisions would reinforce this proclivity. The growth rate of Middle Eastern production sharply declined as a result.[2]

With its rudder firmly in place, the Organization of Arab Petroleum Exporting Countries (OAPEC) in particular, and OPEC in general, assumed a power and capability thitherto absent. Following Saudi Arabia's October 17, 1973, announcement that output would be reduced 10 percent and oil exports to the United States would be banned, material support was given by the other 10 OAPEC members. Kuwait, Abu Dhabi, Egypt, Iraq, Libya, Algeria, Bahrain, Dubai, Qatar, and Syria, acting as a cartel, replicated the Saudi cutback and ban. Oil, more than ever before, was now a political and foreign policy commodity.

Cartels are not easily formed, and their effective operation is even rarer. The crusading fervor against the United States and its pro-Israeli foreign policy in the fourth Arab-Israeli war was an important reason for launching the embargo and for its major psychological, if not physical, effect. But this bitter result of foreign policy was accompanied by a colossal failure of domestic policy.

A second thitherto missing factor transformed the new power of OAPEC and OPEC into an effective cartel, namely, the U.S. price regulation that began in August 1971 (as part of President Nixon's wage and price control program) combined with the oil allocation controls that followed several years later. Domestic price ceilings artificially increased world prices by increasing domestic demand

---

[2]See Walter Mead, "An Economic Analysis of Crude Oil Price Behavior in the 1970s," *Journal of Energy and Development 2* (Spring 1980): 217–24. Also see Ali Johany, *The Myth of the OPEC Cartel* (New York: John Wiley & Sons, 1980). The compound annual growth rate of production of 15 percent from 1970 to 1973 exceeded an 11 percent growth rate between 1960 and 1970 and a 1 percent growth rate between 1973 and 1977.

(which constituted one-third of world demand), discouraging production, and preventing countercyclical inventory strategies by majors and independents alike. Regulated domestic prices, coupled with the refinery entitlements program, which lowered the effective price of foreign crude for domestic refiners, also enhanced demand for foreign oil and raised world prices above the levels an unhampered market would have set.[3] Government intervention, domestically and internationally, played a fundamental role in reversing market conditions away from the consumer.[4]

Virtually all segments of the industry participated in the oil boom. Producers and royalty owners, although restricted from full gains by price regulation and taxation, prospered from a fourfold inflation-adjusted increase in wellhead prices between 1972 and 1981. Refiners, particularly smaller ones qualifying for lucrative regulatory benefits, made regulated margins and, in most cases, much more. The greatest beneficiaries were small refiners. Between 1974 and 1979 alone, 74 new refiners entered the market, only one of which was above 50,000 barrels per day.[5] (What is considered the optimum size is between 100,000 and 200,000 barrels per day.)

---

[3]The refinery entitlements program was adopted in 1974 to equalize crude costs among refiners and thus mitigate a regulation-created inequity. Because of the wide disparity between regulated and unregulated (or less regulated) prices, the program required refiners with average crude costs under the national average to write monthly checks to refiners with average crude costs above the national average. Until its termination in early 1981, the entitlements program effectively raised the cost of regulated oil and lowered the cost (and increased the demand and the price) of unregulated oil, *which prominently included imported crude.* For a description of the genesis of the program, see Neil de Marchi, "Energy Policy under Nixon: Mainly Putting Out Fires," in Craufurd Goodwin, ed., *Energy Policy in Perspective* (Washington: Brookings Institution, 1981), pp. 470–73.

[4]This explanation of the oil boom is also an explanation of the energy crisis. The emphasis on broad governmental factors is different from other explications that mention government intervention in only an auxiliary role (if at all). For example, one textbook writer stated: "The main factors leading up to the 1973 'crisis' were the tremendous growth in world energy demands, the rising share supplied by petroleum, and the increasing role of imports from the Persian Gulf region. In the U.S., additional factors were the environmental constraints on the use of coal, lags in the completion of nuclear plants, and long delays in granting oil and gas leases by the U.S. government." Charles Howe, *Natural Resource Economics: Issues, Analysis, and Policy* (New York: John Wiley & Sons, 1979), p. 180.

[5]*Domestic Refinery Development and Improvement Act of 1979*, Hearings before the Subcommittee on Energy Regulation, U.S. Senate, 96th Cong., 1st Sess. (Washington, D.C.: Government Printing Office, 1980), pp. 71–72.

Taking advantage of not only favorable market conditions but abundant regulatory opportunities, oil resellers proliferated. Whereas prior to May 1973 approximately 60 traditional oil trading/gathering firms existed, between 1974 and 1981 the number swelled past 400 to capitalize on the disparities between regulated prices and prices consumers were willing to pay.[6] Some worked legally within margin constraints by back-and-forth arbitrage trading ("daisy chaining") of physically undisturbed oil; other illegally miscertified oil to escape margin restrictions entirely. This surge of activity created a multibillion-dollar subindustry between the wellhead and refiner and between the refiner and retailer—transactions that generated extraordinary profits.[7] Refiners, oil pipelines, terminal operators, jobbers, and retailers also profited from reselling activity, in addition to profiting from high margins in a "seller's market."[8]

This is not to suggest that *all* firms in *all* periods profited during the "energy crisis" years. Independent gasoline dealers, cut off from traditional major refiner allocations when supply became tight in 1972 and 1973, were badly hurt. Mass closings and threatened closings of these independents, in fact, created the political conditions that led to the Emergency Petroleum Allocation Act, which continued price and allocation controls after the expiration of Phase IV of the Cost of Living Council's wage and price control program.

The great majority of firms in all sectors of the petroleum industry enjoyed an unprecedented decade of prosperity. The tremendous increase in oil prices not only favored wellhead interests, the web of price and allocation regulation redistributed wealth to downstream parties and many new entrants therein. This was most clearly evident in the refining and reselling sectors but was also present elsewhere in the industry nexus.

---

[6]Department of Energy, Freedom of Information Act Request #81-196 to author, October 26, 1981.

[7]The most notorious regulatory reseller, Robert Sutton, miscertified (altered paperwork to relabel regulated oil as unregulated oil to resell at the higher price) an estimated 240 million barrels of oil to become the first "regulatory billionaire" in U.S. history. See Dale Buss, "Little-Known Oilman Charged with Using Resale Scheme in Costliest U.S. Fraud Ever," *Wall Street Journal*, December 2, 1981, p. 31.

[8]See Marvin Reid, "Profiteering," *National Petroleum News*, August 1979, pp. 31–39. Also see Ron Landry, "Considering the Industry Is Regulated, Business Has Been Awfully Good," *National Petroleum News*, April 1980, p. 18.

1. The First Downturn: 1982–83

The reversal of the boom began in 1982 and continued the next year with a fall in wellhead crude prices from a 1981 high of approximately $35 per barrel to approximately $26 per barrel. Two major factors behind weakening prices were (1) increasing conservation of gasoline and other major products in the United States and abroad and (2) increased supply from non-OPEC sources. The lower price level not only falsified investments dependent on peak oil prices but investments predicated on *anticipated* prices at $40 per barrel, $50 per barrel, and higher. The result was a noticeable industry contraction. Although painful, the contraction was recognized by industry veterans as a healthy return to normalcy and a "cleansing" of the excesses of the boom. Nouveau oil resellers and entitlements-spawned small refiners left in droves. Service and supply firms tied to onshore exploration and production suffered disproportionately as drilling activity paused. A death knell was sounded for many highly leveraged firms that could no longer service their fixed costs with diminished cash flows. These victims generally were newer firms, but some established companies were also fatally caught in an overexpansion.

Some statistics will illustrate the reversal of oil-patch fortunes. The Hughes Tool Co. drilling rig count fell from a peak of 4,530 in late 1981 to 2,780 by the end of 1983. Industry employment declined by 140,000 between 1981 and 1983.[9] The economy of the nation's fourth-largest city, Houston, Texas, whose industrial base was closely aligned with the oil and gas industry, lost an estimated 160,000 jobs, equivalent to 10 percent of its work force, in the same period.[10] Revenue of the 21 largest U.S. oil companies fell from $539 billion in 1981 to $451 billion two years later, a 16 percent drop. Profitability of the same major energy firms mirrored the decline in aggregate activity, falling 23 percent, from $27.7 billion to $21.3 billion, in the same period.[11] In sum, the contraction was a painful, albeit necessary, response to a boom that was not sustainable.

[9]American Petroleum Institute, *Basic Petroleum Data Book* (Washington, D.C.: API, 1986), Section 5, Table 2A.

[10]Center for Public Policy, *Handbook on the Houston Economy* (Houston, Tex.: University of Houston, 1985), p. 13.

[11]American Petroleum Institute, "Financial Trends of Leading U.S. Oil Companies: 1968–1985," discussion paper 17-R, October 1986.

2. The Second Contraction: 1986

The period from 1983 to late 1985 was an adjustment period in the industry. The pain was not over; it was simply endured following the cost-cutting. Drilling economics actually improved as crude postings firmed and drilling costs remained depressed.

There was justified worry that prices could slide more after OPEC reduced its benchmark price in the first half of 1983 from $34 per barrel to $29 per barrel. World demand for oil was declining as conservation continued and as non-OPEC production continued to increase because of major investments made during the boom. As swing supplier in OPEC, Saudi Arabia was propping up the cartel's price by repeatedly reducing production. This was not a stable situation, and in the second half of 1985, warnings were heard that oil would reach $15 per barrel should the Saudis relinquish their role and a price war break out. One leading U.S. oilman, T. Boone Pickens, anticipating a major price fall, locked in Mesa Petroleum's 1986 production at $23 per barrel by selling short on the New York Mercantile Exchange's petroleum futures market. This would turn out to be a very sage decision—one that other upstream oilmen wished they had duplicated to weather a tumultuous year.

The "crash of 1986" was traumatic for much of the oil (and gas) industry. Spot prices for West Texas Intermediate crude fell from a November 1985 high of $28 per barrel to a March 1986 low of under $10 per barrel. Posted prices averaged 47 percent lower during the year. Industry income plummeted an estimated $50 billion. Net income for the 25 largest U.S. oil firms fell one-third, to $10.9 billion—equal to 1975's level and a far cry from the 1980 peak of $30 billion. Wellhead interests found their cash flow cut in half virtually overnight and the capital value of their assets correspondingly devalued. The gross value of domestic oil production in 1986 was $85 billion, a 30 percent drop from $121.5 billion, recorded a year earlier.[12] Major companies slashed expenditures by 26 percent, while independents sliced outlays by half. Employment plummeted by 150,000, nearly one-third of upstream industry employment.

Offshore as well as onshore oil and gas service industries suffered an even crueler fate as a virtual paralysis in drilling cut cash flow to the bone. The Hughes rig count, which averaged nearly 2,000 in 1985, fell to a post–World War II low of 663 for the week of July 14,

---

[12]Tom Dougherty, "1986: A Review of a Bad Year," *Petroleum Independent*, February 1987, p. 32.

1986. The yearly average of 964, a 51 percent drop from that of the year before, was the lowest in recent history, eclipsing the 1971 low.[13] Not only did a wipeout of small and most medium-sized companies occur, industry leaders such as Hughes Tool, Baker International, Halliburton, and Cameron Iron Works took unprecedented writeoffs and in some cases merged to shore up shrinking net worths. Mothballed inventory (such as a stack of rigs and related equipment at Sabine Pass, Texas, with an estimated worth of $1 billion), distress auctions, and cannibalized equipment were some realities of an unprecedentedly bad year. Very few oil service companies in the United States made a profit in 1986.

The crash of 1986 was evident in all major oil states except California. Double-digit unemployment rates were experienced in Louisiana and Alaska. Unemployment rates increased noticeably in Colorado, Kansas, New Mexico, Oklahoma, Wyoming, and North Dakota. In Texas, the jobless rate increased to almost 9 percent. Houston, Texas, a barometer of the oil industry's fortunes, lost 90,000 jobs representing 6 percent of its work force. Bankruptcies and bank failures soared in many of the same states. The recession, for many, turned into a depression.

Downstream sectors of the oil industry experienced a far better fate. Refiners enjoyed relief from depressed 1983–85 margins as the decline in refined product prices lagged behind that of crude prices. Oil pipeline companies, in sharp distinction to gas pipeline companies, which had to discount rates to stay competitive with fuel oil in major industrial and powerplant markets, continued to make their former margins. Oil jobbers and marketers not only emerged relatively unscathed in 1986 but as a whole enjoyed the highest sales volumes and margins in years.[14]

B. Calls for Protectionism

1. Independent Refiners Coalition

The opening salvo of the current protectionist debate was launched by a group of independent U.S. refiners under competitive pressure from imported light products, specifically, finished and unfinished gasoline. In late 1984 the Independent Refiners Coalition, consisting

[13]Hughes Tool Company, "Monthly Averages of Rotary Rigs Running in the United States: 1964–1986."

[14]See "Fantastic Margins add Luster to API/SIGMA Meeting," *National Petroleum News*, July 1986, pp. 25–27, 34–36.

of 15 companies and the American Independent Refiners Association (founded in 1962 to represent small refiners), was formed to actively promote trade barriers on gasoline to increase member refiner margins.[15] Since 1979 small refiners had advocated that oil product tariffs, among other government interventions, replace entitlements benefits, but the IRC represented a more-concerted and better-focused lobbying effort.

The IRC argument centered around the national security threat of continued refinery closings as a result of competition from foreign for-export refineries. In a news release of February 21, 1985, the IRC made the following statement:

> America is rapidly replacing its dependency upon imported crude oil for dependency upon foreign gasoline. This development has serious consequences for national security, our economic recovery, and consumers. . . . An import quota on gasoline or a combination of quota and tariff are the appropriate remedy to meet the national security threat posed by increasing gasoline imports.

In testimony before the Subcommittee on Energy and Agricultural Taxation four months later, IRC representatives from Crown Central Petroleum and Ashland Oil urged Congress to "use taxing authority . . . to implement basic energy policy objectives" and cited existing presidential authority under Section 232 of the Trade Expansion Act of 1962 to restrict imports for national security reasons.[16] In IRC testimony before another Senate subcommittee, Ashland chairman John Hall supported countervailing duties and a two-tier tariff, a 10.8 percent *ad valorem* duty on the first 200,000 barrels per day of gasoline imports and a 21.6 percent "national

---

[15]Member companies were Amber Refining, Apex Oil, Ashland Oil, Crown Central Petroleum, Diamond Shamrock, Golden West Refining, MacMillan Ring-Free Oil, National Cooperative Refinery Association, Paramount Petroleum, Placid Refining, Pride Refining, Rock Island Refining, Texas City Refining, Tosco, and Valero Energy/Saber Refining. The American Independent Refiners Association, primarily composed of small refiners (defined as having under 50,000 barrels per day capacity), also was a member of the IRC. The AIRA was composed of 18 refiners, six of which also had individual memberships in the IRC. Representing the IRC was Charls E. Walker Associates, Inc., a consulting firm in Washington, D.C. Joining the IRC several months later were Coastal Corporation, the Indiana Farm Bureau Cooperative Association, and Tesoro Petroleum.

[16]Statement of George Jandacek on behalf of the Independent Refiners Coalition before the Subcommittee on Energy and Agricultural Taxation, U.S. Senate Finance Committee, 99th Cong., 1st Sess., June 21, 1985.

security" tariff on greater amounts.[17] To buttress their argument with academic rigor, the IRC commissioned two studies by consultants in 1985. A Pace Company study documented the existing and potential impact of new Middle Eastern refineries on the domestic industry, and Charles Ebinger of Ebinger International attempted to document a threat to national security posed by unregulated gasoline imports.[18]

Texaco, which had closed five refineries between 1981 and 1985, joined the IRC in castigating gasoline imports but, for public relations reasons, stopped short of recommending trade barriers. In a letter to stockholders dated March 12, 1985, Chairman John McKinley warned of "serious injury to both the economy and national security" from a "flood" of oil product imports from for-export refineries and advocated "conscious policy decisions" to remedy the situation.[19] Another Texaco executive testified before Congress about serious margin problems and the shutdown threat faced by the industry. He suggested that "a policy review should be immediately undertaken by responsible officials to determine at what level increased crude and product imports cease to be prudent from the standpoint of economic policy, energy policy, and national security."[20]

While the American Independent Refiners Association leaned heavily toward the IRC position, the National Petroleum Refiners Association (founded in 1902), consisting of generally larger processing facilities, many owned by the major oil companies, did not formally take a position. However, the NPRA did express an openness to protectionism that it said reflected the views of the "large majority" of its membership:

> Our import control system must be examined in light of a multiplicity of import restrictions in Europe, Japan, and other market-

[17]Statement of John Hall on behalf of the Independent Refiners Coalition, *Impact of Imported Petroleum Products on the Domestic Petroleum Industry*, Hearing before the Subcommittee on Energy Regulation and Conservation, U.S. Senate, 99th Cong., 1st Sess. (Washington, D.C.: Government Printing Office, 1985), pp. 168–69.

[18]The IRC's case for protectionism is analyzed in detail in chapter 3.

[19]Texaco, Inc., *1984 Annual Report* (White Plains, N.Y.: Texaco, Inc., 1984), p. 3. Toward the same end, heightening awareness of refinery capacity shutdowns, Texaco produced a study detailing the problems of restarting idled refineries. See *Protection and Start-up of Idle Petroleum Refining Equipment* (White Plains, N.Y.: Texaco, Inc., 1985).

[20]Statement of William Tell, Jr., *Impact of Imported Petroleum Products*, p. 93.

places for petroleum products so that U.S. refiners are not unfairly disadvantaged. The U.S. government must review tariff levels and clarify existing tariffs on naphtha, gasoline, gasoline blending stocks, and alcohol to insure that these products enter into the U.S. at duty rates which the Congress intends. . . . Some combination of increased tariffs and quotas might ultimately be implemented, dictated by national objectives, with the goal of maintaining a secure domestic refining industry.[21]

In the wake of the crude oil collapse of late 1985–early 1986 and the move for crude oil tariffs by some producing interests, the IRC's policy emphasis shifted from increasing product import tariffs *per se* to ensuring that they would exceed crude tariffs enough to avert a tariff-induced margin squeeze *if* protectionist legislation materialized. The IRC distanced itself as much as possible from advocates of crude oil import tariffs; an unaccompanied crude tariff would be devastating to its interests.

In February 1986 congressional testimony, IRC chairman George Jandacek of Crown Central Petroleum stated, "At this time we take no position for or against import fee legislation in general." However, he did quantify a crude/product differential (111 percent) and a surcharge on nonexempt products to make up for any exempted products.[22]

The shift by the Independent Refiners Coalition from offensive tariffs (product tariffs only) to defensive tariffs (if crude tariffs, then higher product tariffs) has continued into 1987, and the once-aggressive initiative has given way to studied inaction. Not inconsequential in this transformation has been a profitability turnaround starting in late 1985 and continuing into early 1987 for the survivors of the 1981–85 refinery shakeout.[23]

The drive by the Independent Refiners Coalition for product import tariffs in 1985 was effectively countered by independent downstream interests whose competitive viability was directly or indirectly tied to gasoline imports. The Coalition of Independent

---

[21]NPRA, "Products Imports Policy Statement," *Impact of Imported Petroleum Products*, p. 293.

[22]Statement of George Jandacek, Hearings before the Subcommittee on Energy and Agricultural Taxation, U.S. Senate Finance Committee, 99th Cong., 2nd Sess., *Taxation of Imported Oil* (Washington, D.C.: Government Printing Office, 1986), p. 313.

[23]See chapter 3, pp. 108–13.

Petroleum Product Marketers (CIPPM), formed in response to the Independent Refiners Coalition, comprised the Empire State Petroleum Association (New York State independent gasoline and fuel oil distributors), the Independent Fuel Terminal Operators Association (independent operators of tanker terminals involved in importing and marketing), the Independent Gasoline Marketers Council of America (nonbranded independent gasoline marketers), the New England Fuel Oil Institute (New England home heating oil distributors), and the Society of Independent Gasoline Marketers of America (independent gasoline marketers). Their arguments for open trade in the interest of competition and national security were heard by congressional subcommittees alongside the opposite conclusions of the IRC.[24] The Petroleum Marketers Association of America, composed mostly of branded jobbers, was also against the fee but qualified their opposition.[25]   Other groups that countered the IRC before Congress were the Petrochemical Energy Group, the National Council of Farmer Cooperatives, and the Citizen-Labor Energy Coalition.

Despite many hours of loaned executive time and a sizable budget, the Independent Refiners Coalition lobby effort has not to date borne political fruit. An early ray of hope was a speech by Energy Secretary John Herrington before the National Petroleum Council in the spring of 1985, in which he mentioned that President Reagan was "concerned" about the product import situation and promised that "the Administration will not allow the refining industry in this country to be destroyed by product imports."[26] Political inaction, however, was to follow. The political high point came on August 8, 1985, when 43 Republican and Democratic senators representing depressed refining areas asked Commerce Secretary Malcolm Baldrige to conduct a Section 232 investigation on the effect of higher

[24]See, for example, statement of Leonard Steuart on behalf of the Coalition of Independent Petroleum Product Marketers, *Impact of Imported Petroleum Products*, pp. 111–30.

[25]Said PMAA president Dave Robinson, "While PMAA remains unconvinced that available evidence justifies action now to stop imports, we do not intend to bury our heads in the sand. We will be constantly monitoring the situation, and if national security is threatened or if imports began to be the source of a competitive imbalance in the domestic market, then appropriate action may be necessary." Marvin Reid, "Squeeze on Supply Options," *National Petroleum News*, June 1985, p. 41.

[26]Patrick Crow, "U.S. in No Rush to Rescue Small Refiners Hurt by Product Imports," *Oil & Gas Journal*, May 27, 1985, p. 26.

product imports on national security. The Department of Commerce expressed severe reservations about the consumer costs of refiner aid via tariffs and found that higher product imports did not constitute a national security threat, a conclusion shared by the Department of Energy and the Reagan administration.

2. Independent Producers and Related Interests

Before the great price fall that reached its nadir in the first quarter of 1986, scattered industry support for tariffs existed upstream of the independent refiners. One proponent was Hughes Tool chairman J. R. Lesch, who advocated crude oil tariffs to equalize the wide disparity between production costs in Saudi Arabia and the United States.[27] The Independent Petroleum Association of America (IPAA), a national trade association with a membership of 5,200 independent producers, did not rule out tariffs as an option when it stated in May 1985 that "overdependence" on foreign crude is a "legitimate concern of the federal government warranting under extreme circumstances intervention in the marketplace."[28] Later in the year, however, IPAA president Lloyd Unsell would state that protectionism was "counterproductive to the national interest at this time."[29]

The first organized producer support for protectionism came in the summer of 1985 when the Texas Independent Producers and Royalty Owners Association (TIPRO), the largest state independent producing association in the nation, formally endorsed fees on crude oil and oil products. But the producing industry as a whole was not quite ready to endorse the major federal reentry into their business that protectionism would bring. The congressional debate over tax reform, which threatened some sacred deductions for independent producers, was foremost on the political agenda in a time of $25 per barrel oil.

Oil-state congressmen were more vocal about protectionism. In July 1985, Senate budget conferees, led by Pete Domenici (R-N.M.), with support from Senate Majority Leader Robert Dole (R-Kans.), included a $5 per barrel crude oil and a $10 per barrel oil product

[27]"U.S. Oil Import Duty Urged to Bolster Drilling," *Oil & Gas Journal*, August 26, 1985, pp. 40–41.

[28]Quoted in "IPAA Leaders Act on Energy 'Crisis,' " *IPAA News*, August 1, 1986, p. 2.

[29]"Independent Producers Oppose Any Crude Oil Fee," *IPAA News*, October 29, 1985.

import tax as part of a compromise $338 billion budget deficit reduction plan. Staunch opposition from President Reagan and House Speaker Thomas P. O'Neill (D-Mass.) killed the compromise as soon as it was offered, but pro-tariff congressmen would continue the fight unilaterally.[30]

On July 26, the day the Senate budget proposal was presented to Reagan, David Boren (D-Okla.) and Lloyd Bentsen (D-Tex.) introduced S. 1507, which would have enacted the same $5 per barrel and $10 per barrel oil import fees to raise $15 billion and provide a floor should oil prices "plunge sharply to $20 per barrel or even lower."[31] Senators Dole, Malcolm Wallop (R-Wyo.), and Gary Hart (D-Colo.), less inhibited than oil producers about endorsing a major reentry of the federal government into the industry, also saw a union of purpose between revitalizing a lethargic industry and closing record federal deficits, and accordingly introduced oil tariff bills. On the House side, James Weaver (D-Ore.), among others, introduced oil tariff legislation, but as on the Senate side, because of a lack of consumer-state support, none of the bills came close to passage.

On December 10, 1985, Saudi Arabia announced that it was abandoning its crucial support of a fixed cartel price in favor of increasing its "fair share" of the market. From a November 1985 high of $28 per barrel, oil prices plunged below $20 per barrel by year end and fell below $15 per barrel in February 1986. Marketing several million more barrels of daily crude production was accomplished through netback pricing arrangements wherein refiners paid the Saudis a percentage of the refined product price associated with their crude.[32]

Under the prodding of Senators Boren and Bentsen, Wallop called congressional hearings to consider import fee legislation as crude oil prices fell to new lows. In two days of hearings in February 1986, producer unrest was evidenced by an unequivocal call for tariffs by the Texas Independent Producers and Royalty Owners Association to protect stripper well output and other high-cost domestic sup-

[30]Jonathan Fuerbringer, "New Senate Budget Plan Proposes Oil Import Fee," New York Times, July 26, 1985, p. 1; Barbara Saunders, "Oil Import Fee Gaining Hill Support," Oil Daily, July 26, 1985, p. 1; Barbara Saunders, "House Democratic Chiefs Greet Import Fee Idea with Skepticism," Oil Daily, July 29, 1985, p. 1.

[31]David Boren, "We Need an Oil Import Fee," Washington Post, July 29, 1985, p. A–13.

[32]Youssef Ibrahim, "OPEC to Drop Efforts to Prop Up Oil Prices," Wall Street Journal, December 9, 1985, p. 3.

plies from retirement.[33] The Independent Petroleum Association of America, however, testified against protectionism. Although it sanctioned government intervention to reduce import independence "in extreme circumstances," the IPAA concluded that "taxes, tariffs, fees or quotas would be counterproductive to the national interest at this time."[34] Its representatives' reasoning, significant considering that the IPAA was at the forefront of the previous two major oil-protectionist episodes of the century, was not principled but pragmatic, as their testimony made clear:

> The petroleum industry is in the middle of a fight for its life; the "tax reformers" are coming at producers from all directions. Once again, oil and gas producers are whipping boys for many politicians. Any action which would appear to benefit the industry in the short run would inflame those legislators desiring to change the tax treatment of the industry. It would be a poor trade-off if producers were to fight for an import fee whose effects were only temporarily beneficial, if at all, only to find that it had sounded the death knell for statutory depletion and expensing of IDC's by stimulating negative tax action by industry opponents. This is a foreseeable response to any action taken in favor of an import fee.[35]

The IPAA's opposition to tariffs later in the year, with federal tax reform decided and in the face of continuing low prices, would be revised.

In addition to the Independent Refiners Coalition, which advocated an oil product fee to accompany a crude fee, Transco Energy, a natural gas transmission company with a large exploration/production affiliate, testified in favor of tariffs in the February hearing. No other company or trade association of the gas industry testified, and conspicuous by its absence was the largest petroleum trade association in the country, the American Petroleum Institute (API). API's reservations, like the IPAA's, were pragmatic, but the reasons

---

[33]TIPRO representative James Hunt, chairman of a Dallas-based production company, promoted his tariff proposal as "the reverse of the windfall profits tax . . . to protect consumers from the consequences of severe price declines." Remarks by James W. Hunt, *Taxation of Import Oil*, p. 302.

[34]Statement of the Independent Petroleum Association of America, *Taxation of Imported Oil*, p. 281.

[35]Ibid., p. 291. Also see "Independent Producers Oppose Any Crude Oil Import Fee," *IPAA News*, October 29, 1985.

for such opposition ran deeper. Many majors had large foreign reserves, and tariffs would reduce netbacks on these reserves; yet with large domestic output, there was a counter-concern about low prices at home. Like the IPAA, the API would have second thoughts as the price depression lingered on.

In March 1986, prices broke the $10 per barrel barrier, and Vice President George Bush was dispatched to Saudi Arabia to discreetly share the Reagan administration's concern about the plight of the domestic industry. Prices would rebound modestly, but the damage had been done. The industry was aware that the new environment of $10–$15 per barrel crude—if not less—was not an aberration but a return to normal market conditions.

As the year wore on, more and more industry groups and companies, concentrated in the exploration/production sector, implicitly or explicitly supported tariffs.[36] Such prominent industry executives such as Oscar Wyatt of Coastal Corporation, Jack Bowen of Transco Energy, George Mitchell of Mitchell Energy, Fred Hartley of Unocal, and Raymond Plank of Apache Petroleum took a crusading interest in tariffs and urged protectionism at every opportunity. *World Oil* devoted its May 1986 issue to "Why the U.S. Needs an Oil Import Fee." The *Oil & Gas Journal*, which earlier had criticized oil tariff proposals, sympathetically editorialized about a growing consensus within segments of the industry toward endorsing government intervention on national security grounds. In early 1987, editor Gene Kiney, in a state-of-the-industry speech, endorsed

---

[36]Producer trade associations aligning behind tariffs included the Oklahoma Independent Petroleum Association, West Central Texas Oil and Gas Association, Michigan Oil and Gas Association, North Texas Oil and Gas Association, Texas Mid-Continent Oil and Gas Association, Permian Basin Petroleum Association, Louisiana Association of Independent Producers and Royalty Owners, and National Association of Royalty Owners. Other groups aligned with the exploration/production sector supporting a tariff were the Society of Independent Earth Scientists, Petroleum Equipment Suppliers Association, and International Association of Drilling Contractors.

Other energy industry groups that endorsed tariffs in 1986 were the Interstate Natural Gas Association of America (INGAA), whose pipeline members were discounting rates to remain competitive with fuel oil; the nuclear lobby Americans for Energy Independence, which recognized the competitive advantage in higher fossil fuel prices; and the Solar Energy Industries Association, which also sought to close the competitive gap between oil and the fringe energy source.

tariffs as a solution to the industry's plight.[37] *Oil Daily* editorials also warmed up to protectionism as segments of the industry did.

On the government side, the Texas Railroad Commission, the Oklahoma Corporation Commission, and the Interstate Oil Compact Commission, among other oil-state entities, endorsed protectionism for near-term relief. Another political champion for tariffs was Texas governor Mark White, who tirelessly argued for protectionism throughout 1986 in an unsuccessful attempt to win reelection in a state facing huge oil-related budget deficits.

Oil import fees were not the only government intervention advocated by oilmen in 1986 to reverse one of the two worst downturns in industry history. Henry Linden, president of the Gas Research Institute, in addition to repeating his customary call for expanded government subsidies for research and development, proposed government funding and federally guaranteed loans for offshore drilling.[38] The American Institute of Chemical Engineers urged federal authorities to reemphasize synthetic fuels with liberal subsidies.[39] Chevron chairman George Keller called upon the industry to determine a "minimum survival" oil price for the government to legislate.[40] James Stafford, executive director of the National Association of Royalty Owners, petitioned the Oklahoma Corporation Commission to impose a $20 per barrel crude oil floor.[41] Two Dallas independent oil producers persuaded the Texas Railroad Commission to consider reducing the market-demand factor for all oil wells (except for enhanced recovery and stripper output) from 100 percent, where it had been, except for minor deviations, since April 1972, to 90 percent—to prevent "economic waste."[42] The energy writer for the *Houston Chronicle* called upon the Texas Railroad Commission, with its 50 years of experience, to administer OPEC for the purpose of cutting back production sufficiently to return oil

[37]Speech of January 22, 1987, before Bob Spears & Associates, Houston, Texas.

[38]"Alternatives to Oil Import Fees," *Natural Gas Intelligence*, October 27, 1986, p. 8.

[39]"AIChE Calls for Synfuels Funds in U.S.," *Oil & Gas Journal*, November 3, 1986, p. 24.

[40]"API Hears Call for Oil Price Floor, Drops Opposition to Import Fee," *Oil & Gas Journal*, November 17, 1986, pp. 19–22.

[41]"Oklahoma Panel Denies Application for Setting Prices," *Oil Daily*, January 26, 1987, p. 5.

[42]*Oil & Gas Journal Newsletter*, July 21, 1986.

prices to previous levels.[43] Louisiana Land and Exploration chairman E. L. Williamson, after characterizing regulation as inefficient and disjointed, advocated a major intellectual effort to develop an "energy blueprint" from which to implement "strategic national energy planning." One person recommended by Williamson to head the effort was President Carter's former energy czar, James Schlesinger.[44]

These fringe proposals, indicative of waning patience and a quick-fix mentality in parts of the industry, paled in comparison with the growing appeal of oil tariffs. In late 1986 the two largest industry trade groups, the Independent Petroleum Association of America and the American Petroleum Institute, reversed their stand to all but endorse protectionism.

The IPAA's almost apologetic recommendation against protectionism in February 1986 was significant. As prices continued to weaken, small steps toward protectionism were taken. In May, IPAA president Lloyd Unsell accused the majors of "economic vampirism" because of their hard trading with OPEC to lower crude prices.[45] The next month, an IPAA publication reported that petroleum imports exceeded the "peril point" of 30 percent.[46] In August, an Emergency Action Task Force was formed to study appropriate policies to deal with the national security "emergency" of predatory pricing by OPEC.[47] Upon completion of its study several months later, a new policy position conditionally endorsing a comprehensive tariff program was ratified by the general membership, on October 28, 1986. The Task Force report, a compromise victory for moderates viewing tariffs as a last resort over tariff-now proponents, led by Raymond Plank of Apache Petroleum, ended its policy recommendations with the following paragraph:

[43]Barbara Shook, "Let Railroad Commission Run OPEC," *Houston Chronicle*, July 6, 1986, p. 6–1.

[44]E. L. Williamson, "Need for Strategic National Energy Planning," Arthur Anderson Conference, December 8, 1986. Williamson's proposals are similar to former Atlantic Richfield (ARCO) President Thornton Bradshaw's plea a decade ago for "the permanent management of crude-oil prices by the U.S. government" within a national energy plan to replace erratic piecemeal regulation. See Bradshaw, "My Case for National Planning," *Fortune*, February 1977, pp. 100–104.

[45]"Big Oil Blasted for Bidding Down Prices," *IPAA News*, May 21, 1986.

[46]IPAA, *U.S. Energy Update*, June 1986, p. 1.

[47]"IPAA Leaders Act on Energy 'Crisis,' " *IPAA News*, August 1, 1986.

If the dominant Arab OPEC countries continue to hold prices below the level needed for the United States to maintain adequate reserves of oil and gas, we ask the President to take all appropriate actions to prevent OPEC control of our energy supplies and urge the use, whenever needed, of two actions specifically approved by the IPAA:

1) a floor price for crude oil to provide stability,
2) a variable import fee on crude oil and petroleum products, without exceptions or exemptions, to stabilize the price of domestic crude oil and products at an adequate level.[48]

The near-endorsement of tariffs, commented IPAA president H. B. Scoggins in retrospect, "was the long-term effect of deteriorating conditions."[49]

To publicize the perceived threat to national security from oil imports in a way that the media had not, the IPAA simultaneously created the Energy Security Institute of the Jefferson Energy Foundation, named for the third president of the United States, who advocated private mineral rights (but not protectionism) in his early days. This began a two-pronged industry relief effort, one educational and one political, with Congress and the president in mind.[50]

The 5,200-member producer group had now gone about as far as it could without asking Reagan and Congress to immediately enact tariffs. There was still hope that the "last resort" of a major tariff program, with the prospect of the industry fighting bureaucrats on one hand and the public on the other, could be avoided.

The tariff position of the American Petroleum Institute also shifted as the year went on. When oil tariff proposals first took on political life in the summer of 1985, API wrote a letter to the House and Senate budget committee conferees stating that an oil tariff was an

---

[48]*IPAA News*, October 28, 1986. Other interventionist proposals by the national producer group involved natural gas, specifically forcing gas pipelines to ship tendered volumes on a nondiscriminatory basis (mandatory contract carriage) and reducing alleged preferential treatment for gas imports. Other IPAA proposals were noninterventionist—taxation reduction and repeal, natural gas production and consumption deregulation, and expanded access to federal lands for exploration and development.

[49]Judith Crown, "Oilman with a Mission," *Houston Chronicle*, January 19, 1987, pp. 1–4.

[50]See IPAA, *Petroleum Independent*, December 1986, pp. 16–18.

"inappropriate substitute for reduced spending."[51] Earlier, in the February Senate hearings, the API had stayed away, since it realized that the issue was not really politically alive and was not desirous of unnecessarily offending tariff proponents in the independent upstream ranks. By the year-end annual API convention, however, patience and optimism had grown so thin that all policy options, interventionist as well as noninterventionist, were placed on the table. Paced by Chairman George Keller's call for an oil price floor, API dropped its opposition to import fees. The *Oil & Gas Journal* described the about-face as a historic event:

> They swallowed their pride, abandoned their remaining illusions about a free market in oil, and asked the federal government to help them avert the economic and national security disaster wrought by the oil price collapse. . . . What is certain is that the API policy shift is just a first step down a long and treacherous road. . . . Most know that help now probably means a government role in the oil industry forever.[52]

The amended API position did not mean that even major companies laden with foreign reserves and disdainful of federal intervention had capitulated. Some companies, such as Keller's Chevron, Harley's Unocal, Texaco, and Amoco, had abandoned a free-market position because they had domestic-laden oil portfolios. But Exxon, Shell, Mobil, Sun, Standard Oil, and Conoco, among other integrated companies, considered price supports by means of tariffs or other government programs unacceptable. Others, such as Phillips Petroleum, showed a lack of support by not participating in the debate.

In early 1987, the previous year's momentum toward protection-

---

[51]Barbara Saunders, "House Democratic Chiefs Greet Import Fee Idea with Skepticism," *Oil Daily*, July 29, 1985, p. 2. Other evidence of the API position, which remained invariant through most of 1986, was chief economist Michael Canes's *Wall Street Journal* letter to the editor (January 7, 1986, p. 31), which stated: "The American Petroleum Institute has long opposed oil-import levies." Also see API, *Response R-341*, January 21, 1986.

[52]"API's Historic Call for Rescue Should Sound Energy Alarms," *Oil & Gas Journal*, November 17, 1986, p. 17. The new API position was reiterated in a letter to the *Wall Street Journal* (January 5, 1987, p. 13) by API president Charles DiBona. After citing a number of noninterventionist policies that would benefit the industry, he added: "What government actions, if any, should be taken beyond these is not so clear, but until careful consideration is given the gains and costs of various options, we think that no option should be ruled out."

ism continued. In Senate hearings in February, several more major upstream-related trade groups endorsed protectionism.[53] The *National Petroleum News* in early 1987 reported on the continuing move by API toward regulatory relief: "The American Petroleum Institute, while maintaining that it has developed 'no position on an import fee,' has nevertheless launched what is apparently going to be an all-out campaign to get a 'national dialogue' going concerning what it describes as 'the coming energy crisis.' "[54] Interior Secretary Donald Hodel, in a publicized rivalry with Energy Secretary John Herrington, warned of an energy crisis within three to five years with overtures of necessary government intervention.[55] In Congress, Senator Bentsen introduced the Energy Security Act of 1987, which requires the president to project import levels for three years in the future and take action to limit such volumes to 50 percent of domestic production. Reflecting current political realities, the bill's authority for executive action did not specify tariffs or quotas but certainly could include them.

3. Other Support

Support for oil protectionism grew outside the industry, just as it did within the industry, in 1986. S. Fred Singer of the University of Virginia, recently Senior Fellow for Natural Resources Policy at the Heritage Foundation, reiterated his case for a variable oil import fee during the February 1986 hearings before Congress. A study by Chase Econometrics, the forecasting arm of Chase Manhattan Bank, confidently predicted that if oil prices did not improve, a crude oil crisis could be expected by 1991.[56] Other academic support for protectionism was attributable in part to consultant studies underwritten by the tariff lobby to refine and quantify the national security argument against open trade. The Ebinger and Pace studies for the Independent Refiners Coalition are examples.

---

[53]They were the Association of Oilwell Servicing Contractors, the International Association of Geophysical Contractors, and the National Ocean Industries Association. *Oil & Gas Journal*, February 16, 1987, p. 90.

[54]" 'National Dialogue' Sought on Oil Imports," *National Petroleum News*, February 1987, p. 16.

[55]"Hodel Fears Rising Oil Imports Pose Threat to U.S. Security," *Oil & Gas Journal*, December 1, 1986, pp. 27–28; Patrick Crow, "The Secretaries' Rivalry," *Oil & Gas Journal*, March 2, 1987, p. 21.

[56]Chase Econometrics, *The Next Oil Shock: A Planning Guide for World Energy Markets, 1986–2000* (New York: Chase Manhattan Bank, July 1986).

The most prominent academic support for tariffs was a Harvard University study released in late 1986, *Oil Tariff Policy in an Uncertain Market*, which calculated that a fixed tariff between $10 and $11 per barrel was socially optimal.[57] The study, partially underwritten by Raymond Plank and Apache Petroleum's Energy Security Policy, Inc., and unveiled on Capitol Hill to maximize its political impact, was the latest of a series of quantitative economics studies published by Harvard's Energy and Environmental Policy Center favoring an activist role of government toward oil imports. The EEPC, founded in 1980, included among its principal purposes "developing programs to manage the effects of fuel supply disruptions."[58]

The early 1987 hearings before the Senate Finance Committee subpanel on energy taxation found new academic voices for government intervention on a national and even an international scale to prop up oil prices. Philip Verleger, Jr., of the Institute of International Economics announced his "reluctant" support for oil tariffs on national security grounds. Henry Schuler, holder of the Dewey Bartlett Chair on Energy and National Security at the Center for Strategic and International Studies (CSIS), unveiled a striking proposal to have the International Energy Agency coordinate a multilateral (worldwide) oil price floor. Also supporting the proposal were Verleger and Charles Ebinger, now director of energy and strategic resources at CSIS.

Other support for oil tariffs emanated from prominent individuals outside the industry, even before the price collapse of late 1985–early 1986. In addition to numerous oil-state congressmen supporting a levy for national security and deficit reduction reasons, conservative columnist William F. Buckley, Jr., supported oil levies as a "preferred tax" to reduce deficits and as an "economic harassment" to the OPEC cartel.[59] Resurrecting a Carter-era theme of an impending supply crisis, columnist Jody Powell argued for a $10 per barrel oil import fee as a conservation and deficit-reduction

---

[57]The assumptions, methodology, and policy conclusions of the Harvard study are challenged in appendix 4B, pp. 185–94.

[58]One of the earliest products of the Center, primarily funded by the Department of Energy, was a report of the Energy and Security Research Project published as David Deese and Joseph Nye, eds., *Energy and Security* (Cambridge: Ballinger Publishing Company, 1981).

[59]William F. Buckley, Jr., "Go Ahead and Tax Oil Imported from OPEC," *Houston Chronicle*, July 31, 1985, p. 1–28;.

measure.[60] Chrysler chairman Lee Iacocca championed both an oil tariff and Corporate Average Fuel Economy (CAFE) standards in line with his company's major investment in smaller fuel-efficient fleet lines. The higher the price of gasoline, the better Chrysler's competitive advantage over Ford and General Motors, whose product mix favored larger, less fuel-efficient cars.[61] The *New York Times* vehemently editorialized for an oil import tax on national security, revenue, and other grounds.[62] In all, industry protectionists could look to the outside to buttress their argument that a broad-based case for oil tariffs, not one predicated on the self-interest of the upstream oil community, existed.

C. Consumer and Industry Dissent: Is There a Free-Market Alternative?

The growing support that the tariff position received in 1986 did not approach unanimity in the oil industry (or, for that matter, American industry in general), in government, or in academia. In fact, it remained a divisive issue in the petroleum sector and a minority position politically and across broad sectors of the economy.

The self-interest of producers favoring higher oil prices has been countered by oil users advantaged by lower prices. Testifying against oil tariff proposals before Congress were a broad range of consumer groups and energy-dependent sectors making up a majority of the non-oil economy.[63]

Political representatives of the 40 net consuming (net oil-importing) states in Congress stood as a barrier to the representatives of the 10 producing states. To the chagrin of industry protectionists, some oil-state legislators, for example, Sen. Phil Gramm (R-Tex.) and Rep. Tom DeLay (R-Tex.), refused to join the tariff bandwagon.

---

[60]Jody Powell, "Law Putting $10 Tax on Imported Oil Would Help U.S.," *Houston Post*, July 10, 1985, p. B–2.

[61]See, for example, Lee Iacocca, "This Time It's Oil, Not Toyotas," *Houston Chronicle*, May 11, 1986, p. 6–1.

[62]See "In the Name of Sanity, Tax Oil," *New York Times*, December 24, 1985, p. A–16; "Oil and the Crash of '86," *New York Times*, January 26, 1986, p. 20. A front-page *Times* article on February 17, 1987 ("U.S. Oil Shortages Seem Unavoidable to Many Analysts," by Robert Hershey, Jr.), quoted Interior secretary Hodel, former energy czar James Schlesinger, IPAA chairman Raymond Hefner, and Georgetown University's Henry Schuler in another display of strong bias toward the national security threat of unregulated oil imports.

[63]See chapter 5, pp. 210–12, for a summary of these consumer and industry trade groups.

The Reagan administration, the State Department, the Treasury Department, and the Energy Department criticized protectionism as unaffordable for the national welfare. Congress soundly rejected tariff bills that reached a full vote and did little more than debate and redebate the issues on the subcommittee level (owing to the senior positions held by some oil-state legislators).

In the industry, negative opinions toward protectionism continued to emanate from some of the largest oil companies in the country, led by Exxon, Shell, and Mobil. Several other integrated giants with large foreign and domestic output were ambivalent toward a government price floor at best. For self-interested reasons, independent importers, terminal operators, and marketers were solidly against import restrictions. Independent refiners, once at the forefront of the tariff debate, watered down their position from demanding tariffs per se to wanting an adequate product tariff *differential* if crude tariffs were to pass. Even in the exploration and production sector, prominent individuals and firms simply refused to support protectionism or openly criticized tariffs as a Trojan horse for the industry. Tariff critics included T. Boone Pickens of Mesa Petroleum, Michel Halbouty of Halbouty Energy, Harrison Townes of Toklan Oil, Bob Palmer of Rowan Cos., Sherman Norton of Norton Drilling, Ernie Cockrell of Cockrell Oil, Nathan Avery of Galveston-Houston, and Nelson Steenland of Geophysical Exploration.[64] In short, tariffs remained controversial inside, as well as outside, the industry, despite the movement of the API and IPAA toward protectionism.

Despite well-publicized support for the tariff position in academia, dissent, although somewhat muted, also existed. The most prominent example is the case of Emma Brossard, director of policy analysis at the Center for Energy Studies at Louisiana State University. Her antitariff testimony in the February 1985 Senate hearings disturbed a number of independent oilmen connected to LSU. When Sen. J. Bennett Johnston (D-La.) held hearings and a pro-tariff rally in Lafayette, Louisiana, a year later, her criticisms would not be heard again. It was not that she had changed her

[64]See the following issues of *Oil Daily* (all in 1986): September 8, p. 4; September 17, p. 4; September 23, p. 6. Also see *Oil & Gas Journal*, January 12, 1987, pp. 9–10; *Oil & Gas Journal Newsletter*, September 22, 1986; *Houston Business Journal*, May 12, 1986, p. 3A, and September 15, 1986, p. 5; *Houston Post*, March 3, 1986, p. C–9; *Platt's Price Report*, November 10, 1986, p. 1.

mind. She was specifically asked not to give or submit her prepared remarks to the Johnston panel by embarrassed LSU authorities, who were caught in a vise between academic freedom for a faculty member on one hand and the desires of influential university supporters on the other.[65]

Given the great controversy over the governmental approach and the political impasse created by the problem of oil tariffs, the following question may appropriately be posed: Is there an alternative that can provide industry relief *without* injuring consumers and the economy, and can such an alternative remove government intervention rather than increase government involvement in the industry? That is, is there a free-market alternative to protectionism that holds the promise of helping virtually all parties, except, perhaps, those industry, political, and academic constituencies with a vested interest in a new regulatory program?

This question will be answered in chapter 5. But first, it is necessary to understand what the protectionist alternative has been in practice (chapter 2) and what it is in theory (chapters 3 and 4). Only then can the free-market, open-trade alternative be properly evaluated.

[65]Letter from E. B. Brossard to Sen. Phil Gramm, February 10, 1987. Copy in author's files. She ended her letter: "We at the LSU Center for Energy Studies must now shut up, as we will not support an oil import fee; but we are counting on you and President Reagan to prevent this American boomerang from occurring." The rally for oil imports, officially billed as a hearing by the U.S. Senate Energy Committee, was attended by 5,000 people. See Bruce Schultz, "Oil Import Fee Pushed at Lafayette Hearing," *Baton Rouge Morning Advocate*, February 10, 1987, p. 1.

2. The History of Oil Protectionism

This chapter surveys the interventionist past of the oil industry in the United States. It begins with a brief view of petroleum intervention in general before concentrating on oil protectionism. To illustrate the politics and the economic consequences of each, three protectionist episodes, along with intermittent periods of open trade, are studied.

A. An Interventionist Legacy

The U.S. petroleum industry has a 125-year legacy of interventionism.[1] Government involvement with oil since the 1860s and 1870s has consisted of *internal intervention,* intervention fostered within the industry by organized firms and industry coalitions seeking competitive advantage in the political "marketplace," and *external intervention,* intervention fostered by legislators with public support against the will of the industry. Some intervention, particularly in recent decades, rode to victory on both industry and public support.

Most intervention—in over a century of experience—has been internal. That is, if industry parties had not advocated certain measures, they would not have been enacted into laws. The two major protectionist episodes of the present century, for example, were industry-sponsored.

The birth of the U.S. petroleum industry is commonly dated to 1859, the year Colonel E. L. Drake applied salt well drilling techniques to petroleum exploration and discovered the first commercial oil well. Over the next years, a bustle of activity ensued in Pennsylvania, and in a case study of spontaneous economic order engendered by the interplay of self-interest, a major industry consisting of production, transportation, refining, and marketing took shape, to the benefit of consumers and producers alike.

---

[1]This section draws heavily from my forthcoming book, *Oil, Gas, and Government: The U.S. Experience,* to be published in two volumes by the Cato Institute.

27

Market forces, predominant in the first years of the industry, were soon joined by interventionist strands that would take hold in ensuing decades and become more numerous in the 20th century. During the Civil War, as discussed below, the North enacted tariffs on crude oil and oil products. In 1865, a $1 per barrel levy, the most punitive excise tax in industry history, was placed on crude output. This tax led to organized industry protest, and a year later, amid depressed industry conditions, it was repealed.

While the above intervention showed an early proclivity of government to look to the great wealth of oil as a revenue source, other events of that period showed another side of government involvement that would become more common—intervention by industry invitation. It began when oil producers, strained by overproduction and sagging prices, turned to state legislatures to force pipelines to ratably accept their oil for shipment as "common carriers." In the same period, several states, at the bequest of producers, enacted anti-integration laws to lessen the competitive threat of production-pipeline affiliates.

Later in the century, independent producers, joined by independent pipelines and refiners, fought the Standard Oil Trust, which by the 1880s had become the nation's most prominent transporter and refiner of crude. Unable to neutralize Standard Oil's efficiencies in the marketplace, rivals turned to political means for support. (Consumers, with good reason, did not join the independents and their journalist allies—they were enjoying a product that was constantly improving in quality and declining in price.) The Interstate Commerce Act of 1887 was originally drafted by the Petroleum Producers Association to limit Standard's preferential railroad shipping rates. The aforementioned state pipeline regulation was directed at the Trust, as was the 1906 amendment to the Interstate Commerce Act, which began interstate oil pipeline regulation. State antitrust laws were enacted and utilized by independents and opportunistic politicians with the Trust in mind. So was the Sherman Act of 1890, which in a famous 1911 court case was interpreted to dismember Standard Oil into 35 companies.

Other 19th century intervention concerned petroleum leasing on federal lands, which began in 1866; a controversial and consequential monopoly awarded to E. A. L. Roberts by the U.S. Patent Office for rejuvenating oil wells by nitroglycerin explosions (oil well torpedoing); and the beginning of wellhead regulation by oil states to mitigate practices under the "rule of capture" property rights assignment.

The 20th century would witness the broadening and deepening of intervention on all levels of government. This occurred as the government initiated intervention in certain situations and as the industry expanded, became more politically organized, and came to view government involvement in pragmatic business terms.

The breakup of the Standard Oil Trust was the first major episode of the new century (and the most significant and consequential intervention to date). A second episode that cannot be overrated in the history of industry-government petroleum relations came in 1917, when federal authorities established a wartime bureaucracy and appointed an oil czar to regulate the pricing, allocation, entry, exit, and end-use decisions of crude oil and oil products. World War I planning was a new experience to oilmen, but special interests within the industry soon transformed it from external to internal intervention by urging its continuance or extension. In 1919, the petroleum wartime regulations and bureaucracy were dismantled, but the idea of the federal government's place in industry affairs continued. A sign of the new mentality was the reorganization of the major industry wartime advisory group, the National Petroleum War Services Committee, as the American Petroleum Institute in 1919 "to afford a means of cooperation with the government in all matters of national concern."[2]

The 1930s saw major government intervention in the oil industry. Underlying the flurry of state and federal activity was the discovery and development of major Southwest oil fields at a time of stagnant demand during the Great Depression. The result was an unanticipated major price fall from the wellhead to retail. The general industry response was a *quest for stability;* it began with unsuccessful voluntary attempts within the industry to limit oil production and was followed by state regulation in Texas and Oklahoma to limit output to "market demand." Accompanying market-demand proration were well spacing minimums, maximum gas-oil ratios, and field shutdown orders—all intended to limit output and raise prices.

State "conservation" regulation was joined by wellhead-to-pump federal regulation under the New Deal's National Recovery Act from 1933 to 1935. The NRA was also dedicated to industry recovery

[2]Leonard Fanning, *The Story of the American Petroleum Institute* (New York: World Petroleum Policies, 1959), p. 30.

through higher prices. As such, federal regulation was welcomed by industry segments to support fledgling state regulation curbing the flow of illegal "hot" oil (oil produced in excess of state allowables).

Essential to the success of the domestic oil cartel was the restriction of growing volumes of oil imports. This was achieved in the 1930s with comprehensive tariffs and a several-year quota.

World War II petroleum planning was a repeat of the World War I experience but in a more formal and magnified form. It was not a new experience but an almost expected event following World War I and New Deal planning. In addition to familiar price, allocation, and entry/exit regulation, stripper wells were granted cash subsidies, oil wells were assigned a "maximum efficient rate" for regulated production, and civilian gasoline and fuel oil were rationed by coupon.

In the postwar period, state conservation regulation returned to the fore in Texas, Oklahoma, Louisiana, Kansas, and New Mexico to prevent "overproduction." Beginning in 1935, the Interstate Oil Compact Commission, although lacking any regulatory authority of its own, facilitated the effort by pooling information from its oil-state members. The predominance of state over federal regulation was interrupted by the Korean conflict, which led to an almost reflexive reestablishment of a wartime bureaucracy and regulation. It never exerted as primary an influence as did World War II oil planning, however, because of the limited nature and duration of the Korean "police action."

With severely restricted allowables in the oil states (except California, which never adopted market-demand proration), domestic prices were maintained.[3] However, imports were seeping in to replace restricted domestic supply, and for the domestic cartel to survive, a federal complement was required to restrain growing volumes of foreign oil. The result was the Mandatory Oil Import Program of 1959, which set strict importation quotas. As explained below, the program became very complicated and politicized and was finally dismantled in 1973. By that time, overproduction concerns of the proration era were forgotten amid an Arab embargo and oil-product shortages.

The "energy crisis" period from the early 1970s to 1981 spawned a variety of government interventions, primarily at the federal level.

---

[3]See appendix A, pp. 246, for the high degree of price stability in this period.

Major intervention included price ceilings at all industry stages, the supplier-purchaser and buy-sell allocation programs, the refinery entitlements program, conservation regulation, synthetic fuel subsidies, the Strategic Petroleum Reserve, and the Windfall Profits Tax. All of these interventions, except the Windfall Profits Tax and the Strategic Petroleum Reserve, had the support of organized industry in addition to political support. Like preceding intervention, the 1970s' legislation was primarily *internal* intervention.

The 19th-century interventionist episodes mentioned above were by no means the only ones. In 1919, Oregon, with industry support, made a public finance breakthrough by enacting a gasoline tax to underwrite state road construction. Within a decade, every state in the Union had followed suit; this tax was to be increased in future years and was never to be undone. A plethora of local, state, and federal regulations and taxes, virtually all sponsored by service station–dealer coalitions, have governed wholesale and retail gasoline sales, ranging from one-price (minimum markup) laws early in the century and self-service bans in the middle decades to divestiture/divorcement and franchise protection laws in the last decade. The Clean Air Act has limited lead quantities in motor gasoline since 1972 and since 1974 has regulated refinery emissions. State and federal land leasing for petroleum development has been a controversial issue for much of the century. Natural gas regulation, affecting oil industry operations in numerous ways, advanced from the distribution level in the 19th century, to the transmission level in 1938, and to the wellhead in 1954; it remains in flux today.

In short, there has been a multiplicity of intervention in all phases of the oil industry across various eras and at all levels of government. Petroleum taxation has been designed to extract economic rents from the industry to fund certain functions (road building, public education) or support the general treasury. Internal intervention has typically been designed to transfer economic rent within the industry to the politically active parties. Price regulation, on the other hand, generally a mix between internal and external intervention, has been designed to transfer rent from the industry to consumers (although the question of whether this has been accomplished is open to a debate that is beyond the scope of this book). *Thus oil industry protectionism must be seen not as an aberration from the free-market past of the industry but as a complementary intervention in the government quest for revenue and the industry quest for stability and competitive advantage.* This will become more clear as the politics and economics of past protectionist episodes are detailed below.

B. Early Protectionism: 1861–1909

The first period of oil industry protectionism began during the Civil War. To generate wartime revenue, along with many other levies the North placed a $0.10 per gallon tariff on "spirits of turpentine" in 1861. The import tax was set at $0.30 per gallon for all oil products in 1864 and increased to $0.40 per gallon in 1865.[4] The $16.80 per barrel tariff, the highest such fee in industry history, would later prove to be major protection for domestic refiners against growing competition in the world petroleum market.

In March 1863, a 20 percent *ad valorem* tax on imported crude oil joined the product tax. Two years later the crude fee was reset at $0.20 per gallon ($8.40 per barrel), and coal oil was taxed at $0.15 per gallon.[5] In the same year a $1 per barrel excise tax, placed on domestic crude production as a wartime revenue source, not only partly negated the protection but contributed to an industry depression. The wellhead tax, after organized industry protest, was repealed in May 1866.[6]

Pressure from refiners, organized in such trade groups as the Pittsburgh Petroleum Association, kept the unilateral product tariff in effect until 1894. These groups also lobbied successfully to repeal a refinery tax and fended off an attempt to tax refined exports at $0.25 per barrel in 1868.[7] An export levy would not have been of minor significance. By the 1880s, with Standard Oil at the fore, oil became one of the four leading export commodities in the United States, with destinations in the Far East, Germany, Italy, Great Britain, Canada, Belgium, and the Netherlands.[8]

[4] 11 Stat. 292 at 293 (1861); 13 Stat. 491 at 493 (1865). Also see Ralph Hidy and Muriel Hidy, *Pioneering in Big Business* (New York: Harper & Brothers, 1955), p. 6.

[5] 12 Stat. 742 (1863); 13 Stat. 491 at 493 (1865).

[6] 14 Stat. 355 (1866).

[7] 14 Stat. 125 at 167 (1868). Rolland Maybee, *Railroad Competition and the Oil Trade* (Philadelphia: Porcupine Press, 1974), pp. 256–61.

[8] The supporting role of the U.S. government in developing the export trade was acknowledged by John D. Rockefeller: "The Standard is always fighting to sell the American product against the oil produced from the great fields of Russia, which struggles for the trade of Europe, and the Burma oil, which largely affects the market in India. . . . One of our greatest helpers has been the State Department in Washington." John D. Rockefeller, *Random Reminiscences of Men and Events* (New York: Doubleday, Page, and Company, 1909), p. 63.

Although the unilateral product tariff was repealed in 1894, a new countervailing tariff provision in the 1894 law allowed a 40 percent tax on crude oil and oil products if the importing country had a similar duty. The Dingly Tariff in 1897 increased the countervailing tax to 100 percent.[9] Besides its negative effects on U.S. consumers, retaliatory tariffs injured the domestic industry's oil export trade, primarily that of Standard Oil.[10] Domestic producers and key export points such as New York harbor were also disadvantaged by protectionism, unilateral or retaliatory.

A free-trade era was reintroduced for the first time in nearly a half-century when countervailing duties applicable to oil were repealed in 1909.[11] "Standard Oil marketers," as a result, "began . . . to feel more strongly the impact of foreign competition."[12] In the next years, illuminating oil imports surged fivefold, and a similar import growth in lesser products, such as wax, took place. Trade liberalization was also a factor in the decision of Royal-Dutch Shell to set up operations in the U.S. market in 1912, thus contributing to a new competitive era in the American petroleum industry.[13] The new open-trade period would continue for several decades as government officials welcomed, and indeed promoted, the internationalization of the world oil market to alleviate fears of domestic supply shortages.

C. Open Trade: 1909–31

Before the 1920s, officials were greatly concerned that oil consumption might overtake America's endowment of petroleum. This concern was due in no small part to the major role that petroleum had played in World War I: 80 percent of the total used had come from U.S. fields.[14] Contributing to and augmenting this fear was the record petroleum consumption of the automobile age, when the demand for gasoline overtook the traditional (and growing) demand for kerosene and fuel oil. The result was a spate of federal

---

[9]30 Stat. 151 (1897).

[10]See Hidy and Hidy, *Pioneering in Big Business*, p. 235.

[11]W. W. Thornton, *The Law Relating to Oil and Gas*, vol. 1 (Cincinnati: W. H. Anderson Co., 1925), p. 121.

[12]Hidy and Hidy, *Pioneering in Big Business*, p. 452.

[13]Ibid., pp. 452–53.

[14]Edward Chester, *United States Oil Policy and Diplomacy* (Westport, Conn.: Greenwood Press, 1983), p. 5.

activity that preceded protectionist programs in oversupply periods and, later, subsidy programs in short-supply periods.

Following the advice of the head of the U.S. Geological Survey, George Otis Smith, who warned of an imminent exhaustion of oil reserves, President Theodore Roosevelt in 1909 and 1910 withdrew millions of acres of oil-laden government lands in the western United States for future development. As part of the conservation effort, four Naval Petroleum Reserves were withdrawn from private development in California, Wyoming, and Alaska between 1912 and 1923 and reserved for later use by the U.S. Navy. Federal officials, also in the name of conservation, established the Petroleum Division within the Bureau of Mines in 1915 and began subsidizing oil research two years later. In 1924, President Calvin Coolidge created the Federal Oil Conservation Board to "study the government's responsibilities [and] enlist the full cooperation of representatives of the oil industry [to] safeguard the national security through conservation of our oil."[15]

Periodic reports, sounding the conservation alarm, influenced policy decisions at the highest level. One example was a report issued in 1919 by the director of the Bureau of Mines, Van Manning, which estimated that 40 percent of the nation's oil had been spent and that within five years production would irrevocably decline.[16]

In addition to conservation through public land withdrawals and bureaucratic stipends, national leaders followed another strategy to deal with petroleum supply uncertainty. Again at the urging of Smith, Manning, World War I oil czar Mark Requa, and other government officials familiar with oil, a "vigorous national policy" commenced to encourage U.S. firms to gain foreign concessions to explore for and produce oil for importation to the United States.[17] The "open door" policy involved State Department support to gain footholds in foreign territories and neutralize unpredictable nationalistic elements. By 1920, U.S. firms had become the leading producers in Canada, Colombia, and Mexico. Development in the United States by British, Dutch, German, and French oil firms,

[15]The text of Coolidge's letter is reprinted in Samuel Pettengill, *Hot Oil: The Problem of Petroleum* (New York: Economic Forum Co., 1936), pp. 209–11.

[16]"Crude Production to Reach Maximum in Two to Five Years," *National Petroleum News*, October 29, 1919, p. 51.

[17]John Ise, *The United States Oil Policy* (New Haven: Yale University Press, 1926), p. 480.

however, was not welcomed if they did not reciprocate. Fear of unilateral control and depletion of U.S. resources by foreign powers led to inclusion of a clause in the Mineral Leasing Act of 1920 (a comprehensive federal public land leasing law written by Secretary of the Navy Josephus Daniels) barring foreign citizens from acquiring leases on public lands if U.S. individuals and firms were restricted.[18] Following a Federal Trade Commission report issued in 1923 detailing foreign oil holdings in the United States, an application to lease Indian land in Oklahoma for petroleum development by Royal Dutch Shell was denied by the Department of Interior.[19] Reciprocity requirements were the lone foreign-trade restrictions in the free-trade era of the 1920s.

Conservation of domestic reserves through international development and importation was a policy not free of controversy. With aggressive exploration in Mexico, Venezuela, Colombia, and Peru leading to major discoveries, crude exports to Gulf Coast refineries and other U.S. destinations increased from under 40 million barrels in 1918 to 130 million barrels in 1922. While this was the intention of federal oil policy, small producers tied to domestic production were less than supportive. In January 1917, the Gulf Coast Oil Producers Association unsuccessfully lobbied for a tax on Mexican crude on equity grounds, maintaining that domestic output paid taxes while imported oil bore "no share of the government's expense."[20] In 1921, an attempt at a comprehensive tariff by domestic producers was defeated by Harding administration opposition. The Mid-Continent Oil and Gas Association, which complained about the "demoralization of the oil industry . . . due to the great companies," nearly spearheaded a comprehensive tariff bill into law a year later before the strength of the opposition won out. Not only was the Harding administration staunchly against tariffs on conservation, national security, and international grounds, but importing oil companies, Southwest railroads busy with Mexican crude, New England manufacturers, shipping firms, and the U.S.

---

[18]"Citizens of another country, the laws, customs, or regulations of which, deny similar or like privileges to citizens or corporations of this country, shall not by stock ownership, stock holding, or stock control, own any interest in any lease acquired under the provisions of this act." Public Law 146, 41 Stat. 437 (1920).

[19]Harold Williamson and Arnold Daum, *The American Petroleum Industry*, vol. 2 (Evanston, Ill.: Northwestern University Press, 1963), pp. 518–19.

[20]The trade group's petition is reprinted in *Oil & Gas Journal*, January 18, 1917, p. 36.

Shipping Board (the world's largest oil consumer) lobbied against tariffs on self-interested grounds.[21]

The return of the United States from a net importing country to a net exporting country in 1923, reflecting a 47 percent decline in imports between 1922 and 1927, quelled protectionist sentiment. This would prove to be only a temporary reprieve, however, as the next section will substantiate.

The record of imports and exports in the period under study is summarized in Table 2–1 below.

Several trends and conclusions may be noted. While crude imports were cyclical, refined imports and exports and crude exports steadily increased, with few exceptions, in the 12 years under study. Increasing trade volumes (the sum of imports and exports) underscored both a growing role of the United States in the world petroleum market and product demand growth at home and abroad in the automobile age. A second observation is the return of the United States from a net importing country to a net exporting country in 1923—a change

Table 2–1

PETROLEUM IMPORTS AND EXPORTS: 1918–29
(thousand barrels per day)

Year	Crude Oil		Refined Product		Total	
	Imports	Exports	Imports	Exports	Imports	Exports
1918	103	16	3	173	107	188
1919	145	17	4	158	148	175
1920	290	25	7	192	297	218
1921	343	26	9	171	353	197
1922	357	30	16	175	373	204
1923	225	48	48	232	273	280
1924	213	50	46	271	258	321
1925	169	37	45	276	214	312
1926	165	42	57	321	223	363
1927	160	43	37	346	197	390
1928	218	52	32	372	250	423
1929	216	72	82	375	298	447

SOURCE: Energy Information Administration, U.S. Department of Energy

[21]Gerald Nash, *United States Oil Policy: 1890–1964* (Westport, Conn.: Greenwood Press, 1968), pp. 53–55.

due not only to steadily rising exports but to a decline of record imports after 1922. In the next decade, the United States would continue to export more than import but, for political reasons, would reduce its presence in the international market.

D. The Revenue Act of 1932: Rescuing Oil-State Proration

The fear of declining U.S. oil production and reserves was rudely reversed by events of the 1926–31 period. It began with the Seminole field in Oklahoma, which by mid-1927 was pouring out half a million barrels of crude oil per day. As more Oklahoma and Texas megafields were uncovered and "overproduction" drove prices down, a quest for stability began.[22] To reverse "overproduction" and falling prices, producers unsuccessfully attempted to set voluntary quotas for individual wells in the new large fields. To shore up the minicartels, proponents of production restraint and price stability sought a declaration of waste by the state conservation commissions whereby *field* production ceilings could be mandated.

A fundamental change in the meaning and practice of conservation was now taking place. Instead of conservation of domestic reserves through public land withdrawals and foreign development, the new conservation movement centered around reduced domestic output to create and maintain prices necessary to support ("conserve") marginal wells.

Spearheading the drive for proration field orders were generally major companies who gained more from higher prices for their national output than they lost from restricted output in the prorated fields. Opposed to government production orders were small independents who relied on flush output from a few wells in the prorated areas.

Field proration orders were first issued by the Oklahoma Corporation Commission and the Texas Railroad Commission in 1927 for major fields. However, as seen below, effective regulation soon required the cutbacks to extend across the state.

While domestic output reached new heights, imports, principally from South America, returned to previous highs set in the early 1920s. In 1928, crude imports increased one-third from a year before, and in 1929 product imports more than doubled. While small midcontinent producers chafed under prorated output and prices that

[22]See Norman Nordhauser, *The Quest for Stability: Domestic Oil Regulation 1917–1935* (New York: Garland Publishing, 1979).

dropped nearly by a third between 1926 and 1929, such major companies as Standard Oil (New Jersey), Standard Oil (Indiana), Gulf, and Shell offset the same problems handsomely with their import, refining, and marketing profit centers. This disparity, and the political situation surrounding it, would lead to *cumulative intervention* (that is, intervention prompted by the results of previous intervention).

Independents, feeling that their sacrificed output was being replaced by competitor imports, acrimoniously split from the American Petroleum Institute in the fall of 1929 to form the Independent Petroleum Association of America. IPAA founder Wirt Franklin, an Oklahoma producer whose own company was severely strained, stated the sentiments of the small Southwest producer:

> The true intent and purpose of those who had been fostering and promoting the so-called conservation program is to shut in domestic production and to turn the markets for petroleum in the United States over to a few large companies engaged in exploiting the petroleum reserves of South America and in importing the production thereof into the United States.[23]

While the majors sought to persuade the independents that regulation of flush output required an interstate association to bring uniformity, and hence equity, to conservation orders, the independents' legislative priority was to remove oil from the "free list." Meetings between API board members and Franklin, however, failed to find a compromise between conservation (proration) and protectionism. The majors wanted to continue to import South American crude to Atlantic refineries; the independents felt strongly they had an economic right to the same market for Gulf Coast shipments of midcontinent and Southwest crude instead.

In July 1929, hearings were held before the Senate Finance Committee on a proposal to levy a $1 per barrel tax on imported crude with an unspecified higher levy on refined product imports. The tariff proposal was sponsored by a delegation of Louisiana independent producers supported by Governor Huey Long, the Producers and Royalty Owners Association of Texas, the new-born IPAA, and the National Coal Association (founded 1917). Testimony was heard that while the posted price for crude had declined by 29 percent since 1921 to demoralize independent producers, the

---

[23]Nordhauser, *Quest for Stability*, pp. 48–49.

major Standard Oil companies were prospering as major importers, refiners, and marketers. "A failure to place a tariff on petroleum," stated E. B. Howard for the Louisiana delegation, "will be a great victory for the Standard Oil Company and of practically no benefit to any other American citizen."[24]

Although traditional opposition to oil tariffs kept the independents from victory, continuing price pressure from increasing imports on the one hand and domestic proration on the other increased the resolve of independents to reach their legislative goal. After Jersey Standard and New York Standard lowered posted crude prices in early 1930, "Mr. Independent Oil" Wirt Franklin called a mass meeting in Tulsa, Oklahoma, to mobilize support and raise $100,000 for a lobbying effort in the nation's capital. Several days later, over two hundred midcontinent and Southwest producers boarded a chartered train for Washington, D.C., to personally plead their case. The Hawley-Smoot Tariff Act was under debate, and the independents wanted oil included with the myriad other articles that were about to receive protective duties. The political novices, however, were no match for the counterlobbying of the big internationals— Gulf, the Standard companies, and Royal-Dutch Shell.[25] Three tariff proposals were defeated in the Senate. The final one, a watered-down demand for a $0.40 per barrel crude oil fee and a 20 percent *ad valorem* product tax applicable only if the posted price was below $1.50 per barrel and if gasoline in the New York area was under $0.20 per gallon, lost by a close vote.

Domestic proration by the Texas Railroad Commission and the Oklahoma Corporation Commission expanded from field orders to statewide orders in 1930 to end the practice of unregulated output increasing to fill the gap created by the prorated fields. The situation was far from "fixed," however, by expanded regulation. In late 1930, the East Texas field was discovered, and with well after well striking oil in shallow pockets over a several-hundred-mile area, it was realized that the largest contiguous oil reservoir in the United States had been found. Controlling the East Texas field to stabilize

[24]A. E. Heiss, "Standard and Other Big Companies Lead in Opposing Tariff, is Claimed," *National Petroleum News*, July 24, 1929, p. 23.

[25]For a description of the Washington, D.C., excursion and controversy surrounding the independents' lobbying effort, see the reprint of Wirt Franklin's Senate speech in *National Petroleum News*, March 26, 1930, pp. 32–33, and "IPAA's First Trip to Capitol Hill," *Petroleum Independent*, February 1979, pp. 30–34.

prices was a task that took five years of arduous effort by the Texas Railroad Commission, federal regulators, and supportive industry groups. The Oklahoma City field simultaneously created difficulties for the Oklahoma Corporation Commission, although these were not as great as the problems encountered in the East Texas "hot oil" war. But these efforts would have been futile had it not been for another piece of the cartelization puzzle. Output restriction that had gone from the well to the field to statewide had to go to the international border to quiet the flow of crude and product imports that constituted an "East Texas" in its own right.

The close call with an oil tariff in 1930 increased the conciliatory mood of the importing majors. In early 1931, with proration entering its most crucial phase with the East Texas field, the aforementioned four majors, accounting for 95 percent of imports, announced a voluntary plan to reduce their export shipments to the United States between 25 and 50 percent. Negotiating the effort was Secretary of Commerce Robert Lamont, appointed by President Herbert Hoover for the task. The motivation of the majors was to win independent support for market-demand proration during a desperate hour. In 1931, not only did imports drop noticeably from a year earlier—24 percent for crude oil and 11 percent for products—the IPAA's debt of $40,000 was quietly retired by some of the same major companies.[26] A principal lobbyist for one of the importing majors underscored the political quid pro quo when he stated to the independents that "our cooperation [with import restraint] will be as permanent as your cooperation [with domestic proration]."[27]

The compromise of 1931 would not be enough because of the huge production emanating from the Southwest. The East Texas field, which after seven months of open production was approaching a million barrels per day (over one-third of national output), was declared a military zone, placed under martial law, and shut in by Texas governor Ross Sterling, former chairman of Humble Oil. Humble, an affiliate of Jersey Standard, was the most active company in the field with more than a thousand wells. Leading the troops in East Texas was the general counsel of Texaco, Jacob Walters. Only two weeks before (August 14, 1931), Oklahoma governor

---

[26]William Kemnitzer, *Rebirth of Monopoly: A Critical Analysis of Economic Control in the Petroleum Industry of the United States* (New York: Harper & Brothers, 1938), p. 135.

[27]Nordhauser, *Quest for Stability*, p. 79.

William Murray took the same drastic action with the Oklahoma City and Seminole fields, which he vowed not to reopen until "we get dollar oil."[28]

After the fields reopened under strict allowables, enforcement problems continued to frustrate the price goals of the state governments, federal officials, and industry supporters. Under such pressure, just about any quantity of imports was controversial. A tariff was still to come.

Although a tariff was again rejected by the Senate in 1931, political support for a duty intensified. In March, the governors of Oklahoma, Texas, Kansas, and New Mexico formed the Oil States Advisory Committee to lobby President Hoover to negotiate import reductions with the major importers and pass a protective tariff. The former was accomplished through Commerce Secretary Lamont; the latter was accomplished on June 6, 1932, when Hoover signed the Revenue Act of 1932, which taxed oil and other imported goods to close a then-record federal budget deficit. Effective June 22, imported crude and heavy oil products not destined for export were taxed at $0.21 per barrel, gasoline at $1.05 per barrel, and lubricating oils at $1.68 per barrel.[29]

The loss for U.S. consumers, the importing majors, and foreign countries from the tariff was the gain of four constituencies. For domestic wellhead interests, a crude tariff comprising 25 percent of the posted price equalized the transportation-adjusted cost advantage of foreign crude and reinforced the major importers' voluntary quota. For independent refiners, the sizable product tariff differential offered a protective barrier against imported products that were streaming to the United States from several 200,000 barrel per day U.S.-owned refineries in South America and elsewhere. For oil-state governments, more domestic output at higher prices meant more royalty revenue and severance tax income. And for the federal government, the act was the "bill-which-balanced-the-budget."[30] But even the majors' loss was offset by domestic refinery protection, and proration would be reluctantly and controversially supported by the independents—particularly as they began to organize politically to shape it their way.

---

[28]Ruth Knowles, *The Greatest Gamblers* (New York: McGraw-Hill, 1959), p. 265.

[29]47 Stat. 169 at 259–60 (1932).

[30]George Stocking, "Stabilization of the Oil Industry: Its Economic and Legal Aspects," *American Economic Review*, March 1933, p. 62.

On September 2, 1933, a formal quota for oil and oil products under the National Recovery Act joined the tariff and voluntary quota. Section IV of the Code of Fair Competition for the Production Industry tied import ceilings to the volume imported during the second half of 1932 as part of an overall supply allocation plan administered by the Petroleum Administration Board. The PAB quota averaged 98,000 barrels per day, an amount that constituted about 4.5 percent of national consumption. The quota, aided by the tariff, was adhered to without the necessity of resorting to individual firm allocations.[31]

The new quota was restrictive. Imports in the base period were depressed, not only by the tariff and the voluntary quota but by the fact that imports were abnormally high during the first half of that year in anticipation of the midyear restriction.

The *Schecter* decision of May 1935 annulled the quota (along with the rest of the National Recovery Act) to leave the voluntary quota and the tariff as the barriers to imports.[32] With the help of a reclassification to close a product loophole, the tariff had its intended effect of continuing what began with the quota compromise of 1931. Imports in the 1930s, particularly crude but also product, would not reach previous highs set in the preprotectionist era; exports, however, increased as a result of growing domestic refinery investments and the escape valve of foreign markets for hot oil in addition to legally produced oil. Nonetheless, exports, like imports, would have been substantially *higher* without the trade barriers—to the benefit of both the industry and world oil consumers. As it was, foreign crude and product displaced from U.S. markets were diverted to markets formerly served by U.S. exports.[33]

Yearly trade volumes from 1930 to 1938 are summarized in Table 2–2 below.

Compared to the last free-trade year of 1929, crude imports declined first from the voluntary quota in 1930–31, second from the tariff in

[31]Northcutt Ely, "The Government in the Exercise of the Power over Foreign Commerce," in *Conservation of Oil & Gas*, ed. Blakely Murphy (Chicago: American Bar Association, 1949), p. 657.

[32]*Schecter Poultry Corp.* v. *United States*, 295 U.S. 495 (1935).

[33]For an example involving gasoline, see A. E. Mockler, "World Gasoline Trade Shifting with Protective Legislation by Various Countries a Factor," *Oil & Gas Journal*, November 3, 1932, p. 13. For a case of a foreign refinery sale between U.S. firms to replace U.S. product sales with foreign sales, see C. C. McDermond, "U.S. Tariff Has Little Effect on Venezuela's Output," *Oil Weekly*, January 30, 1933, p. 14.

Table 2–2

PETROLEUM IMPORTS AND EXPORTS: 1930–38
(thousand barrels per day)

Year	Crude Oil Imports	Crude Oil Exports	Refined Oil Imports	Refined Oil Exports	Total Imports	Total Exports
1930	170	65	119	364	289	429
1931	129	70	106	271	236	341
1932	122	75	81	208	204	282
1933	87	100	37	192	124	292
1934	97	113	41	201	138	314
1935	88	141	56	212	144	353
1936	88	137	68	224	156	361
1937	75	184	81	289	157	474
1938	72	212	76	319	149	531

SOURCE: Energy Information Administration, U.S. Department of Energy

1932, and third from the NRA quota in 1933. As theory would suggest, product imports also dropped significantly owing to major trade barriers. Exports, on the other hand, had a mixed fate. Despite tariffs and quotas that usually hurt exports as much as imports, crude oil exports increased significantly in the period. The reason was that other things were not equal; the huge East Texas field and the general "oversupply" situation allowed U.S. crude to outcompete foreign crude kept from the U.S. market. The consequence of import restrictions on exports was more clearly evident with *oil products*, however. Product exports fell over 40 percent between 1929 and 1935 before recovering to 85 percent of preprotectionism levels in 1938.

An unambiguous result of 1930s protectionism was a diminution of the United States in the world petroleum market. With the drop in crude oil and refined imports and the drop in product exports, the United States substantially reduced its role in the world market, reaching its nadir in 1933. The level of oil trade in 1933 plummeted to less than one-half of 1929 levels before recovering to 91 percent by 1938. Without protectionism, import growth from foreign investments and significant export growth from prolific Southwest production would have increased, not decreased, U.S. participation in the world oil trade. The intended and unintended effects of foreign-trade restrictions were not to be denied.

In the 1939–49 period, the United States relaxed some of the trade barriers created the decade before. Unlike the situation earlier in the decade, market-demand proration was politically and operationally secure, and marginally expanded imports were not seen as threatening.

The Trade Agreements Act of 1934, strongly endorsed by Secretary of State Cordell Hull, who favored expanded world trade, allowed the president to lower tariffs by 50 percent in exchange for similar concessions abroad.[34] In 1939, a reciprocal trade agreement with Venezuela, the leading oil exporter to the United States, reduced tariffs on crude, topped crude, fuel oil, and gas oil by 50 percent for quantities below 5 percent of U.S. supply.[35] The Netherlands and territories, Colombia, and other smaller areas qualified with Venezuela for the reduction. As a result, imports surged from under 5 percent to nearly 7 percent of domestic output. In 1943, the reduction was extended to volumes above 5 percent, introduced for kerosene and liquid asphalt, and granted to Mexico.[36] Gasoline and lubricants, however, remained under the sizable tariffs established in 1932, and both the 1939 and 1943 revisions contained "escape clauses" to revert to 1932 duty rates. Independent refiners still enjoyed a higher product differential, and the independent producer lobby was keeping protectionism alive in anticipation of a postwar return to prorated output and price instability.

World War II and the abrupt switch from supply restrictions to supply maximization did not result in tariff reduction or repeal. The problem faced by oil imports was not the remnants of the Revenue Act of 1932 but safe transportation from German submarines. Wartime planning would be primarily concerned with regulating exports as part of a supply control program, while federal officials worked to increase oil output and gain new concessions in foreign lands.[37]

In 1947, with concern over supply availability continuing to predominate over overproduction and price stability, a third reduction in the 1932 tariff occurred. The General Agreement on Tariffs and Trade (GATT), signed by the United States and 22 other countries, reduced the gasoline and lubricant duties by half and stated that

[34]48 Stat. 943 (1934).

[35]54 Stat. 2375 (1939).

[36]57 Stat. 833 (1943).

[37]See John Frey and H. Chandler Ide, *A History of the Petroleum Administration for War* (Washington, D.C.: Government Printing Office, 1946), pp. 24–25, 250–87.

"in no event shall the rate of import tax . . . to topped crude petroleum, or fuel oil devised from petroleum, be less than the rate of such tax applicable to crude petroleum."[38] The importance of this reduction was stated by IPAA general counsel Russell Brown when he retrospectively stated that "for thirteen years the tariff proved a great help."[39]

In 1950, trade liberalization went the other way when the Mexican Trade Agreement of 1943 expired, causing this country's oil tariff structure to revert to rates set in the Venezuelan Trade Agreement of 1939.[40] However, a supplemental trade bill with Venezuela in 1952 lowered tariffs by half to $0.0525 per barrel for crude oil and residual oil under 25° API gravity, and these provisions also applied to Mexico.[41]

The result of trade liberalization in the decade under review, shown in Table 2–3 below, was a surge of crude imports after the

Table 2–3
PETROLEUM IMPORTS AND EXPORTS: 1939–49
(thousand barrels per day)

Year	Crude Oil		Refined Product		Total	
	Imports	Exports	Imports	Exports	Imports	Exports
1939	91	197	71	323	162	520
1940	117	141	112	216	229	356
1941	139	91	127	207	266	298
1942	34	93	65	228	99	320
1943	38	113	136	298	174	411
1944	122	94	130	474	252	567
1945	204	90	108	411	311	501
1946	236	116	141	303	377	420
1947	267	127	169	324	437	451
1948	353	109	161	259	514	367
1949	421	91	224	236	645	327

SOURCE: Energy Information Administration, U.S. Department of Energy

[38]61 Stat. Volume 5, Schedule XX (1947).

[39]Fanning, *Story of the American Petroleum Institute*, p. 136.

[40]15 *Federal Register* 6063, September 9, 1950; 16 *Federal Register* 109, January 5, 1951.

[41]Douglas Bohi and Milton Russell, *Limiting Oil Imports: An Economic History and Analysis* (Baltimore: Johns Hopkins University Press, 1978), p. 231.

early World War II transportation problems were overcome. Product exports peaked in 1944 and 1945 before settling at prewar levels in the postwar period. The 1948 shift from a net exporting nation to a net importing nation (for the first time since 1922) began a trend that would accelerate in the postwar period and beyond.

Also evident with the relaxation of trade barriers was a resurgence of the United States in the world petroleum market. Total international oil trade involving the United States, the sum of imports and exports, reached nearly a million barrels per day in 1949, the highest to that point.

E. Discontent and "Voluntary" Import Restrictions: 1949–58

Near-shortages of fuel oil, attributable to a government anti-inflation campaign exhorting oil companies to "hold the line" on prices, lingered until early 1948 but marked the final stanza of the scarcity era. For the next 23 years, the domestic upstream industry again would be engaged in an arduous quest to maintain price levels.

In response to (regulatory-induced) domestic supply problems, imports almost tripled between 1944 and 1949. Consequently, the United States became a net oil importer for the first time since the early 1920s. With a postwar drilling and production boom, the Texas Railroad Commission and other state agencies began to lower allowables below the "maximum efficient rate," a telltale sign of a reestablished buyer's market. Also in 1949, the IPAA reverted to old ways and appealed to Congress for new protectionist legislation based on national security:

> The nation's security and welfare of these many independent producers, their employees, and suppliers cannot be made subservient to the will of the ten principal importing companies. . . . Petroleum reserves may be developed and refining facilities may be built in the theaters of future hostilities, but those will be of little value in time of war.[42]

In 1930, Wirt Franklin supplemented his antimonopoly tune by raising the national security argument, which was hypothetical at best. In the post–World War II period, the same argument seemed to have some basis in fact. National security, however, was a broad

---

[42]Quoted in Stuart Long, "The Oil Men's War," *The Nation*, September 17, 1949, p. 272.

and nebulous argument with different implications. For regulatory advocates, it not only meant restricting imports to keep the domestic industry at a high level of activity but prorating output from flush wells to create prices necessary to preserve marginal wells should a sudden event require their contribution. For others, as will be seen, conservation meant welcoming imports to husband domestic reserves and predicating the domestic producing industry on flush-well output. Norman Nordhauser has remarked that conservation "was a ubiquitous word, a word which appeared over and over again in the rationalization offered by government officials and industry leaders for the policy for the moment, be it laissez-faire or government sponsored planning."[43] So was, and so would be, "national security."

The period from 1949 until 1958 was a winter of discontent for domestic producers. Inflation, particularly pronounced in the post–World War II and Korean conflict periods, reduced tariffs in real terms, thus contributing to record imports of both crude and products. In the early 1950s, independents—through the IPAA and local and state organizations—increasingly pressed for tariffs; in this they were joined by coal interests and a Texas citizen group interested in maintaining public sector programs dependent on oil revenue.[44] The 81st Congress (1949–50), strongly influenced by the oil-state delegation, conducted three investigations, and the Federal Trade Commission another, to see if imports were injuring independent domestic producers. In M. A. Adelman's estimation, "All four groups failed to uncover any respectable evidence" but "not for lack of effort."[45] Although legislation was not imminent, governmental suasion came into play when the Small Business Committee of the House of Representatives called for voluntary import restrictions. The major accomplishment of the flurry of congressional interest, however, was to bring imports out into the open; who the importers were and how much, when, and from where they were importing—all was now part of the public record.[46]

Petroleum demands of the Korean conflict swung concern away

[43]Nordhauser, *Quest for Stability*, p. 163.

[44]"Imports Roundup," *Oil & Gas Journal*, February 2, 1950, p. 25; *The Nation*, April 22, 1950, p. 358.

[45]M. A. Adelman, *The World Petroleum Market* (Baltimore: Johns Hopkins University Press, 1972), p. 150.

[46]Ibid.

from the independents' complaints, but by 1953 they were back on the offensive. The Texas Railroad Commission entered the picture in January 1953 by requiring importers to keep meticulous records of both their actual and planned imports. Such information, now part of the market-demand process for determining allowables, was more than simple estimating and reporting. Noted Adelman:

> The large importers . . . made [their] intentions known to all the others in advance in great detail. These reports constituted an agreement between the commission and each importer to limit imports, which amounted also to an agreement among the importers themselves. The subsequent record of actual imports constituted a compliance report.[47]

As a result, the major importers, attuned not only to the Texas Railroad Commission's import reports but to the independents' plight as market-demand proration factors fell to new lows in Texas, Oklahoma, Louisiana, Kansas, and New Mexico, began voluntarily to curb imports.[48]

Unlike the situation in 1932, the tariff drive in the 1950s found the federal government cautious and deliberate. In the fifth year of the IPAA's drive (1954), President Dwight Eisenhower established a cabinet-level Committee on Energy Supplies and Resources Policy to study oil demand and supply conditions "with an aim of strengthening the national defense, providing orderly industrial growth, and assuring supplies for our expanding national economy and for any future emergency."[49] In February 1955, the Committee recommended that crude and fuel oil be restrained to previous-year levels and hinted at mandatory controls should voluntary controls

---

[47]Ibid., p. 152.

[48]In the 1950s, market-demand proration factors fell from 71 percent to 33 percent in Texas, from 93 percent to 33 percent in Louisiana, from 30 percent to 23 percent in Oklahoma, and from 74 percent to 50 percent in New Mexico. Source: Respective State Conservation Commissions.

[49]Quoted in William Peterson, *The Question of Governmental Oil Import Restrictions* (Washington, D.C.: American Enterprise Association, 1959), p. 18. The year 1954 was a turning point for the independent producers' effort even without Eisenhower's concession. In this year, a ruling was made by federal officials that domestic watchmakers required protection from their Swiss counterparts on national security grounds. This led IPAA general counsel Russell Brown, "quick to see the advantage, [to hitch] the IPAA's star to 'national security.' Indeed lobbyists from every other domestic industry rushed to Washington to get on the 'national security' bandwagon." Fanning, *Story of the American Petroleum Institute*, p. 138.

fail. "As a result," Adelman concluded, "the work of the Texas Railroad Commission was taken over by the Office of Defense Mobilization."[50]

Several importers, led by Jersey Standard, announced cooperation with the Committee finding and continued their previous policy of voluntary import restraint. In the same year the government stepped closer to formal protectionism by enacting standby authority for the president to "adjust" imports on national security grounds. Section 7 of the Reciprocal Trade Agreements Extension Act of 1955 provided that

> whenever the Director of the Office of Defense Mobilization has reason to believe that any article is being imported into the United States in such quantities as to threaten to impair the national security, he shall so advise the President, and if the President agrees that there is reason for such belief, the President shall cause an immediate investigation to be made to determine the facts. If, on the basis of such investigation . . . the President finds that the article is being imported into the United States in such quantities as to threaten to impair the national security, he shall take such action as he deems necessary to adjust the imports of such articles to a level that will not threaten to impair the national security.[51]

Over the next five years, with the "club in the closet," the federal government embarked on a more formal "voluntary" program to limit oil imports. It began in late 1955 with import data requests and specific reduction requests from the Office of Defense Mobilization. When imports continued to rise, primarily as a result of new entry by importers (some of whom had no domestic output to worry about) and major new Canadian crude capacity, the IPAA and 18 other domestic producer organizations petitioned the ODM to activate Section 7 of the Reciprocal Trade Agreements Extension Act. On April 23, 1957, the month tanker traffic resumed on the Suez Canal to end the Suez crisis, the ODM issued a finding to President Eisenhower that crude was being imported in quantities threatening to impair national security. Eisenhower in turn appointed a Special Committee to Investigate Crude Oil Imports, which on July 29 of the same year warned that "excessive . . . reliance [on imported crude] in the short run may put the nation in a long-term vulnerable

---

[50]Adelman, *World Petroleum Market*, p. 153.
[51]69 Stat. 162 (1955).

position."[52] In response, a second phase of voluntary import controls was implemented by the newly created Oil Import Administration. The de facto planning effort divided the country into five PAD districts, named for the Petroleum Administration for Defense, which during the Korean conflict used the geographic divisions for regulatory purposes. A quota of 90 percent of 1954–56 import quantities was assigned for seven "established" importers (Atlantic, Esso, Gulf, Mobil, Sinclair, SoCal, and Texaco), and a residual corresponding to present (July 1957) import levels was divided among 15 newer importers. This applied to the entire country except for the West Coast area (District V), which was vitally dependent on imports to meet demand.

It would not be long before the program fell victim to market pressures—self-interest by another name. The phase-in period was bombarded by requests for exceptions. Some imports that normally came through Districts I–IV (East of the Rockies) came through less-scrutinized District V instead. Savvy importers brought in slightly refined oil that was just enough "crude" to escape higher product tariffs but just enough "product" to escape the crude quota. New firms entered to import crude with and without permission from the Oil Import Board. At the same time, output in Kuwait in particular and the Persian Gulf in general was rapidly increasing, thus keeping the import pressure on.

To combat these problems, loopholes were closed, and new laws were enacted to strong-arm compliance. The Trade Agreements Act of 1958 empowered the president to ensure compliance.[53] The Buy American Act of 1933 was amended to require firms that sold oil to the U.S. government, the world's largest single oil-consuming entity, to have a Certificate of Compliance from the Oil Import Administration.[54] But these measures were too little and too late. Noncompliance was quickly spreading, since imported foreign oil was nearly 20 percent cheaper on a landed basis than domestic crude.[55] At the end of 1958, imports jumped by more than one-third to exceed a

---

[52]Quoted in William Barber, "The Eisenhower Energy Policy: Reluctant Intervention," in *Energy Policy in Perspective*, ed. Craufurd Goodwin (Washington, D.C.: Brookings Institution, 1981), p. 239.

[53]72 Stat. 673 (1958).

[54]23 *Federal Register* 2067, March 28, 1958.

[55]See Kenneth Dam, "Implementation of Import Quotas: The Case of Oil," *The Journal of Law and Economics*, April 1971, p. 11.

million barrels of oil per day. Threatened producers demanded another national security finding, and on February 27, 1959, the Office of Defense Mobilization reported that "crude oil and the principal crude oil derivatives and products are being imported in such quantities and under such circumstances as to threaten to impair the national security."[56] A new phase of oil protectionism was set to begin.

The record of imports and exports in the "winter of discontent" is summarized in Table 2-4 below.

The statistics of the period show an unrelenting increase in crude and product imports in absolute and net (of exports) terms. Exports grew unevenly until falling off dramatically in 1958. Aggregate imports and exports set new highs throughout, primarily reflecting growing domestic and world demand for oil products.

While the above import growth appears to suggest an open-trade situation, it should be remembered that de facto import regulation was present. Without informal import regulation from 1949 forward, imports (and exports) would have been *higher* than actually

Table 2–4
PETROLEUM IMPORTS AND EXPORTS: 1950–58
(thousand barrels per day)

Year	Crude Oil Imports	Crude Oil Exports	Refined Product Imports	Refined Product Exports	Total Imports	Total Exports
1950	487	95	363	210	850	305
1951	491	78	354	344	844	422
1952	573	73	380	359	952	432
1953	648	55	386	347	1,034	402
1954	656	37	396	318	1,052	355
1955	782	32	466	336	1,248	368
1956	934	78	502	352	1,436	430
1957	1,023	138	552	430	1,574	568
1958	953	12	747	264	1,700	276

SOURCE: Energy Information Administration, U.S. Department of Energy

[56]Reprinted in Cabinet Task Force on Oil Import Control, *The Oil Import Question* (Washington, D.C.: Government Printing Office, 1970), pp. 207–10.

experienced.[57] The sharp drop in exports in 1958 signified that more than free-market forces were at work.

F. The Mandatory Oil Import Program: 1959–73

On March 10, 1959, President Eisenhower, under pressure from the independent lobby, imposed mandatory oil import quotas by executive order.[58] His decision was not without reservation. In a cabinet meeting where he made his decision, Eisenhower expressed concern about the "tendencies of special interests in the United States to press almost irresistibly for special programs" which were "in conflict with the basic requirement on the United States to promote increased trade in the world."[59] The unfolding turns and consequences of this decision, like another reluctant decision to not deregulate natural gas production sold in interstate commerce three years before, would be cause for regret.

The Mandatory Oil Import Program (MOIP) began as a "clean" program; it had relatively uniform standards rather than politically tailored ones. The 50 states were divided, as they were under the voluntary program, into five PAD Districts. In Districts I through IV, imports of crude and all oil products except residual fuel oil were limited to the lower of 1957 levels or 9 percent of total demand, as estimated semiannually by the Bureau of Mines in the Department of the Interior. Quotas for residual fuel oil were subject to the discretion of the Secretary of the Interior, a concession to the Northeast and a precaution against the near-shortages that occurred after World War II. District V, covering the area west of the Rockies, was more leniently treated. Crude and finished products were allowed to be imported in quantities equal to 1957 volumes. Unfinished oil, on the other hand, could not exceed 10 percent of allowed crude and product imports. Puerto Rico, outside the PAD Districts, was given a straight quota of 1958 import volumes for all petroleum,

---

[57]M. A. Adelman has commented: "Imports into the United States have never been free since World War II. No company was free to consult its own interests and its own profit. To suppose that the mandatory oil import program of 1959 forced the world oil industry into surplus, or did anything but hold the line, ignores the documented record." *World Petroleum Market*, p. 155. This statement can be amended to begin in 1949 rather than 1946.

[58]Proclamation 3279, "Adjusting Imports of Petroleum and Petroleum Products into the United States," 24 *Federal Register* 1781, March 12, 1959.

[59]Quoted in Barber, "The Eisenhower Energy Policy: Reluctant Intervention," *Energy Policy in Perspective*, p. 251.

subject to changing demand. All firms had to obtain import licenses from the Oil Import Administration in the Department of the Interior.

Determining aggregate quotas was only the beginning of the regulatory decision-making. The quotas had to be allocated among firms. The decision was reached to allocate 80 percent of allowables to historic importers and distribute the remaining 20 percent to nonimporting (inland) refiners. The "sliding scale" allocation favored small refiners, ranging from 12 percent of throughput for refineries under 10,000 barrels per day to 4 percent for refineries over 300,000 barrels per day in Districts I–IV. In District V, the bias was even more skewed toward small facilities.[60] This bias began a series of government subsidies to small refiners that would continue until 1981.

Quota tickets distributed to nonimporting inland refiners could not be sold for cash to coastal importing refiners. This would quantify the subsidy and forgone consumer benefit to detract from the "national security" basis of the program. Noncash trading also prevented third-party speculation with quota tickets. Instead, quota rights had to be used by the original recipients, whether, as explained below, with virgin imported oil or domestic oil obtained in an exchange with a coastal refiner.

To avoid unloading and transportation costs, inland refineries would exchange their quota of foreign crude for inland crude sold by the coastal importing refiners. If the coastal refiner did not have its own crude near the refiner from whom it was utilizing the quota ticket, an additional step was necessary to effectuate the swap. First, the inland refiner sold crude at an interconnected point to the coastal refiner, whereupon the latter sold foreign crude to the former, who officially imported the oil. Then the final transaction—the exchange—was made: the inland refiner gave the foreign crude to the coastal refiner as "domestic" crude and received back "imported" crude run with the quota ticket. All legal and logistical requirements were thus met, and "the biggest spate of horse trading in the history of the oil business" ensued.[61]

---

[60]The sliding scale concept was credited to Under Secretary of Commerce Frederick Mueller and State Department consultant Herbert Hoover, Jr. Barber, "The Eisenhower Energy Policy: Reluctant Intervention," *Energy Policy in Perspective*, pp. 245–46.

[61]Henry Ralph, "Crude Oil Men Are Having a Field Day," *Oil & Gas Journal*, April 27, 1959, p. 83.

Because cheaper foreign crude demanded a premium over domestic crude adjusted for quality and location, inland refiners received more barrels in the exchange. This was the small-refiner subsidy that characterized the small-business bias of the program. One economist, calculating exchange differentials and using an estimate by an involved company, pegged the subsidy at between $0.65 and $1.25 per barrel.[62]

For a variety of reasons, which pointed out its vulnerable underbelly, the program did not restrict imports to anticipated levels in its first few years. A combination of industry ingenuity and political modification that created regulatory gaps was responsible for this outcome.

The negative impact of the protectionist program on Western Hemisphere exporters to the United States, in light of an obvious lack of national defense justification, led to the first major exemption for petroleum "entering the United States by pipeline, motor carriers or rail from the country of production."[63] This helped not only Canada and Mexico but also Venezuela. In eastern Canada, Canadian crude, which was displaced from U.S. markets, was threatening to crowd out Venezuelan crude, thus adding to the latter's North American problems under the quota program.

The creation of a regulatory gap only five weeks into the program would have both predicted and unpredicted consequences. Canadian imports resumed their traditional role with northern tier U.S. refineries. But given the profit opportunities of the artificial situation, both Canadian and Mexican imports rose well above pre-MOIP levels. In one of the most striking circumventions of regulatory constraints in U.S. history, Mexico increased its U.S. exports sixfold, despite an absence of overland transportation facilities. In 1961, a routine began whereby Mexican residual oil was shipped by tanker to Brownsville, Texas, unloaded for export (thus making it exempt from the quota), trucked across the Mexican border, trucked back after a U-turn, and reloaded on tankers for East Coast delivery. The "Brownsville shuffle" was tolerated by U.S. author-

---

[62]Torleif Meloe, *United States Control of Petroleum Imports* (New York: Arno Press, 1968, 1979), p. 245.

[63]Proclamation 3290, 24 *Federal Register* 3527, May 2, 1959.

ities who feared that without exploitation of the overland exemption, PEMEX oil would go to communist Cuba.[64]

Other factors kept imports high despite program intentions. Residual fuel oil imports, which were separately regulated to appease District I (East Coast) political interests, were leniently treated. Overestimated demand for District V by the Bureau of Mines allowed incremental imports, which in turn made their way to more restricted eastern districts. By selling domestic oil, furthermore, additional imports were allowed to make up the deficit between demand and available supply. In the first year alone under the MOIP, petroleum sales between District V and Districts I–IV doubled.[65] Increased natural gas liquids production, which was counted as domestic output to increase the quota, liberalized allowable imports. Refineries were constructed in Puerto Rico, which was a mini free-trade zone, for quota-free importation to the contiguous United States. Finally, the Oil Import Appeals Board, made up of representatives from the departments of Interior, Defense, and Commerce, permitted special quotas for firms demonstrating "hardship, error, or other relevant consideration." These adjustments were subtracted from the aggregate quota to leave other firms with less allowables, but the aggregate quota was simultaneously increasing. Other factors, such as military purchases abroad and overestimated refinery runs to secure more quota tickets, kept the ratio of imports to domestic production higher than the statistics showed.

These leaks in the dike doubled crude imports as a percentage of domestic production in the first two years of the program. Product imports, led by residual fuel oil (which jumped 45 percent between 1958 and 1962), were substantially higher. "The victory for the producing interests represented by the mandatory program," commented Douglas Bohi and Milton Russell, "was slipping away."[66]

In a protectionist counterattack, program revisions in the 1960–65 period succeeded primarily in closing loopholes. This did more

[64]Eventually Mexico would be granted a quota to end what was also called "el loophole," but to aid Brownsville's unemployment problem, the requirement remained that oil had to be unloaded and reloaded on tankers for the East Coast trip. See Bohi and Russell, *Limiting Oil Imports*, pp. 132–34.

[65]Rene Manes, *The Effects of United States Oil Import Policy on the Petroleum Industry* (New York: Arno Press, 1961, 1979), pp. 111, 139–42.

[66]Bohi and Russell, *Limiting Oil Imports*, p. 107. For the IPAA's defensive political agenda, see Manes, *Effects of United States Oil Import Policy on the Petroleum Industry*, p. 143.

to bring the program to the new realities facing it than to actually reduce imports. The 9-percent-of-domestic-demand quota was replaced with a 12.2 percent quota.[67] Several rule changes restricted opportunistic District V sales east to Districts I–IV.[68] A quota was established for residual fuel oil and Puerto Rican crude imports and product exports to the United States.[69] The overland exemption was brought within the aggregate 12.2 percent ceiling.[70] Stability, however, would not follow these tightening amendments. Political pressures created the program; political pressures would continue to modify it.

The third and final phase of the Mandatory Oil Import Program, before changed market conditions made quotas obsolete, was characterized by increasing complexity. The quota pie would be divided into more slices as more constituencies invaded the program, while the purported goal of national security became more distant.

In 1966, petrochemical plants were granted quotas for foreign oil to put them on a more equal footing not only with refineries but with themselves.[71] Nearly 40 percent of U.S. petrochemical plants had already received quotas because of their refining facilities— and now they all had quotas. Puerto Rico and the Virgin Islands received preferential quotas to aid economic development.[72] "Bonus" quotas were awarded to refineries across the country that distilled low-sulfur residual fuel oil.[73] Inflation concerns and consumer pressure for lower prices led to relaxed quotas for fuel oil in District I, and asphalt and home heating (#2) oil across the entire country.

The above administrative changes led to broader thoughts about the quota program itself. After a decade of experience, neither proponents nor opponents of protectionism were satisfied. National security was a tired theme that aroused little fervor.

In the spring of 1969, President Richard Nixon called for a thor-

---

[67]Proclamation 3509, 27 *Federal Register* 11985, December 5, 1962.

[68]Proclamation 3541, 28 *Federal Register* 5931, June 13, 1963; Manes, *Effects of United States Oil Import Policy on the Petroleum Industry*, pp. 141–42.

[69]Proclamation 3389, 26 *Federal Register* 507, January 20, 1961; 30 *Federal Register* 15459, December 16, 1965.

[70]Proclamation 3509, 27 *Federal Register* 11985, December 5, 1962.

[71]Proclamation 3693, 30 *Federal Register* 15459, December 16, 1965.

[72]Proclamation 3693, 30 *Federal Register* 15461, December 16, 1965; Proclamation 3820, 32 *Federal Register* 15701, November 15, 1967.

[73]Proclamation 3994, 32 *Federal Register* 10547, July 19, 1967.

oughgoing study of the program. The result was a recommendation that quotas be scrapped in favor of tariffs (or, more precisely, an increase in the tariffs established in the Revenue Act of 1932).[74] In the debate that followed, the IPAA and the Texas Independent Producers and Royalty Owners Association argued that whatever the choice between tariffs and quotas, protectionism was essential for the domestic industry. With increasing inflation and Nixon's price control program in August 1971, however, the price effects of protectionism came under increased scrutiny. In 1971 and 1972, the quota program was further liberalized, and the end seemed near. Market-demand factors in Texas, Oklahoma, Louisiana, and several other states increased toward "maximum efficient rate" production for the first time since World War II, and consumer interests were stepping up the attack on protectionism. On April 18, 1973, President Nixon ended speculation with the following announcement:

> The current Mandatory Oil Import Program is of virtually no benefit any longer. Instead, it has the very real potential of aggravating our supply problems, and it denies us the flexibility we need to deal quickly and efficiently with our import requirements.[75]

Another phase of import management was set to begin.

The record of the period, shown in Table 2–5, verifies the tremendous growth of crude and product imports as the MOIP began to sag under the weight of self-interest and political modification. Also at work near the end of the period was price regulation that encouraged imports as the incremental supplier to an "overheated" market. Stagnant exports were the flip side of import regulation and signified growing supply problems at home.

G. Tariffs and Supplemental Fees: 1973–Present

Tariffs enacted in 1932 survived World War II, the postwar period, the Korean conflict, and the quota program. In this four-decade period, modifications that reduced the levies were made in 1939,

---

[74]Cabinet Task Force on Oil Import Control, *The Oil Import Question, A Report on the Relationship of Oil Imports to the National Security* (Washington, D.C.: Government Printing Office, 1970), p. 129.

[75]Message from the President of the United States Concerning Energy Resources, April 18, 1973. Reprinted in Lester Sobel, ed., *Energy Crisis*, vol. 1 (New York: Facts on File, 1974), p. 148.

Table 2-5

PETROLEUM IMPORTS AND EXPORTS: 1959-72
(thousand barrels per day)

	Crude Oil		Refined Product		Total	
Year	Imports	Exports	Imports	Exports	Imports	Exports
1959	965	7	814	204	1,780	211
1960	1,015	8	799	193	1,815	202
1961	1,045	9	872	165	1,917	174
1962	1,126	5	955	163	2,082	168
1963	1,131	5	1,000	203	2,130	208
1964	1,198	4	1,060	198	2,259	202
1965	1,238	3	1,229	184	2,468	187
1966	1,225	4	1,348	194	2,573	198
1967	1,128	73	1,409	234	2,537	307
1968	1,291	5	1,549	226	2,840	231
1969	1,409	4	1,757	229	3,166	233
1970	1,324	14	2,095	245	3,419	259
1971	1,681	1	2,245	223	3,926	224
1972	2,222	1	2,532	222	4,754	223

SOURCE: Energy Information Administration, U.S. Department of Energy

1943, 1947, and 1952. In 1962, the fees were reorganized and perpetuated in the Trade Expansion Act.[76] Upon the termination of the MOIP, modifications to the fee structure would begin again.

On April 10, 1973, President Nixon by executive order introduced a complicated set of "license fees" that were applicable to volumes above January 1973 quota levels in place of prior fees.[77] The fees began at $0.105 per barrel for crude oil with differential product fees (for domestic refiner protection) of $0.15 per barrel for fuel oil and $0.52 per barrel for motor gasoline. Asphalt, butane, ethane, and propane were duty-free, as was Canadian crude (for one year, after which smaller fees were payable) and Puerto Rican exports. To continue the 14-year subsidy to small (generally inland) refiners, fee-free allocations were awarded by the Office of Oil and Gas (which in March 1969 replaced the Oil Import Administration within the Department of the Interior) to all existing quota holders.

[76]Public Law 87-794, 76 Stat. 877 (1962).
[77]Proclamation 4210, 38 *Federal Register* 9645, April 19, 1973.

This initially covered about 7 million barrels of imported crude and product and was scheduled to drop each April 30 to 90 percent of allocations in 1974, 80 percent of allocations in 1975, 65 percent in 1976, 50 percent in 1977, 35 percent in 1978, 20 percent in 1979, and 0 percent in 1980. New refining capacity was also given an exemption on the crude tariff equal to 75 percent of inputs, but for five years only. Canadian, Puerto Rican, and Virgin Island imports were given lenient treatment. Fee exemptions could be granted by the Oil Imports Appeals Board of the Office of Oil and Gas, which began with a 50,000 barrel per day allocation. As before, the allocations had to be used by the recipient either with imported oil or domestic oil obtained in an exchange. This was modified in late 1975 to allow the sale of oil import licenses within the antispeculation guidelines. The purpose of this modification was—in the words of the Federal Energy Administration, which now administered the program—to "eliminate much of the cumbersome paperwork that has heretofore characterized transfers of this sort."[78]

The two major characteristics of the new fee program were its complexity, akin to the program it replaced, and its primary motivation of continuing the small-refiner subsidy rather than protectionism per se.

As the fee-exempt allocation wound down, small refiners would not lose their preferential treatment. In December 1974, the old oil refinery entitlements program began with benefits (bonus entitlements) inversely correlated with throughput capacity. This sliding scale, noticed Bohi and Russell, was "a mirror image of the import quota."[79]

The license-fee program would be supplemented by another tariff several years later. Its genesis was a January 14, 1975, letter from Treasury Secretary William Simon to President Gerald Ford, pursuant to Section 232 of the Trade Expansion Act of 1962, that stated:

> As a result of my investigation, I have found that crude oil, principal crude oil derivatives and products, and related products from natural gas and coal tar are being imported in the United States in such quantities as to threaten to impair the national security. . . . I therefore recommend that appropriate action be taken to reduce such imports.[80]

[78]40 *Federal Register* 59195, December 22, 1975.
[79]Bohi and Russell, *Limiting Oil Imports*, p. 226.
[80]40 *Federal Register* 4457, January 30, 1975.

In response, President Ford began a new era of import management by introducing supplemental license fees on oil. Effective February 1, a $1 per barrel surcharge was placed on crude and product imports, excluding asphalt and natural gas liquids. Increases were scheduled to be $2 per barrel on March 1 and $3 per barrel on April 1.[81] The president's motivation was not so much to protect the industry but to reduce dependence on foreign crude, which he pegged at 38 percent of supply. Another motivation was to give Congress a bitter pill to swallow to persuade the Northeast delegation, in particular, to enact his energy plan.

With major criticism from Congress and fuel-user constituencies, Ford voluntarily rescinded the March increase several days after it took effect, postponed the April increase 60 days, and postponed it again on May 1. On June 1, Ford increased the fees to $2 per barrel for crude oil and $0.60 per barrel for products because Congress had, since February, "done nothing positive to end our energy dependence."[82] On September 1, however, the product fee was rescinded, and the crude fee was revoked in the Energy Policy and Conservation Act later that year.[83] This left the longstanding fees antecedent to the Revenue Act of 1932, which were deductible under Ford's fees. Fee-free imports, however, were reduced from 80 percent (of 1973 levels) to 65 percent in 1976 and 1977, 50 percent in 1977 and 1978, and 20 percent in early 1979, except for residual fuel oil imports to District I. This program was a reduced phase-out from that originally set in 1973. Meanwhile, "hardship" exemptions continued to be granted by the Federal Energy Administration and, after 1977, by the Department of Energy.

With supply problems looming, President Carter went the other way and temporarily abolished tariffs effective April 1, 1979, with a reactivation point set well above current import levels. For the first time in nearly a half-century, free trade (except for the formality of obtaining a license from the Interior Department) in petroleum held sway.

Stripped of both their protective differential and small-refiner

<hr/>

[81]Proclamation 4341, 40 *Federal Register* 3965, January 23, 1975; 40 *Federal Register* 4771, January 31, 1975.

[82]The political battle between President Ford and the Democratic Congress over tariffs and a national energy plan is chronicled in Lester Sobel, ed., *Energy Crisis*, vol. 2 (New York: Facts on File, 1975), pp. 114–21.

[83]89 Stat. 871 (1975); 41 *Federal Register* 1037, January 6, 1976.

preference, small refiners, organized as the Domestic Refining Group, lobbied for a quick reimposition.[84] The suspension was extended for a second six-month period, however, before the import fees were reinstated on April 1, 1980.[85]

President Carter's earlier decision to remove tariffs was purely pragmatic. His approach to the energy question was interventionist, bordering on national planning. So it was with import management. In July 1979, four months after Treasury Secretary W. Michael Blumenthal made a finding, under Section 232 of the Trade Expansion Act of 1962, that a threat to national security existed, Carter floated the idea of limiting imports to 8.2 million barrels per day so that the United States "will never use more foreign oil than we did in 1977."[86] In 1980, he implemented a $4.62 per barrel "conservation fee," which immediately brought court action and a congressional override.[87]

With the tariff suspension removed in 1980, tariffs reverted to previous amounts last amended in the 1950s. It is this tariff structure, supplemented by a superfund tax of $0.118 per barrel and an *ad valorem* Customs Department user fee of $0.22 percent effective January 1, 1987, that has been the target for reform by protectionists.[88]

The record of imports and exports in the post-MOIP period did not reflect market forces. This time, however, *the bias was toward imports* (despite on-and-off tariffs) and explicitly against exports. While government foreign-trade policy has historically discouraged imports (and indirectly exports) to protect domestic industry, from 1974 through 1981 the refinery entitlements program *subsidized* imported oil by requiring refiners running price-regulated oil to write monthly checks to refiners running unregulated oil. Domestic price regulation from 1971 through 1981 also encouraged imports

[84]*Oil & Gas Journal*, May 28, 1979, p. 48. Among the most vocal companies for reimposition was Ashland Oil, a perennial proponent of government intervention for competitive advantage.

[85]45 *Federal Register* 41899, June 23, 1980.

[86]Joseph Yager, "The Energy Battles of 1979," in *Energy Policy in Perspective*, ed. Craufurd Goodwin (Washington, D.C.: Brookings Institution, 1981), p. 625. Also see "The Oil Quota May Backfire," *Business Week*, August 13, 1979, p. 99. Secretary Blumenthal claimed that his finding was even more compelling than Secretary Simon's four years before. 44 *Federal Register* 18818, March 29, 1979.

[87]45 *Federal Register* 22864, April 3, 1980; 94 Stat. 439 (1980).

[88]See chapter 5, pp. 221–22, for a review of existing tariff fees.

by discouraging domestic output. Foreign crude was the most prominent unregulated oil, and its effective price was reduced by the per barrel amount of entitlement income, generally above $5 per barrel. With the end of the entitlements distortion and with declining demand in the period of deregulation, imports reversed their upward trend until 1986, when Saudi Arabia abandoned its role as swing supplier.

Exports began to be regulated in 1973 under the Export Administration Act to retain price-regulated crude for the domestic market.[89] Quarterly quotas were instituted by the Office of Export Administration in the Department of Commerce the next year. A second export-control law was passed the same year in the Trans-Alaska Pipeline Authorization Act, which limited exports of domestic oil that passed over federal domain.[90] Alaskan North Slope oil was at issue, and in 1977 amendments to the Export Administration Act effectively banned its export.[91] This ban, which forced Prudhoe Bay and other Alaskan oil to the West Coast (or Gulf Coast through the Panama Canal), preventing its exportation to the Pacific Rim, was the result of domestic supply concerns in the wake of the Arab embargo and heavy lobbying by U.S. shipping interests, which by law (the Jones Act) claimed all tanker business between U.S. destinations.[92]

The results of regulation-subsidized imports and regulation-discouraged exports in the 1973–81 period are summarized in Table 2–6 below.

Record-setting imports peaked in the 1977–79 period and declined thereafter because of declining U.S. demand and phased decontrol of the price and allocation regulations responsible for subsidizing imports. Despite the Alaskan and West Coast export ban, East and Gulf Coast exports grew after decontrol in early 1981.

Total U.S. participation in the world oil market peaked in 1979, with imports leading the way, and then fell until 1986, when Saudi Arabia increased its for-export liftings by several million barrels per day. Full participation in world oil trade, however, was prevented by the West Coast/Alaska export ban. By locking California and

---

[89]38 *Federal Register* 34442, December 13, 1973.

[90]Public Law 93-153, 87 Stat. 584 (1973).

[91]Public Law 95-52, 91 Stat. 235 (1977).

[92]Export regulation is also reviewed in chapter 5, pp. 235–37.

Table 2–6
PETROLEUM IMPORTS AND EXPORTS: 1973–86
(thousand barrels per day)

Year	Crude Oil Imports	Crude Oil Exports	Refined Product Imports	Refined Product Exports	Total Imports	Total Exports
1973	3,244	2	3,012	229	6,256	231
1974	3,477	3	2,635	218	6,112	221
1975	4,105	6	1,951	204	6,056	209
1976	5,287	8	2,026	215	7,313	223
1977	6,615	50	2,193	193	8,708	243
1978	6,356	158	2,008	204	8,364	362
1979	6,519	235	1,937	236	8,456	471
1980	5,263	287	1,646	258	6,909	545
1981	4,396	228	1,599	367	5,995	595
1982	3,488	236	1,625	579	5,113	815
1983	3,329	164	1,722	575	5,051	739
1984	3,426	181	2,011	541	5,437	722
1985	3,201	204	1,866	577	5,067	781
1986	4,111	154	1,950	618	6,061	772

SOURCE: Energy Information Administration, U.S. Department of Energy

Alaska oil into U.S. markets, not only exports but imports were artificially discouraged.

H. Summary: The Harvests of Protectionism

What has each of the protectionist episodes rendered for the national interest? Three unequivocal negative consequences, shared by each, have been to raise prices for domestic consumers, accelerate the depletion of U.S. reserves (and postpone the depletion of foreign reserves), and lose export markets for U.S. oil. In addition, each program created unpredicted consequences that worked against protectionist interests and national policy.

1. Early Tariffs: 1861–1909

Nineteenth-century oil tariffs began as a revenue source. But from the late 1880s forward, the tariffs gave the Standard Oil Trust shelter from its foreign refining rivals, principally from Russia.[93] Ironically,

[93]For the prominent role of Russia in the world oil trade, see Williamson and Daum, *The American Petroleum Industry*, vol. 1, chap. 24.

while the U.S. government was preoccupied with dislodging the Trust from its preeminent position through regulatory policies and judicial challenges, it aided the Trust through international trade barriers. Although the economic performance of Standard refineries was exemplary, as demonstrated by declining prices, improved product quality and safety, and expanding output, artificial discouragement of product imports was nonetheless a notable distortion of market competition and consumer sovereignty. Another irony was that Standard Oil was the biggest *loser* from product protectionism, as well as its biggest beneficiary. Standard was the world's largest product exporter, and with foreign oil displaced to foreign markets, the Trust's export opportunities were narrowed. Standard also faced foreign tariffs and quotas that in part were in retaliation for U.S. tariffs.

2. Tariff and Quota Regulation in the 1930s

The Revenue Act of 1932 was a far more blatant protectionist episode than the previous experience with product tariffs. It was not justified on the grounds of stemming a "flood" of imports—imports had fallen from a decade before, and the country as a whole exported more oil than it imported. Its seminal purpose and effect was to rescue a notoriously inefficient and corrupt wellhead proration system in Texas and Oklahoma and foster its expansion in 1935 to Louisiana, New Mexico, and Kansas. In the same year, the Interstate Oil Compact Commission was created with an antitrust exemption from Congress to coordinate the multistate effort, and Section 9(c) of the invalidated National Recovery Act was replaced by the Connally Hot-Oil Act to prohibit interstate commerce of oil illegally produced under state statutes. The "bailout" of state (and federal) conservation regulation by tariffs, politically as well as economically, would be consequential not only in the early 1930s but in future decades.

The forgone alternative to state regulation (market-demand proration, well spacing minimums, field shutdowns) and protectionism (tariffs, quotas) was *the unfettered operation of market processes* to combat real or perceived problems of overdrilling and overproduction. Without state and federal intervention, the inefficiencies and price consequences of open-flow production in the big fields, with wasteful above-ground storage and distress sales substituting for underground (reservoir) storage and calculated depletion, would have been self-correcting. If the National Guard had been employed to keep order in the fields by enforcing private property rights rather than violating them through martial law shutdowns in the watershed period preceding the 1932 tariff and 1933 quota, asset transfers from distressed open-flow operators to better capitalized firms could have taken place. The survivors, prominently including major companies, would have been capable of entering legal agreements to produce cooperatively in accordance with new theories of reservoir mechanics and with attention to the inventory and price situation. As it was, production was arbitrarily curtailed through the vagaries of government agencies, and even then proration barely survived its own economic and political shortcomings.[94]

The 1930s protectionist experience cannot be evaluated without describing its contradictions. A forgotten fact was that *the United States was exporting more oil than it was importing during the heyday of 1930s protectionism.* The Texas Gulf Coast was the oil export center of the world. Far from dumping foreign oil in the United States, involved firms were importing crude oil, primarily from Latin America (Venezuela, Mexico, and Argentina), and exporting crude to Canada, Japan, France, Italy, and Germany, among other nations. On the product side, imports also originated primarily from Latin America and were exported to such destinations as Japan, Britain, Germany, the Netherlands (Europe and West Indies), France, China, and elsewhere.[95] The interruption of imports that occurred from the 1932 tariff and the New Deal quota also reduced export opportunities, most evident with oil products, and *unintentionally* kept oil in home markets to add to the domestic glut and price demoralization.[96]

Exports fell approximately one-third between the late 1920s and 1933, while imports fell over 50 percent in the same period. However, because exports were consistently greater than imports, the net effect was a marginal increase in net exports. In other words, the stiff import duties had virtually no effect on domestic oversupply except to raise domestic oil prices and lower world prices.

---

[94]See, for example, "Is Proration Doomed?" *Oil & Gas Journal,* January 5, 1933, p. 18.

[95]Williamson and Daum, *American Petroleum Industry,* vol. 2, pp. 717–35.

[96]Stated Norman Nordhauser: "Independent well owners in Texas and Oklahoma . . . remained indifferent to the loss of such foreign markets. Their horizon was limited to their immediate buyers, the American refiners." Nordhauser, *Quest for Stability,* p. 52. Also see Chester, *United States Oil Policy and Diplomacy,* p. 16.

Coupled with the fact that the proration programs of the Southwest oil states increased prices to *encourage* imports at the same time that tariffs discouraged imports, the conclusion can be reached that *the combination of federal and state regulation worsened the oversupply and import "problems" from the U.S. independent's point of view.* Thus the nation's first bona-fide protectionist experience failed from the perspectives of economic efficiency, the consumer, national security, the domestic industry, and the world oil market. The only "winners" were those beneficiaries of market-demand proration.

The stringent operation of market-demand proration during the 1950s and 1960s, chastised by such economists as M. A. Adelman and Alfred Kahn as a multibillion dollar drain on the economy and an affront to efficient resource use predicated upon maximum output from low-cost wells, was the long-term consequence of oil import protectionism in the 1930s.[97] Without protectionism and without proration, rearranged entrepreneurial control of the great Southwest fields would have better met the challenges under the rule of capture, and the monumental wastes of both regulatory programs would have been avoided.[98] Furthermore, with lower-cost and more efficient production, domestic supply could have gained market share by better competing with foreign oil. Proration regulation *created* the conditions that led to further regulation, a theme common to U.S. petroleum regulation.

A final irony of 1930s protectionism, alluded to above, was con-

---

[97]For example, see M. A. Adelman, "Efficiency of Resource Use in Crude Petroleum," *Southern Economics Journal,* October 1964, pp. 101–22.

[98]A major misconception of the state conservation movement was that entrepreneurs were helpless to overcome the "common pool" problem under the rule of capture and that mandatory output constraints and forced cooperative development of oil reservoirs were required. This conclusion severely underestimates the barriers and disincentives that government intervention placed in the way of entrepreneurial reform. Such intervention included state and federal antitrust law that discouraged cooperative strategies, common-carrier and common-purchaser pipeline law that promoted overdrilling and overproduction, depletion-allowance incentives for offset drilling, corporate (double) tax discouragement of pooling and unitization, field shutdowns to annul market forces and protect anticonservation "mom and pop" producers, and proration assignments rewarding overdrilling. There was also, in the 1930s as later, an open scientific debate over how many wells were necessary to efficiently drain a reservoir and what the optimal extraction rate should be. This counterthesis, coupled with the failure of the political solution to overdrilling and overproduction, is developed at length in my forthcoming book, *Oil, Gas, and Government: The U.S. Experience,* chapter 4.

tinued demoralization of the independent sector. One firm that could not be saved belonged to IPAA founder Wirt Franklin—"Mr. Independent Oil." Franklin, who lobbied for the law in early 1932 with the words "there is hardly an independent company not now in the hands of its bankers," found his company in receivership over a year after protectionism was enacted. A lesson was involved: protectionism was not nirvana for inefficient firms.

3. The Mandatory Oil Import Program

In contrast to the subtle distortions of the previous two protectionist episodes, the problems of the Mandatory Oil Import Program were readily identifiable. A National Petroleum News prediction that March 10, 1959, would be "a day the oil industry will regret" would be on the mark.[99]

The litany of distortion and political reshaping of the program left national security, by anyone's definition, in its wake. Quotas were allocated on welfare grounds to Puerto Rico and the Virgin Islands, on environmental grounds to reward low-sulfur residual fuel oil distillation, and on macroeconomic-policy grounds to fight inflation. Equity considerations expanded allocations in unforeseen directions. Politicization and complexity characterized the program; its 23 major "resource consuming adjustments" contributed, along with market conditions, to its demise.[100]

The legacy of the Revenue Act of 1932 was oil-state proration; the legacy of the Mandatory Oil Import Program was the Organization of Petroleum Exporting Countries (OPEC). As Emma Brossard, an authority on Venezuelan oil, stated:

> The most direct result of government import quotas was the creation of OPEC in 1960. Venezuela was the largest exporter and the hardest hit by the quotas. The quotas turned an abundance of non-U.S. oil into a world glut that forced international oil companies, led by Standard Oil of New Jersey (Exxon), to cut the posted price abroad and ultimately to reduce the revenues of

[99]"A Black Day for the Oil Industry," National Petroleum News, April 1959, p. 109.

[100]Robert Goodwin, "Regulation of Imports and Exports," in Petroleum Regulation Handbook, ed. Joseph Bell (New York: Executive Enterprises Publications, 1980), p. 230; Yoram Barzel and Christopher Hall, The Political Economy of the Oil Import Quota (Stanford: Hoover Institution Press, 1977), p. 34.

producing countries. The producing countries fought back and formed . . . OPEC.[101]

Douglas Bohi and Milton Russell, in the most thorough study of the Mandatory Oil Import Program to date, similarly wrote:

> The difficulties [Venezuela] faced in marketing its crude, even at lower prices, and at a time when it was undertaking extensive economic development programs, led to new sympathy toward organizing with other oil-exporting nations to achieve better terms of trade for oil. Indeed, Perez Alfonso, the Venezuelan oil leader, apparently in part in response to the frustrations involved in seeking freer access to the U.S. market, was willing to join and in fact led in the formation of OPEC; it is certainly true that the more experienced and better trained Venezuelan oil establishment supplied much of the analysis and impetus in the early, somewhat floundering years of that organization.[102]

It is also true that as the MOIP went on, Middle Eastern oil became increasingly discriminated against as federal regulators tilted the quota toward Canadian, Mexican, and, finally, Venezuelan supply. The primary market for Persian Gulf oil was Western Europe and Japan, both of which benefited from depressed oil prices from the U.S. market exclusion. In fact, the MOIP served as an "Oil Marshall Plan" for contributing to the differential between U.S. oil at $2.80 per barrel and Western Europe landed crude at $1.80 per barrel.[103]

The exclusionary "favor" of protectionism would be returned by Middle Eastern producers once conditions went from an importers' market to an exporters' market. In the 1960s, U.S. authorities told Persian Gulf producers that they did not want to buy oil; in the 1970s, Arab OPEC governments would tell the United States that they did not want to sell oil.

In a real sense, the voluntary import regulation followed by the MOIP gave oil-state proration a *third* life. Three congressional investigations and an FTC study into oil imports in 1949 and 1950 began

---

[101]Emma Brossard, *Petroleum—Politics and Power* (Tulsa: PennWell Books, 1983), pp. 63–64. The initial quota program was damaging; the overland exemption five weeks later, which deregulated oil imports from Canada and Mexico, hurt Venezuela even more.

[102]Bohi and Russell, *Limiting Oil Imports*, pp. 134–35.

[103]Brossard, *Petroleum—Politics and Power*, p. 127.

a series of events that had a subtle but crucial effect on state regulation to reduce production. Noted M. A. Adelman:

> The real threat was: faced with eventual collapse of the proration
> system, the states would bolt out—each state for itself. The
> congressional investigations were at once a reassurance to the
> states and a threat (not a bluff) to the companies that if they did
> not keep imports down to a very low figure, legislative action
> would be taken. And so long as Congress did their share, the
> states could make would-be importers think twice; for against the
> chance of Congress allowing them to import in the future, they
> had to weigh the chance of having wells shut in on one pretext or
> another, on the bulk of their current production.[104]

4. After the MOIP: Contradiction and Complexity

The opposing influences of government policy toward imports
in the 1970s reflected the ambivalence that regulators themselves
felt—they needed imports but did not want them. Imports were at
once the savior of domestic regulation, which artifically discouraged
supply and encouraged demand, but the messenger of bad news
(the plight of domestic regulation) and artificial import dependence.
Thus, while tariffs and quotas were bandied about to reduce imports
and foreign oil dependence, U.S. regulation, stretching from price
controls to the entitlements program, jammed the door open for
imports. Only with decontrol in early 1981 would the import bias
be removed, leaving modest tariffs and export prohibitions in the
way of a nondistorted foreign-trade market from the U.S. side.

The license fee program that replaced the quota program in 1973
borrowed the latter's political biases and, thus, its problems. Commented Thomas Preston:

> By 1973, the Mandatory Program had become so complex and so
> torn by the pressures of diverse interests that no one could hon-
> estly maintain that it was a program with a distinct philosophy
> and direction. Yet incredibly, the license fee system was estab-
> lished with the same kind of crippling special interest provisions.
> Just as with price protection or the fee-free allocations, the accom-
> modation of special interests reflects an effort to by-pass normal
> market forces.[105]

---

[104]Adelman, *World Petroleum Market*, p. 150.

[105]Thomas Preston, "National Security and Oil Import Regulation: The License
Fee Approach," *Virginia Journal of International Law*, Winter 1975, p. 417.

The lesson learned from the fee program, of significance to the current debate over tariff protectionism, was that tariff/fee structures as well as quotas could be politicized.

5. Open Trade, by Contrast

In sharp contrast to protectionism, the open-trade period witnessed increasing internationalization of the world oil market, with attendant geographical diversification of reserves and deliverability. A less quantifiable benefit was goodwill between nations. Not only did U.S. industry play a major role in expanding world supply, an intricate web of interdependent import and export patterns based on transportation cost-efficiencies was fostered. Consumer sovereignty was advanced. This benefited domestic oil because of not only profitable foreign production and exportation to the United States but the encouragement given to foreign sales. It may be asked what would have happened if U.S. policy in formative open-trade periods (1909–31, post–World War II) had been replaced by oil nationalism, exclusively emphasizing domestic discoveries and consumption at the expense of foreign oil. Not only would U.S. consumers have paid a heavy premium, the high-cost U.S. reserve base would have been that much more depleted and foreign reserves that much more preserved. Such a policy would have indeed raised unsettling questions from a patriotic, utilitarian viewpoint. But this hypothetical thought is mentioned out of turn. The next two chapters, within a wide-ranging analysis of protectionism, examine another side of national security and the national welfare with a different set of policy implications.

Part II

The Case for Protectionism Reconsidered

Introduction

History has shown that insofar as national security and the national interest are concerned, protectionism has been counterproductive. In the current debate, both academic and industry advocates of protectionism remain largely silent about the historical record, implicitly acknowledging this fact.

Indeed, there is reason for protectionists to "start over" and "start clean." Each of the three previous episodes offers little inspiration for a fourth.[1] It is difficult to conclude that nineteenth and early twentieth century tariffs had redeeming social consequences to offset higher prices for consumers and protection from foreign refiners and marketers for the Standard Trust. The tariff walls of the 1930s turned foreign oil markets previously served by U.S. oil to other sources, rescued market-demand proration in the Southwest oil states, and put the industry on a political basis for decades to come. By salvaging wellhead proration, the tariff also led to the next protectionist experience, which was also instigated by worsening proration restrictions. The Mandatory Oil Import Program, formalizing "voluntary" trade barriers, destroyed U.S. export markets, became disoriented from its "national security" goals, and inspired the formation of OPEC. The program's negative experience, in fact, has single-handedly banished quotas as a policy alternative to tariffs in the current debate and offers a penultimate case study for avoiding exceptions and exemptions in any adopted program.

This section contains a historical, theoretical, institutional, and political analysis of the arguments for oil protectionism that have emanated from industry and academia. Historically, the experiences and lessons of past petroleum interventionism in general,

[1]License-fee tariffs during the Nixon, Ford, and Carter administrations are not considered a protectionist episode because they were enacted for conservation reasons and not for domestic industry protection. Conservation tariffs, however, like protection tariffs, were intended to increase the market-share of domestic production.

and tariffs and quotas in particular, are referenced where applicable in the current debate. Another important historical question in the national security debate is how the world petroleum market of the 1980s is different from the "energy crisis"-era industry. Theoretically, economic insights (the logic of "profit maximizing" human action) are interwoven into the analysis to describe the role of entrepreneurship in prospective oil crises and identify some of the effects on the U.S. economy of a tariff. The "externality" case for oil import restrictions, critically reviewed in appendix 4B, probes deeply into economic methodology and theory to unmask a problem-fraught, albeit sophisticated, call for major oil tariffs.

Institutionally, the question is, To what extent can a major exporting country effectively embargo a major importing country or engender concerted production cuts to "shock" the market? Asked another way, To what extent can the diversity and complexity of the institutions composing the world petroleum market frustrate any such effort? Politically, finally, the question is whether a new protectionist program can insulate itself from the special-interest modifications that were so prevalent in recent regulatory experience and that have proven so debilitating to the stated goals of the program.

3. The Case for Refiner Protectionism Reconsidered

A. The IRC Argument Revisited[2]

The argument presented to lawmakers, the trade press, and the industry by the Independent Refiners Coalition in late 1984 and 1985 was based on the national security implications of a large shutdown of distillation capacity. In the past, the national security argument had been the domain of crude oil producers; now, with foreign refinery capacity replacing domestic capacity at an "alarming" rate, a companion national security argument swept into prominence.

Between 1981 and 1985, more than a hundred oil refineries, mostly independents, were idled, with a loss of over 5 million barrels per day of primary and secondary capacity. These closings represented one-fourth of national refining capacity. While many refiners in the first several years were small, inefficient "topping" plants unable to compete without the government subsidies that ceased with the termination of the entitlements program in early 1981, many more-recent closings have involved technically advanced units. These units, many modernized to make light products in the decontrol era,[3] were victimized by growing imports of gasoline and gasoline blendstocks that drove prices to unprofitable levels. Without profitable gasoline sales, refining itself ceased to be profitable; approximately 80 percent of U.S. refinery output consists of light products, and these margins often subsidize the output of heavier (residual) byproducts.

[2]This section supplements the previous discussion in Chapter 1, which concentrated on the membership, politics, and policy positions of the Independent Refiners Coalition.

[3]U.S. refiners as a group spent an estimated $12 billion to refine heavier crudes into lighter products. Statement of John Hall (Ashland Oil) on behalf of the Independent Refiners Coalition, *Impact of Imported Petroleum Products on the Domestic Petroleum Industry*, Hearing before the Subcommittee on Energy Regulation and Conservation, U.S. Senate, 99th Cong., 1st Sess., June 4, 1983, p. 155.

Between 1980 and 1985, gasoline imports rose approximately 175 percent to 381,000 barrels per day, while unfinished product imports, including gasoline feedstocks, surged proportionally. As a percentage of domestic demand, gasoline and related blendstock imports nearly tripled between 1980 and 1985 (before falling in 1986), as seen in Table 3-1 below.

The growth in imports of oil products, except for light products, was nominal. Total product imports in 1985 and 1986 approximated 1979 levels, and as can be seen in Table 3-2, compared to 1980-83 levels, product imports actually declined. Between 1983 and 1985, the IRC argued, the changed *composition* of U.S. imports—away from residual fuel oils exported from Western Hemisphere sources and toward lighter products exported from the Middle Eastern and European refiners—produced negative margins for domestic refiners and displaced 1.5 million barrels per day of downstream capacity.[4] With these "second wave" closings, the argument continued, distillation capacity was at the national security minimum; any new shutdowns would leave the industry below the capacity necessary to meet domestic demand in the event of an import cutoff or military

Table 3-1
GASOLINE IMPORTS: 1979–86
(thousand barrels per day)

Year	Finished Gasoline	Gasoline Blendstocks	Total Gasoline	Percent of Total Market*
1979	184	N/A	184+	2.6+
1980	140	N/A	140+	2.1+
1981	157	24	181	2.7
1982	197	42	239	3.7
1983	247	47	294	4.5
1984	299	83	383	5.7
1985	381	48	429	6.3
1986	296	68	363	5.2

*Total gasoline consumption in the United States was 7 million barrels per day in 1979, 6.6 in 1980 and 1981, 6.5 in 1982, 6.6 in 1983, 6.7 in 1984, 6.8 in 1985, and 7.0 in 1986.
SOURCE: Energy Information Administration, Department of Energy

[4]Statement of John Hall, *Impact of Imported Petroleum Products*, pp. 156–57.

Table 3–2

PRODUCT IMPORTS: 1979–86
(thousand barrels per day)

Year	Gasoline & Blendstocks	Distillate Fuel Oil	Residual Fuel Oil	Other	Total
1979	181	193	1,151	195	1,720
1980	140	142	939	210	1,431
1981	181	173	800	202	1,356
1982	239	93	776	292	1,400
1983	294	174	699	364	1,531
1984	383	272	681	482	1,818
1985	429	200	510	540	1,679
1986	363	235	650	460	1,708

SOURCE: Energy Information Administration, Department of Energy

mobilization (which could increase product demand from 500,000 barrels per day to as much as 2 million barrels per day).[5]

The urgency of the refiner group's testimony was not only a response to record gasoline imports that were setting unprofitable prices. It also reflected the increased foreign competition on the horizon. Both developments resulted from a strategy of oil exporting nations beginning in the 1970s to refine overabundant crude into products for home and foreign markets. In the 1975–80 period, the world refining industry enjoyed robust margins, and with projections of increasing product demand, particularly for light products, cash-laden Middle Eastern oil powers added or scheduled over 2 million barrels per day of new capacity. Major new for-export refineries in Saudi Arabia and Kuwait, in particular, geared to turn heavy crudes into light products with catalytic cracker, hydrocracker, delayed coker, and visbreaker units, inspired competitive concerns by the Independent Refiners Coalition. In mid-1985, a Pace Company study commissioned by the IRC predicted that by 1990, increased imports, reaching nearly 13 percent of domestic gasoline demand, would retire 1.4 million barrels per day of domestic capacity, thus leaving the United States short of light products

[5]Ibid., p. 162.

by the same amount in the event of a major supply disruption.[6] One million barrels per day of this amount was predicted to be idled as early as 1987. The national security implications, it was emphasized, were independent of the size of the Strategic Petroleum Reserve (SPR) and other domestic crude stocks because virgin crude cannot fuel civilian or military motor vehicles. Only refined products can, necessitating an adequate home industry to turn the SPR's raw material into useful products.

A linchpin in the refinery protectionism argument is the contention that the world petroleum market has discriminated against U.S. refiners both on the production side and the marketing side. Free trade has been neither free nor fair and, in fact, is to blame for the national security predicament.

Foreign refineries, calculated by the IRC to be less economical than their U.S. counterparts on a stand-alone basis, were being subsidized into superiority by their respective governments through crude-feedstock discounting. By arranging special processing, netback, and barter deals, state-owned plants around the globe received feedstock below the official OPEC prices that U.S. refiners—especially independents, since netback arrangements were being made only with the former ARAMCO partners—had to pay.[7] Thus new for-export facilities were able to penetrate U.S. markets as the incremental supplier and create unprofitable conditions for U.S. refiners.

The argument concerning crude-feedstock subsidization was part of a wider argument against state-owned integrated operations responsible for 60 percent of product imports in 1984. The IRC identified the state-owned refining branch as a "loss leader" in the integrated organization, while U.S. independents had to be a stand-alone profit center.[8]

Other advantages enjoyed by foreign refiners were tax "holidays" and avoidance of pollution control expenditures that burdened U.S. refiners. Although less emphasized by the IRC than feedstock discounts, these incremental obligations raised the effective cost of U.S. refining compared to the international market. Discounted or

[6]The Pace Company, *The Effect of Increasing Petroleum Products Imports on the United States Refining Industry*, June 1985, pp. 3, 5.

[7]For a summary of some of these early feedstock arrangements, see Charles Ebinger, *Oil Product Imports: A Threat to U.S. National Security* (Washington D.C.: Ebinger International, October 9, 1985), pp. 11–13, 16.

[8]Statement of John Hall, *Impact of Imported Petroleum Products*, p. 158.

no-interest government loans, finally, rounded out the IRC's complaint list of foreign subsidies.[9]

In gasoline marketing, relatively strict trade barriers in the two major non-U.S. gasoline markets, Western Europe and Japan, made the United States, in the IRC's estimation, the "international dumping ground for the world's surplus refined product."[10] In Western Europe, a 6 percent *ad valorem* tax was applicable to nonpreferential gasoline and kerosene imports, which included exports from the United States, Eastern Europe, and the USSR. Heavy oils were taxed at 3.5 percent. Preferential imports from the Middle East and North Africa, duty-free below certain levels, crowded out European output, which was then sent to the United States. Saudi and African imports above a specified level were taxed at an estimated tariff rate of $1.66 per barrel, which made the U.S. duty of $0.525 per barrel relatively attractive for these incremental supplies also.

Japan, through tariffs, quotas, and informal agreements, has discouraged gasoline imports altogether. This policy also directed incremental world gasoline shipments toward the United States, at once the most free and largest gasoline market in the world.

Table 3–3 compares relative tariff rates of the world's three major

Table 3–3
RELATIVE OIL PRODUCT TARIFFS
(dollars per barrel)

Product	United States	European Economic Community*	Japan
Gasoline	0.525	1.66	2.22
Naphtha	0.105	—	0.08
Heating Oil	0.105	1.13	1.75
Residual Fuel Oil	0.105	1.00	1.40

*Applies to imports from the United States., Canada, and most Soviet-bloc countries only.
SOURCE: National Petroleum Council, *U.S. Petroleum Refining*, October 1986, p. 131.

[9]Statement of George Jandacek on behalf of the Independent Refiners Coalition before the Subcommittee on Energy and Agricultural Taxation, Senate Finance Committee, February 27 and 28, 1986, p. 15.

[10]Statement of John Hall, *Impact of Imported Petroleum Products*, p. 21.

markets for gasoline and other major products, based on 1985 prices. U.S. levies are the lowest, with Western Europe second and Japan third.

A related national-security implication raised by refinery protectionists is the dispersed location of independent refiners and their specialized sales to the U.S. military. "Because they are dispersed geographically and are small enough to tailor production for specialty products," an IRC publication stated, "independent refiners are vital for America's military fuel supply."[11] In fact, independents with approximately one-fourth of national refining capacity have supplied the military with 50 percent of its fuel requirements.[12] A loss of this capacity, consequently, could interfere with military procurement with regard to either product type or convenience.

The purpose of the commissioned research and political lobbying by the Independent Refiners Coalition was either to persuade Congress to enact protectionist legislation (as successfully done by independent producers in 1932) or to inspire a national security finding by the president to impose a tariff or quota (as done by President Eisenhower in 1959). Another policy initiative was to close "loopholes" in present tariffs that allowed near-products, such as gasoline blendstocks, to qualify for the crude tariff of $0.105 per barrel rather than the $0.525 per barrel gasoline tariff.

With the great price fall in early 1986, the protectionist debate shifted from independent refiners to independent producers. The goal of the Independent Refiners Coalition consequently changed to ensure that *if* a crude tariff was enacted, product tariffs would be higher to protect their interests.

Despite the "demotion" of the IRC position, their original arguments are serious and, in the event of another prolonged situation of negative refiner margins, could very well reemerge. It is not an exaggeration to say, moreover, that the small refiners' national security argument is at least as plausible as the producers' national security argument, which is currently at center stage.

B. Refinery Protectionism Reconsidered

Much has happened since John Hall, George Jandacek, Charles Ebinger, and the Pace Company put forth the above arguments in

[11]Independent Refiners Coalition position paper, "Independent Petroleum Refiners and Gasoline Imports," p. 3.

[12]Ebinger, *Oil Product Imports: A Threat to U.S. National Security*, p. 28.

the heyday of the Independent Refiners Coalition in 1985. Not only are the criticisms of the IRC position still as valid today as they were in 1985,[13] the passage of time has produced a situation very different from the crisis anticipated by the refiner lobby.

The proposition that there is a national security threat from current and anticipated world oil market conditions, most elaborately developed in the Ebinger study, is questionable on many grounds. The analysis begins by placing the Independent Refiners Coalition in political perspective as yet another attempt to regain government subsidies in the post-entitlements period. The refiners' national security case is then reinterpreted as applicable to East Coast gasoline imports only. Conservation is emphasized as much more important than import growth in refinery closings, demonstrating the myth of a "second wave" of refinery shutdowns. A "national security" minimum of refining capacity is found to be highly ambiguous. The role of market entrepreneurship is entirely neglected. Three IRC arguments for protected domestic capacity are examined and found wanting: the unfair competition/subsidy argument, the Strategic Petroleum Reserve complement argument, and the military service argument. The ability of the world oil market to circumvent selected embargoes and the sizable capacity of Western Hemisphere refining both call into question the "worst case" scenario of the protectionists. Finally, new developments in 1986 have contradicted many of the ominous trends emphasized by the IRC.

1. Old Song—New Verse

When President Reagan ended the refinery entitlements program on January 27, 1981, the retirement day came for many undersized refiners whose capacity could process only heavy products such as residual fuel oil instead of lighter products such as gasoline. These refiners' profitability depended on monthly entitlements income, regulated access to price-controlled crude, or a combination of both. With decontrol, much of the 4 million barrels per day of capacity built between 1974 and 1981 to reap regulatory rewards now had little choice but to exit. They did not do so without a political fight, however, and their battle cry was familiar—*national security.*

---

[13]See Robert Bradley, Jr., "Oil Protectionism: The New Threat," *Cato Policy Report,* September/October 1985, pp. 12–13, 15; idem, "Taxing Imported Oil: Consumers Beware," reprinted in *Taxation of Imported Oil,* Hearings before the Subcommittee on Energy and Agricultural Taxation, U.S. Senate, 99th Cong., 1st Sess. (Washington, D.C.: Government Printing Office, 1985), pp. 238–47.

In June 1979, two months into the 18-month phased termination of the entitlements program, a group of senators from small-refiner states, led by J. Bennett Johnston (D-La.) and Lloyd Bentsen (D-Tex.), lobbied Energy Secretary James Schlesinger for "a national policy for domestic refineries."[14] The newly formed Domestic Refiners Group, joined by the established small-refiner trade groups, American Petroleum Refiners Association and the Independent Refiners Association of America, argued that President Carter's crude oil decontrol program required compensating product tariffs, federal loan guarantees, and other government subsidies to their members.

As the entitlements program wound down, another group of vulnerable refiners organized the Emergency Small Independent Refiners Task Force to seek a crude oil tariff from which they would be exempt. Another refiner lobby group led by political juggernaut Ashland Oil, the Committee for Equitable Access to Crude Oil, was formed in the same period to reactivate the buy/sell allocation program.[15] The banner of national security was frequently waved by the refiners during their complaints about the transition from regulation to the free market. Raymond Bragg of the American Petroleum Refiners Association, for one, warned that decontrol would "leave our economy vulnerable to increasing imports of foreign refined products."[16]

Threatened independent refiners have been sounding the national security alarm since the free market made its appearance in 1979. Thus John Hall's statement in mid-1985 that "the U.S. cannot afford to lose any more of its refineries" is not unique or particularly convincing.[17] It is a special-interest statement in its seventh year.

[14]*Domestic Refinery Development and Improvement Act of 1979: Part I*, Hearings before the Subcommittee on Energy Regulation, U.S. Senate, 96th Cong., 1st Sess. (Washington, D.C.: Government Printing Office, 1980), p. 3.

[15]See Tom Alexander, "Day of Reckoning for Oil Refiners," *Fortune*, January 12, 1981, p. 40. A third splinter refiner group, the Alliance of Independent Crude Producers and Refiners, took a market-oriented approach by lobbying for exemptions from the Windfall Profits Tax.

[16]*Wall Street Journal*, March 18, 1981, p. 48.

[17]Statement of John Hall, *Impact of Imported Petroleum Products*, p. 153. In 1979, Louisiana Senator J. Bennett Johnston was not ready to lose a single refiner, *at least in his home state*. In a flagrant display of parochialism, he stated: "I think many [refiners] probably came in at the invitation of the Government through the entitlement program but they are there now and I think we have got to see that they

2. Narrowing the "National Security" Problem

The refinery national-security debate is not about petroleum imports per se. It is about the importation of a particular product. Noted a study by the Resource Systems Institute:

> The level of imports at present is not exceptional in a historical setting either in absolute terms or relative to consumption. . . . Much of the concern of U.S. refiners over growing imports is actually a response to a simultaneous change in the composition of imports.[18]

The supply of middle distillates (home heating oil, kerosene, and naphtha) and heavy oils (residual fuel oil, lubricating oil, petroleum waxes, asphalt, and road oils) was not perceived by the refiner lobby to be currently inadequate or potentially so. *The product at issue is gasoline and gasoline feedstocks.* Indeed, while the refiners may *like* to include the entire output slate on the endangered list, they cannot look to imports to make their case. As shown in Table 3–2 above, product imports other than gasoline, led by residual fuel oil, have fallen since 1979. What was responsible for this decline was fundamental changes in consumer demand, propelled by *conservation* and *alternate-fuel switching*. Increasing efficiency in oil-burning furnaces and power plants, and the ability of many of these same facilities to switch to coal or natural gas on short notice, preclude any serious discussion of a national security threat from an interruption of these imports.[19]

A look at the composition of gasoline imports into the United States reveals that not even gasoline imports per se are the problem. It is gasoline imports into the eastern states (PAD District I) that has taken its toll on many refining investments.[20] While these imports reverberate on PAD District III and to a lesser extent on PAD District II refineries, District IV and V refineries are largely insulated. Western U.S. refineries, and in particular environmentally driven

---

survive, at least those in Louisiana." *Limiting Oil Imports,* Hearing before the Subcommittee on Energy Regulation, U.S. Senate, 96th Cong., 1st Sess. (Washington, D.C.: Government Printing Office), p. 92.

[18]Patrick Crow, "U.S. in No Rush to Rescue Small Refiners Hurt by Product Imports," *Oil & Gas Journal,* May 27, 1985, p. 27.

[19]See appendix 4A (pp. 173–83) for further discussion about the promoted role of natural gas, coal, and other fuels in the U.S. energy picture.

[20]National Petroleum Council, *U.S. Petroleum Refining,* October 1986, p. 4.

refineries in the Los Angeles Basin, are far removed from Middle Eastern concerns and indeed constitute a separate industry. Their protectionist battle has been fought and won against unfinished Chinese gasoline, a separate issue completely.[21] Refineries in Japan, China, Singapore, and Australia, unlike their European and Middle Eastern counterparts, are geared toward fuel oils, not gasoline, and are thus less of a threat to PAD District V members. This is not to say that West Coast refiners would not benefit from higher gasoline tariffs (which explains why several District IV and V refiners joined the IRC) but that the IRC case applies east of the Rockies.

The contrasting import situation of U.S. refining regions as of 1985 is illustrated in Figure 3–1 that subtracts exports from imports to determine net imports per PAD district. The situation of PAD Districts II–V imports is very different from that of PAD District I imports.

The refiners' national security argument pertains only to *gasoline imports into the Eastern seaboard*. Thus if the refiner lobby argues for *comprehensive* product tariffs on national security grounds, they would have no case. A geographical tariff on gasoline and gasoline blendstocks imported into PAD District I, which would be fully consistent with their arguments, on the other hand, would be a logistical nightmare, as cargoes would be rerouted to free-trade destinations and for-export gasoline refineries would spring up in the Pacific Rim. Instead, the IRC has taken the middle ground and advocated comprehensive gasoline tariffs only. But the question still must be asked: Why should there be gasoline tariffs into the Western states any more than there should be "national security" tariffs on heating oil, diesel oil, lubricating oil, residual oil, kerosene, asphalt, road oils, petroleum coke, and lesser products? Such a policy would load consumers, both motorists in the West and heating oil users in the Northeast, with higher prices *without* a national security justification.

3. Gasoline Imports: A "Whipping Boy"?

One trend that the IRC correctly emphasized was the decline of U.S. refining capacity from 1981 until 1985. Net refinery deactiva-

---

[21]The Chinese gasoline issue resulted in the Customs Department reclassifying unfinished gasoline from China. As gasoline, it had been subject to the $0.525 per barrel tariff; reclassified as a chemical, it was taxed between $3 and $4 per barrel. See "Chinese Gasoline Imports Reach Financial Crossroad," *National Petroleum News*, September 1984, p. 28.

Figure 3–1:

U.S. PRODUCT IMPORT-EXPORT BALANCE

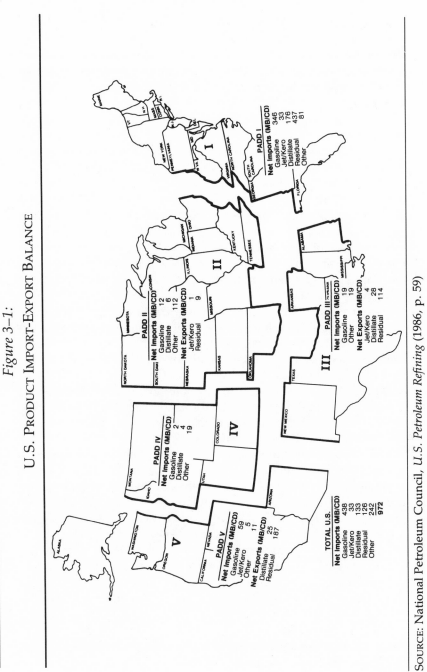

SOURCE: National Petroleum Council, *U.S. Petroleum Refining* (1986, p. 59)

tions totaled 875,620 barrels per day in 1981, 1,668,990 in 1982, 1,349,764 in 1983, 1,280,220 in 1984, and 380,826 in 1985.[22] In the IRC literature, the explanation for "first wave" closings is the end of government subsidies under the entitlements program; gasoline imports—and subsidized imports at that—are blamed for "second wave" closings.

While the end of entitlements revenue did mean the end for many "teakettles" in the first years of decontrol, and while gasoline imports did increase their market-share in the 1981–85 period, the most important factor in refinery closings was *conservation*. Between 1979 and 1985, petroleum product demand fell by 17 percent, led by a 44 percent drop in demand for residual fuel oil. This is more clearly seen in volumetric terms. Between 1979 and 1985, total product imports decreased by 71,000 barrels per day, while total demand fell more than 2.5 million barrels per day. In the same period, gasoline imports increased by 200,000 barrels per day, while decreased gasoline demand totaled 433,000 barrels per day. *Market* conservation, as a result of higher prices, and *mandatory* conservation, as a result of federal and state regulation and subsidies, were having a major effect that refineries could not escape.[23] The same painful adjustment to lower demand was experienced by sophisticated European refineries that could not make the margins necessary to stay in business.

Despite the import surge, many marginal refineries here and abroad would have survived had demand been steady, and many more could have survived with demand growth. This would be the case in 1986, as will be discussed below.

The IRC's complaints about for-export facilities suggest that there is something inherently wrong with refineries that produce in excess of domestic needs. For-export refineries in the United States have been artificially encouraged by regulation—Caribbean Basin refiners during the Mandatory Oil Import Program and a recently proposed Alaskan for-export refinery to serve the Pacific Rim countries, given the Alaskan crude export ban—but this is not necessarily the case abroad. For-export facilities represent specialization and interdependence in the world refining market, traits that are characteristic of a mature industry such as refining. But such facilities also

---

[22]See appendix C, pp. 250–54.

[23]See, for example, "Refiners/Marketers Adjusting to Lower U.S. Products Demand," *Oil & Gas Journal*, June 1, 1981, pp. 46–48.

represent overcapacity relative to home markets, making it necessary for excess products to find more distant markets, despite transportation costs.

While much of the import threat is imaginary, it should be kept in mind that U.S. intervention in the refining marketplace has penalized domestic firms and thereby subsidized product imports. The current tariff structure requires U.S. refiners to pay either a $0.0525 or $0.105 per barrel levy for crude imports, while European and Canadian refiners escape such feedstock costs.[24] The heavy environmental regulations imposed on U.S. refiners, affecting siting, emissions, and lead gasoline content, are a uniquely domestic burden that encourages foreign refining and exportation to the United States. This has been particularly true in PAD District 1 where product demand is the greatest. Some small refiners able to make only leaded gasoline have been driven from the market by the lead phasedown requirement;[25] others have survived by purchasing substitute octane blendstocks (reformate, alkylate) abundantly produced by foreign refiners. (Unleaded requirements have *benefited* generally larger refineries, however, by closing off this market from foreign refiners who do not make unleaded gasoline because it is not required in their countries.) The high differential between crude and gasoline tariff rates ($0.0525/$0.105 versus $0.525 per barrel) has also encouraged gasoline blendstock imports (qualifying as crude for tax purposes) from 1980 forward.[26]

Occupational Safety and Health Act (OSHA) regulations impose costs on the domestic industry not shared by foreign competitors. Superfund taxes, in addition to regular corporate taxes, reduce net income and discourage production decisions at the margin. Tradi-

[24]National Petroleum Council, *U.S. Petroleum Refining*, p. 130. The crude-product tariff differential makes up for this penalty, however.

[25]Mark Emond, "Phasedown, Diesel Sulfur Limit Push Small Refiners Closer to Edge," *National Petroleum News*, January 1986, pp. 20–21. The same article also stated that the "combination of the lead phasedown and lower-sulfur requirement is potentially deadly for small refiners." Quoting an industry source, the article continued: "Only companies with large internal sources of funds can 'afford' to spend the money necessary to adequately respond to the continuously changing legal requirements, even when there is no return on investment."

[26]See Emma Brossard, *Protectionism and the U.S. Refining Industry* (Baton Rouge: Louisiana State University, Center for Energy Studies, October 1985), p. 17. Brossard notes the irony of the IRC complaints against gasoline blendstocks since such imports were vitally needed by independents as a lead substitute.

tional Interstate Commerce Act regulation of entry and rates, while relaxed for railroads and trucking in the last decade, has embarked on a new phase with interstate oil pipelines; such regulation, now administered by the Federal Energy Regulatory Commission (FERC), threatens future expansion of this cost-effective transportation from the wellhead to refinery gate and from the refinery gate to points of consumption. The Jones Act raises shipping costs by restricting shipments between U.S. destinations to U.S.–flag vessels, which are higher cost than foreign-flag vessels. All of these things discourage domestic refining capacity and output, while simultaneously encouraging foreign capacity and exportation. They are candidates for policy reform in their own right, not arguments for tariffs or quotas.[27]

4. OPEC Gasoline Dependence: A Paper Tiger

Gasoline imports from OPEC are a paper tiger. In 1985, record gasoline imports of 429,000 barrels per day comprised 6.3 percent of total U.S. gasoline consumption of 6.8 million barrels per day. Of total gasoline imports, OPEC nations comprised 23 percent or only 1.4 percent of national consumption. This figure, small as it is, becomes infinitesimal when reduced to Arab OPEC, the potential trouble spot according to the IRC literature. (The difference between OPEC and Arab OPEC is primarily Venezuela, the most secure U.S. supplier in the world, with gasoline exports to the United States of over 60,000 barrels per day.) Arab OPEC gasoline imports, totaling 34,452 barrels per day, supply 0.5 percent of U.S. gasoline consumption: 0.4 percent from Saudi Arabia, 0.07 percent from the United Arab Emirates, and 0.006 percent from Libya. This means that the average U.S. automobile, which consumed 549 gallons of gasoline in 1985, used only 2.7 gallons of Middle Eastern fuel. Seen another way, of the nearly 10,000 miles traveled by the average American car in 1985, fewer than 50 miles were on fuel provided by "unstable" Persian Gulf sources. The threat of gasoline lines from a Middle East cutoff could not be more remote.

The increase in Saudi refining capacity in particular and Arab OPEC in general was the target of national security concern by the Independent Refiners Coalition. A list of major post-1982 "for export" facilities showcased by the IRC shows over 2 million barrels per

---

[27]See chapter 5, p. 232, for policy reform for refining.

day of incremental distillation capacity on-stream or planned, boding ill for the future if not the present.[28]

The *prospective* threat of Middle Eastern gasoline has also been highly exaggerated by the IRC. Gasoline imports from the Persian Gulf were even smaller in 1986 and early 1987 than in 1985. Not only would some of the referenced facilities be postponed because of unfavorable prospects—a self-correction of world refining overcapacity—but the primary market of Middle Eastern refineries has been Western Europe, not the United States. Moreover, the new plants are geared toward heavy products, not gasoline. Stated one major study:

> Although some of the recent refineries in the Middle East have been designed to produce a slightly lighter product slate, on the average the Middle East refineries produce a heavier product slate than a typical U.S. refinery. This yield structure tends to put more economic pressure on free-world, private-sector topping refineries than on free-world, private-sector cracking refineries.[29]

Hence any prospective for-export "threat," quantity aside, is concentrated on products that cause no national security concern. U.S. demand for residual fuel oil has drastically declined, as have such imports. Should residual fuel oil imports suddenly become unavailable, natural gas and coal are available to substitute in industrial and powerplant markets.

---

[28]These new refineries as of 1985 were as follows (in barrels per day):
Saudi Arabia
Yanbu: 250,000 (1984); Rabigh: 325,000 (1986); Jubail: 270,000 (1985); Buraidah: 160,000 (forthcoming).
Kuwait
Mina Abdulla: 156,250 (1986); Mina Al Ahmadi: 170,000 (1984) and 100,000 (1986).
Qatar
UMM Said II: 50,000 (1984).
United Arab Emirates
Ruwais II: 185,000 (forthcoming); Ajman: 171,000 (1987).
Oman
Salalah: 200,000 (forthcoming).
Libya
Ras Lunuf: 228,000 (1986).
[29]National Petroleum Council, *U.S. Petroleum Refining,*October 1986, p. 129.

5. Product Exports: The Forgotten Byproduct

The flip side of imports is exports. This is true for foreign trade in general and true in the particular case of U.S. participation in world oil trade. When oil imports are encouraged, foreign markets become more accessible to U.S. oil exports. Foreign currency is also made available to facilitate international trading. The link between reciprocal foreign trade was clearly seen when oil import restrictions sharply curtailed oil exports during the 1930s.

Relatively open trade with oil imports in recent years has allowed U.S. refiners to seize export opportunties. The National Petroleum Council brought attention to the domestic industry's neglected place in the world refining market when it stated:

> The United States has become a significant exporter of finished products. Product exports have reduced the United States' net dependence on finished product imports to approximately 1.0 MMB/CD in 1985. The increase in product exports is the result of a rebalancing of product demands. Major exports from the United States are high-sulfur residual oils and high-sulfur petroleum coke, which reduces net imports of residual-type fuels to 126 MB/CD by 1985. In 1985, the United States also exported 67 MB/CD of distillates. As a result, net motor fuel and distillate imports now comprise 60 percent of net product imports.[30]

Certain sections of the country, in fact, have been net exporters of certain products (see Figure 3–1 above): PAD District II with residual fuel oil and jet fuel/kerosene, PAD District III with residual, distillate, and jet fuel/kerosene, and PAD District V with residual and distillate.

One critic, pointing to a 300 percent increase in U.S. oil exports within the last decade, has taken the IRC to task for ignoring the other side of robust oil imports in the United States:

> Ever since the last quarter of 1984, a great deal of rhetoric has been spent on the "the alarming growth in oil products imports, particularly gasoline." What is *never* mentioned by these alarmists and advocates of shutting the doors to foreign oil imports through quotas or taxes are the U.S. *exports* of petroleum products. . . . One might even accuse the Independent Refiners Coalition of diversionary tactics.[31]

[30]National Petroleum Council, *U.S. Petroleum Refining*, p. 56. MMB/CD is million barrels per calendar day; MB/CD is thousand barrels per calendar day.

[31]Brossard, *Protectionism and the U.S. Refining Industry*, pp. 26, 28.

6. The Myth of "Second Wave" Closings

With the end of government subsidies in early 1981, many refiners unable to turn varying crude grades into light products had to modernize or close. Those who modernized, however, were not automatically saved by their expenditure. Refineries that closed between 1983 and 1985 with gasoline capacity ("second wave" closings) did not represent a market aberration creating a national security threat. Their fate was indicative of a realignment of the world refining market in response to declining product demand and, to a lesser extent, growing product imports as long-planned foreign refineries came on stream. Some closings also were the result of high debt service at a time of squeezed margins. If equity capital had been used to lower fixed costs, more refineries would have survived. Indeed, small refiners who made incorrect business choices should have recognized that demand was falling (it began to fall in 1979) and that foreign refineries were being planned or were actually under construction.[32] In brief, *such refinery closings reflected failings of entrepreneurial foresight, not a foreign conspiracy or acts of God.* Evidence of this failing was confined not only to veteran refineries that, in retrospect, should have retired after a long and lucrative existence. (Twenty-six refineries that closed in 1981 and 1982 were at least 25 years old.) Upstart refineries were also hard hit by misestimating the future configuration of costs and revenue. Approximately 35 refineries that shut down between 1981 and 1986 were in operation for five years or less.[33]   Others, like the $650 million state-of-the-art Saber (Valero) refinery that began production in 1983, have struggled due to an unanticipated narrowing of heavy and light crude oil prices and questionable economies of scale. The Saber experience reflects the primordial fact that of the wide range of *technological* successes, a smaller subset are also *economic* successes as demonstrated by profitability. Refinery conversions in the early 1980s were no exception.

A close look at the first wave and second wave of refinery closings

---

[32]For evidence of these refiner challenges, see "Tariffs, Subsidies, Small Refiner Aid Draw Fire," *Oil & Gas Journal*, September 22, 1980, pp. 68–69; Marvin Reid, "Refinery Shock: Only the Strong Survive," *National Petroleum News*, April 1981, pp. 43–45, 61. In September 1979, Senator Johnston remarked in hearings that "the Saudis and others want to get into the refining business. They have tentative plans to get into business in a very big way." *Limiting Oil Imports*, p. 90.

[33]See appendix D, p. 255, for a table of refinery closings and length of service.

does not reveal a clear division between "expendable" (unsophisticated) refiners prior to 1983 and "nonexpendable" (sophisticated) refiners from 1983 forward. Close examination of the 121 plant closings since 1981 (and 20 plant reactivations in the same period) reveals a variety of characteristics that are inconsistent with the IRC's argument. Small and large refineries closed after 1982 as before 1983. Some second-wave idled plants had small primary production by first-wave standards (Shore, Inc., 550 B/D; Silver Eagle, 1,500 B/D; Flint Chemical, 1,500 B/D; and others), while some first-wave closings were large by second-wave standards (Dow Chemical, 190,000 B/D; Amoco Oil, 185,000 B/D; Phillips Petroleum, 156,700 B/D; among others). Table 3–4 demonstrates the similarity of primary capacity between both waves of closings.

Similarly, sophisticated plants closed in the first wave as unsophisticated plants shut down in the second wave. Of 64 closings in 1981 and 1982, 21 had downstream capacity to produce light products. Of 57 closings from 1983 through 1985, 20 did not have any downstream capacity to make light products. Table 3–5 compares the secondary capacity of first- and second-wave refiners.

Table 3–4

PRIMARY CAPACITY COMPARISON
1981–82 versus 1983–85 Shutdowns

(000 B/D)	0–50	50–100	100–150	150+	Total
First Wave	57	3	3	1	64
Second Wave	50	6	0	1	57
Total	107	9	3	2	121

SOURCE: Appendix C

Table 3–5

DOWNSTREAM CAPACITY COMPARISON
1981–82 versus 1983–85 Shutdowns

(000 B/D)	0	1–50	50–100	100–150	150+	Total
First Wave	43	13	2	3	3	64
Second Wave	20	26	7	3	1	57
Total	63	39	9	6	4	121

SOURCE: Appendix C

The fact that 65 percent of 1983–85 shutdowns had secondary capacity while only 33 percent of 1981–82 closings had the same is the grain of truth in the IRC argument. But there are too many exceptions and contradictions to make the rule. A variety of factors *besides* imports—conservation, fixed costs, location, distribution network, and management—explains the diversity of results. Another reason was unusually high gasoline imports associated with the British coal strike from April 1984 through February 1985. With world refiners (including U.S. refiners) producing as much as 550,000 barrels per day of residual oil to replace coal for this incremental market, the byproduct of gasoline was also produced and found its way to the world's largest gasoline market—the United States. With the end of the strike, coal replaced British fuel oil demand and gasoline exports were reduced.

New refining capacity was reactivated in the second-wave period in response to *opportunities* created by the marketplace. Not once in the IRC literature is mention made of reactivated or new refinery entry; the picture is misleadingly painted to give the impression that gasoline imports were creating an industry death spiral that not only shut down plants but foreclosed selected capacity *additions*. In fact, 2 refineries were added in 1984, 6 refineries joined the active list in 1985, and 12 refineries entered in 1986. Some, like a New Jersey Amerada Hess unit with 68,000 B/D, had sizable primary capacity; one, Hill Petroleum with 62,000 B/D, had large secondary capacity. Other restarts were small unsophisticated units such as Virginia Oil & Refining (1,000 B/D) and Primary Oil & Energy (2,000 B/D). As with refinery exits, determining a first and second wave of refinery entry is difficult. The heterogeneity of product demand and market factors defies simplistic divisions.

A look at IRC-member refineries reveals that they are not much different from the first- or second-wave victims of the 1981–85 shakeout in crude distillation and downstream capacity. Thus John Hall's aforementioned statement in mid-1985 that "time was of the essence" and not one more refinery could be lost without compromising national security can be appreciated as protecting the membership's flank. In fact, not all members could be saved. One member, Amber Refining, shut down permanently in 1985.

Only parochialism can explain the argument that post-1982 closings were part of the sophisticated refiner population that the national interest required to stay operable and operating. One example concerns the leading IRC member, Ashland Oil. From 1981 to 1982, no refineries were deactivated by Ashland. In 1984, Ashland closed four plants, one with 106,500 B/D of downstream capacity to produce gasoline. While this may explain why the position was adopted by the IRC, it does not substantiate the thesis. Refineries owned by Phillips, Texaco, Dow Chemical, and Evangeline closed prior to 1983 with *more* downstream capacity than Ashland's Buffalo, New York, plant. All totaled, 1.27 million barrels per day of downstream capacity was idled in 1981 and 1982 compared to 1.58 million barrels of similar capacity lost during the second wave.

7. Is There a Quantifiable "National Security" Refining Minimum?

F. A. Hayek, in his 1974 Nobel Memorial Lecture in Economics, warned his fellow social scientists of a "pretence of knowledge" in investigating social phenomena. Unlike the natural sciences in which complexity can be simplified by laboratory experiments under *ceteris paribus* conditions, the social world offers unique, fleeting historical events that do not allow empirical testing and repeatable, independent verification. Quantitative certainty is absent in the realm of human action. Consequently, estimating minimum national security refining capacity or any capacity optimum per se is wholly different from determining, for example, at what temperature a particular crude oil turns into a refined product. This methodological point was implicitly acknowledged in a major National Petroleum Council study that spoke of the "tension" between simplicity for the sake of analysis and complexity for the sake of realism in applying quantitative analysis to the U.S. refining market.

> For purposes of the study of refining markets, there is a tension between finding an acceptable level of detail for describing the issues, and preserving a manageable framework for estimating the effects of different policies. A highly aggregated accounting might be easy to manipulate, but it would risk obscuring many of the most important problems. A detailed description of all refining products and relative economics, similar to those used within individual refineries, would overwhelm the analysis when extended to the breadth of the world market.[34]

The effort of the Independent Refiners Coalition to estimate a national security configuration of refining capacity, with national policy hanging in the balance, is an attempt Hayek warns against—

[34]National Petroleum Council, *U.S. Petroleum Refining*, p. 113.

an attempt that entails claiming to have a particular knowledge that *no one has or can have.*[35] Only the market, the collective expression of consumers and entrepreneurs, can "know" what aggregate capacity and the relative configuration of refineries "should" be. The market, however, is not perfect, as evidenced by losses and forgone profits. But neither is it unreliable and backward-looking in its economic function. Nor is there reason to believe the protectionist assumption that government intervention can systematically outperform market outcomes. As explained in the next section, entrepreneurship and consumer decisions are forward-looking, intelligent modes of action in an inherently uncertain world.

This methodological error finds expression in the particular application of a national security determination by the IRC. While IRC representatives before Congress pegged the national security refining floor at present operating capacity, Charles Ebinger went further to define the minimum as the ability to refine all domestic crude and natural gas liquid production, an uninterrupted level of crude imports, and sufficient quantities of Strategic Petroleum Reserve oil to supply all U.S. and NATO military requirements and civilian requirements at 85 percent or more of previous levels. With this definition, Ebinger determined that domestic refining capacity was insufficient and would be more so with predicted import growth and more closings. With the Department of Energy estimating operable capacity at 15.6 million barrels per day and operating capacity at 14.6 million barrels per day, Ebinger's operating minimum would fall somewhere between.[36]

The assumptions behind Ebinger's refining floor are open to debate. In a later section, critical examination is made of the cavalier postulate that because the Strategic Petroleum Reserve exists, it *ipso facto* requires congruent refining capacity.[37] Here it is appropriate

---

[35]Paraphrasing Hayek to fit the present example: "Because we, the observing scientists, can thus never know all the determinates of such a [national security] order, and in consequence also cannot know at which particular structure [of refining] demand would everywhere equal supply, we also cannot measure the deviations from that order; nor can we statistically test our theory that it is the deviations from that 'equilibrium' system . . . which make it impossible to [meet national security]." Hayek, "The Pretence of Knowledge," *New Studies in Philosophy, Politics, Economics, and the History of Ideas* (Chicago: University of Chicago Press, 1978), p. 27.

[36]Ebinger, *Oil Product Imports: A Threat to U.S. National Security*, p. vi.

[37]See pp. 106–7.

to examine the assumption of fixed civilian and military demand.

The notion of fixed demand is a disservice to economic analysis. By banishing the element of change, the crucial function of the price system (and market entrepreneurship, as discussed in the next section) is neglected.

Prices shift with the level of consumption and production; thus, there is no independent level of optimal refining but a *dependent* constellation of capacities associated with particular levels of price (existing and anticipated). Prices, consumption, and refining throughput are not exogenous and fixed but endogenous, moving with the actions of market participants. Such change can quickly reveal that what was "right" before is "wrong" now, and vice versa. Thus any statement that we need all *present* capacity, a *certain* number of refineries, a *certain* quantity of capacity, or a *certain* locational dispersion is arbitrary. Ebinger's particular definition of necessary capacity errs in this regard. Meeting "all" military demand begs the question of *how much* demand; this, in turn, begs the question of *at what price*. (It also neglects the dependence of foreign U.S. military requirements on foreign petroleum.) Meeting 75 percent of civilian demand similarly begs the questions of how much demand and at what price. Precrisis demand and price are no longer "right" with import disruptions, a sudden demand surge, or other "worst case" assumptions. Supply must be anchored to demand, and demand must be anchored to supply. Changing prices coordinate this link. Abstract optimalities, on the other hand, do not exist in the dynamic reality of the economic realm.

The function of the price system is critical in the national security debate. It is price that coordinates supply and demand in normal times and in abnormal times. Yet Ebinger gives short shrift to the fact that *at some price* there will be ample gasoline (or any product) for civilian and military use in any emergency. Consumers (including the military) will have to pay more for supply and *economize*, but supply will be available. (This has become more true with today's vigorous spot market.) Without government intervention to the contrary (price and allocation controls, in particular), marginal uses will be displaced by conservation. *Increased scarcity*, not *shortages* as experienced under 1970s regulation, is the worst-case scenario. M. A. Adelman made this point in relation to the exaggerated use of "national security" when he stated:

"National security" is a phrase often used, seldom explained. I submit that the only possible consistent meaning is: the probability or hazard of a sudden production cut. A permanently lower level of production, or to use the misleading popular phrase, production "not enough for our needs" is just another way of saying "higher prices." This is an economic burden, but not a security problem.[38]

The fact is that *in the 125-year history of the American oil industry, there have never been product shortages when the market was free of federal price and allocation regulations*.[39] Credit for this belongs to the "spontaneous order" of the market engendered by the price system and entrepreneurship.

Oil protectionism shares a problem common to all forms of government planning, whether for a sector of the economy or for the economy as a whole. The problem, though subtle, is based on a rather obvious fact: quantitative precision, upon which protectionist policy is based, is subjective and necessarily arbitrary. For example, the Independent Refiners Coalition has emphasized that the absolute minimum operating capacity for national security is approximately 14 million barrels per day. Yet cannot reasonable minds disagree that this estimate is too high (or too low) by, say, 10 percent? Is it not improper to say that there are plenty of able and willing consultants who can modify their assumptions and interpretations to fit a preconceived notion different from 14 million barrels per day? Charles Ebinger, who calculated such a minimum for the IRC, began his quest with the following reservations:

> The problem is that there is no consensus either as to what constitutes an adequate level of refinery capacity or what criteria should be employed to make that determination. The debate is further clouded by contradictory policy goals that appeal to different constituencies. . . . Still another dimension of the problem is the changing nature of the international crude oil and refined product markets.[40]

Indeed 14 million barrels, as previously discussed, is a preconceived notion. It just happens to correspond to the entire operating refining

[38]Adelman, *Limiting Oil Imports*, p. 98.

[39]For a detailed look at previous oil shortages in U.S. history, see chapter 4, pp. 129–39.

[40]Ebinger, *Oil Product Imports: A Threat to U.S. National Security*, p. 32.

capacity in the United States. A lower figure would have confirmed the existence of excess capacity, even belonging to an IRC member.

Just as there have been studies showing that refining capacity is at or below the national security level, there have been other studies showing a comfortable surplus of capacity over feedstock availability. A study released in April 1986 by the U.S. General Accounting Office concluded that

> present U.S. crude oil refining capacity would likely exceed domestic crude supplies during an oil emergency and still leave about 3 MMBD capacity to refine available crude imports. Since available crude imports would probably be substantially lower than this level during a world wide shortage, we can conclude that domestic refining capacity would likely be sufficient to refine all the oil the United States could reasonably expect to obtain.[41]

Is there a national security minimum for distillation capacity and a national security maximum for product imports as a percentage of consumption? As Ebinger hints, *there is no correct, unambiguous answer.* It depends on assumptions and the interpretation of individual minds. For a policy alternative such as protectionism based from start to finish on quantitative estimates of domestic capacity and a corresponding *base* import quota or tariff *amount*, this is a glaring deficiency. The open trade position, conversely, is based not on any particular configuration but on a continually changing constellation of profitable opportunities. It is this "uncoordinated" unknowable aggregate of economic decisions in the market that is more intelligent than the inevitably limited knowledge of consultants and would-be government planners.

8. Entrepreneurship and the Market Process

A glaring deficiency in the Ebinger study, also evident in the less systematic presentations of IRC spokesmen before Congress, is the disregard of market entrepreneurship and its role in the economic system. *Market entrepreneurship, through the discovery and exploitation of profitable opportunities, anticipates and mitigates surprises and "shocks" in the economic system.* Where market processes are unimpeded, the emergencies hypothesized by protectionists present profitable opportunities. Examples of entrepreneurial alertness to profit

---

[41]GAO, *Effects of Imports on U.S. Refineries and U.S. Energy Security,* April 1986, p. 50.

opportunities in an oil import disruption include eliminating slack capacity to reach full refinery utilization, modifying existing units to increase capacity, "tilting" runs toward relatively scarce products (such as from residual fuel oil to distillates or gasoline), building up inventory of the threatened product(s), and constructing or reactivating refinery capacity to refine feedstocks into the product(s) perceived to become relatively scarce. Consumers too can increase their inventory holdings of products in question and can alertly economize usage (whether by car pooling to reduce gasoline usage, wearing warmer clothing indoors to stretch fuel oil supply, or fuel switching to replace residual oil with natural gas). These available opportunities to producers and consumers are more than sufficient to meet conceivable product import disruptions potentially reducing quantities from a base amount of only 5 or 6 percent of national consumption.

By stocking at low prices and unloading at high prices, speculators serve themselves while, unintentionally, stabilizing price and supply availability in the market. With gasoline, for example, a major inventory buildup in primary (refinery), secondary (service station, farm tank), and tertiary (automobile) storage can create a sizable buffer against temporary disruptions. Combined with the fact that product tankers from the Persian Gulf require over a month's travel time to reach U.S. destinations, an adjustment period is afforded that mitigates the hardship. But even assuming that such a major interruption could occur may be conceding too much.

Both the Arab embargo of 1973 and the Iranian crisis of 1979 were not sudden arbitrary events but the predictable, cumulative result of U.S. foreign policy misadventures. The Organization of Arab Petroleum Exporting Countries (OAPEC) warned the United States to stop subsidizing the Israeli war effort or else face an embargo and higher world oil prices. The United States did not alter its pro-Israeli policy, and the threats were carried out. The Iranian cutoff followed several decades of Central Intelligence Agency (CIA) involvement in Iran that increasingly created an unstable internal situation. The 69-day oil field worker strike that ended on March 5, 1979, which halted exports and contributed to the overthrow of the U.S.-backed Shah Mohammed Riza Pahlevi, and the fragile resumption of exports thereafter, was another bitter and unintended result of foreign policy. Whatever the foreign policy implications of these episodes, what is important for this analysis is that oil crises in the past have not been sudden "acts of God" but the result of a process that entrepreneurs can be expected to be alert to. The fact that entrepreneurship did not do more than it did to mitigate the hardship of these previous "oil shocks" is a sad commentary on U.S. petroleum regulation, which discouraged "speculation" and "profiteering" when it was needed the most.

This neglect of the role of entrepreneurship is different from the *theoretical* neglect by economists who obliterate the entrepreneur by assuming perfect knowledge and instantaneous adjustment in their models. Whether in applied economics or economic theory, however, sound analysis and policy inferences must take into account the contributions of market entrepreneurship. Commented Israel Kirzner, "To make the error of imagining that there is nothing for entrepreneurs to do, that economic processes are somehow propelled without the entrepreneurial spirit and genius for discovery, is to fall prey to a way of thinking that can harmfully affect social policy."[42] This neglect can lead not only to recommendations for government intervention that unintentionally stifles alertness to socially desirable profit opportunities (as repeatedly occurred in the 1970s with oil), but also to a misdiagnosis of a market situation to encourage intervention (such as recommending oil-product tariffs).

9. Embargo Circumventions

An inherent problem limits the effectiveness of nation-to-nation embargoes of crude oil and oil products. Because of the interrelated world petroleum market and the complexity and secrecy therein, selective embargoes can be easily circumvented by diverting cargoes to embargoed nations where, if the embargo is having any effect, prices and profits are greater. For example, if country *A* embargoes country *B*, country *C* can divert its regular product imports (or export domestic refined output) to country *B* and take new cargoes from country *A* or elsewhere. This breaks the embargo by new trading patterns, albeit at higher transportation cost. Alternatively, country *C* can simply re-export cargoes from country *A* to country *B*. In October 1973, the decision by Saudi Arabia and other OAPEC members to embargo the United States and the Netherlands left other importing nations and major company intermediaries to break the embargo. The OAPEC production cutback, consequently, was evenly shared between embargoed and nonembargoed countries.

---

[42]Kirzner, *Discovery and the Capitalist Process* (Chicago: University of Chicago Press, 1985), p. 92.

The obstacles that limited the effectiveness of the Arab embargo in 1973–74 have not gone away—rather, they have been magnified. Given the greater role of spot cargoes and middleman trader activities today than in the 1970s, selective embargoes will be even more difficult to effectuate than in the past—whether with crude oil or petroleum products. In chapter 4, the embargo problem will be revisited and the real threat, *a concerted production cutback*, will be evaluated. For purposes of the present discussion of oil products, and gasoline in particular, a look at the configuration of "friendly" versus "nonfriendly" refining will suffice.

10. Western Hemisphere Refining and "National Security"

A bulkhead against a gasoline import crisis from the Middle East is the sizable, sophisticated refinery centers in North America (U.S. territories, Canada, and Mexico), South and Central America, Western Europe, and the Far East and Oceania. Unfriendly or potentially unfriendly capacity would include refineries located in Eastern Europe, the Soviet Union, the Middle East, and Africa. In addition

Table 3–6

WORLD REFINING CAPACITY AS OF JANUARY 1, 1986
(thousand barrels per day)

Region	Number of Refineries	Primary Capacity	Secondary Capacity	Total Capacity
Friendly:				
North America	253	18,584	12,083	30,667
South/Cen. America	68	5,491	1,634	7,125
Western Europe	124	14,516	5,203	19,719
Far East/Oceania	128	12,262	2,351	14,613
Total Friendly	573	50,853	21,271	72,124
Suspect:				
Soviet Union	38	12,200	N/A	N/A
Eastern Europe	45	3,150	N/A	N/A
Middle East	36	3,831	685	4,516
Africa	43	2,521	503	3,024
Total Suspect	162	21,702	N/A	N/A
Total:	735	72,555	N/A	N/A

SOURCE: Energy Information Administration, Department of Energy

to approximately 15 to 16 million barrels of primary refining capacity in the United States today, friendly capacity totals approximately 35 million barrels per day, while "suspect" primary capacity totals around 22 million barrels per day. A comparison of downstream capacity between East and West is hampered by the unavailability of capacity figures for the USSR and Eastern Europe.

It is widely recognized that there is spare refining capacity in many countries friendly to the United States. Through processing agreements and exchanges, gasoline and other products could be refined for export to the United States to mitigate unanticipated product interruptions from the Middle East.

Table 3–7 demonstrates the diverse supply sources that supplied the United States with gasoline and gasoline feedstocks last year. The top four suppliers, Venezuela, Virgin Islands, Netherlands, and Canada, accounted for a secure 48 percent of the market. Three

Table 3–7

LEADING GASOLINE EXPORTERS TO THE U.S. IN 1986
(thousand barrels per day)

Rank	Country	Volume	Percent of Total Imports
1	Venezuela	76	21
2	Virgin Islands	35	10
3	Netherlands	32	9
4	Canada	29	8
5	Romania	25	7
6	Brazil	25	7
7	Italy	22	6
8	China	18	5
9	Saudi Arabia	17	5
10	Hawaii (T. Z.)	8	2
11	Netherlands Antilles	7	2
12	Belgium	5	1
13	France	5	1
14	Mexico	4	1
15	Germany	3	1
Other		51	14
Total:		363	100

SOURCE: Energy Information Administration, Department of Energy

possible adversaries in the top 15 suppliers, Romania, China, and Saudi Arabia, accounted for only 17 percent. The diversity and market share of these exporters, combined with the gasoline import aggregate of only 6 percent of national consumption, make a national security threat from a gasoline cutoff virtually unimaginable.

11. The Unfair Competition/Subsidization Argument

Competition from product imports, the IRC emphasized, has been an unfair aberration of true market rivalry because of the government-sponsored advantages of foreign refiners over U.S. refiners. In addition to less taxation, less pollution-control expenditure, and fewer pollution-control restrictions, foreign refineries are distinctly advantaged by government integration whereby crude prices can be discounted to keep refining profitable under a wide range of adverse conditions.

The first critical point regarding the above is to note that U.S. refiners have an important inherent advantage over their foreign counterparts, particularly with light products. Gasoline is a particularly expensive cargo to ship great distances. It is a highly volatile, dangerous cargo and, accordingly, pays high insurance premiums. It cannot be shipped in large crude tankers; smaller vessels, with special compartments to avoid contamination and evaporation, are required. As more expensive cargo, it has higher inventory costs than cheaper crude shipments to U.S. destinations. In short, domestic refiners enjoy a major natural advantage over for-export facilities by being nearer their market.

Turning to the subsidization charge, the incremental (lifting) cost of foreign crude for many state-owned firms is a fraction of the cost of crude output in the United States. In Saudi Arabia, to use the most pertinent example, the marginal cost of production is under $1 per barrel. Thus feedstock discounting to meet the pricing requirements of product markets simply ensures that there are two profitable centers instead of one. Secondly, at the time the IRC made this argument, OPEC crude prices were widely recognized as artificially high. Low-priced product was more reflective of reality than "official" OPEC crude pricing. The final price, in any case, not the transfer price, is key. As I argued in 1985:

> It is generally recognized that official OPEC crude-oil prices are higher than market-clearing levels and that aggressive entry into product markets by Saudi Arabia, Kuwait, and other cartel members merely disguises this fact. The exact transfer price from the

field to the refinery is ultimately irrelevant; the quantity and price of the resulting products are what matter in the world petroleum market.[43]

The transfer-price complaint, at base, is not an argument against integrated government oil concerns. It is an argument against integration per se. It is as applicable to Exxon, Chevron, Texaco, Shell, and the other integrated majors as it is to Saudi Arabia, Kuwait, and other for-export state refineries with home production. Any integrated firm can either take a bookkeeping loss on refining and stay in business by virtue of wellhead (or marketing) profitability or make an accounting change to give its refining branch "paper profits." Consequently, the refiners' argument against foreign competition has the unsettling implication of being an argument for divorcement and divestiture of domestic integrated competitors. If integration is advantageous, as much evidence in the 125 years of the U.S. oil industry suggests, each nonintegrated refiner has the option to integrate by buying another firm, being bought by another firm, or establishing a production or marketing affiliate. In 1978, Ashland went from an upstream integrated refiner to a nonintegrated refiner by selling their production properties, reasoning that if they needed crude and it was too expensive or unavailable, they could petition regulators to force another company to give it to them. Ashland soon found itself without access to low-priced crude, regulators acquiesced, and the company that bought Ashland's production properties, among others, was forced to sell crude back to the refiner at less than its purchase price.[44] For Ashland (as the IRC leader) to condemn integration as unfair competition after choosing to disintegrate is rank hypocrisy.

The unfair-competition argument of the IRC against the Saudi refiners is little more than chagrin at the sight of the world's dominant producer also becoming a dominant refiner. In retrospect, the Saudis may have built too much capacity for their own good, but then so did many U.S. and European refiners. (The Saudis have also postponed construction of scheduled projects, demonstrating the limits to "subsidization.") But to deny the Saudis the right to

[43]"Oil Protectionism: The New Threat," p. 15. For a rebuttal of the subsidy argument by an OPEC official, see Marvin Reid, "Looking Things Over," *National Petroleum News*, September 1985, p. 5.

[44]Alexander, "Day of Reckoning for Oil Refiners," p. 41.

integrate forward, both to satisfy increasing internal product demand and pentrate foreign markets, is unrealistic. Their decision to integrate was based on estimates of growing internal and external demand, a long history of forward integration by successful private firms, strategies as the "dominant" firm in a cartel, and their *own vulnerability to oil product cutoffs*. Emma Brossard has identified several logical reasons for OPEC's integration:

> There was a considerable need within OPEC countries to build their own refineries. Not only were their own domestic consumption needs rising (Saudi Arabia with a population of 7 million in 1983 consumed 424,900 b/d, compared to Venezuela with a population of 16 million whose consumption was 346,000 b/d), their vulnerability to being cut off from imports, in time of crisis, was no less than any other country's. Furthermore, they had their own funds to pay Western construction and consulting companies to build or upgrade their refineries, and the West was anxious to sell the machinery and technology to them. Now, when the plants have reached the production stage, the West's attitude changes. One has to ask the hard question, why should OPEC, or any producing country, not have the opportunity to increase the value of their oil by moving downstream?[45]

The subsidy argument would evaporate in 1986. Selective crude discounting was a forerunner to the OPEC price war that broke out when Saudi Arabia increased crude output from 2 million barrels per day to 5 million barrels per day. To move these incremental volumes, de facto integration was resorted to whereby the Saudis (and other oil-exporting countries) sold their crude to U.S. refiners at a "netback" price guaranteeing the latter a certain margin.

12. The SPR Refining Argument

The IRC has effectively used the Strategic Petroleum Reserve as an argument in their favor. Exclusive emphasis on the SPR to mitigate a national security emergency with oil is, after all, mis-

---

[45]Brossard, *Protectionism and the U.S. Refining Industry*, p. 10. Douglas Bohi and William Quandt, citing "substantial political and economic advantages" from Saudi integration into refining, identify several other advantages: use of previously flared gas and scale economies of "package deals" with crude oil, oil products, petrochemicals, and transportation. A disadvantage of OPEC refining from their point of view, on the other hand, is that it complicates price and quantity agreements within the cartel. Bohi and Quandt, *Energy Security in the 1980s: Economic and Political Perspectives* (Washington, D.C.: Brookings Institution, 1984), pp. 6–7.

placed. The United States must have the *refining facilities* to complement the SPR drawdown level of 3 million barrels per day (and potentially 4.5 million barrels per day) to complete the national security exercise.

This argument possesses a self-contained logic, but it is a nonsequitur when presented as an argument for refiner protectionism. It is as much an argument against the existence of the SPR in its present form than it is an argument for product tariffs.

The SPR has been a sacred cow among interventionist-minded energy economists since its beginning in 1975. Yet it has suffered from all the problems that could be expected from a massive government storage program enacted in the haste of the energy crisis. In its 12 years it has never been used. The Iranian cutoff and price explosion of 1979–80, which was as much a crisis as the SPR can hope to counter, did not result in any drawdowns; it resulted in a decision to suspend purchases temporarily because crude prices were too high. The average acquisition and storage cost of the $15 billion "insurance premium" is approximately $30 per barrel, well above the current market price for crude oil. It has experienced major cost overruns, overpayments, disruptive reorganizations, design problems, schedule misestimations, quality control breakdowns, lavish extracurricular expenditures, burdensome congressional oversight, environmental problems, and a safety mishap that resulted in a loss of life. It has turned into a foreign-aid program for Mexico with a secretive long-term contract that included $1 billion of up-front money. Relatedly, there is concern that too much heavy crude has been purchased (from Mexico) rather than lighter (Middle Eastern) crudes that can be processed by more refineries. Domestic crude purchases for the reserve are now required to aid the ailing U.S. industry, and legislative proposals have been made to require future purchases to be from U.S. stripper wells and the Naval Petroleum Reserve. (Note the irony of extracting the government's NPR oil in the Western United States to return to the ground in the Southwest.) The SPR has experienced drawdown problems on the technical side and remains without a *politically sanctioned* drawdown plan. Since May 1981, moreover, it has been financed off-budget to mask its continuing contribution to federal deficits.

Granted that these are sunk costs, the question is whether SPR oil has a fundamental role to play in a future supply emergency. In public hands, the answer is not certain. The reserve is a *political asset*, which is not necessarily the same as a national security asset.

With such unanswered questions as *when* should the oil be distributed, *at what rate* should the oil be drawn down, and *who* gets (or does not get) such oil facing political barriers, there is uncertainty about whether excess refining capacity should stand ready for utilization in a drawdown. Another fundamental question is whether "extra" refining capacity is necessary for the reserve since *if* there is a drawdown, it theoretically would be replacing crude that is temporarily unavailable. In short, the political and economic uncertainties of the Strategic Petroleum Reserve do not qualify it as an integral part of the private oil market and "national security."

The addition of "national security" refining to the crude reserve does not complete the national security structure of production. The need for an effective *distribution* system opens up another government protection/subsidization issue. Yet because the competitive viability of so many independent gasoline wholesalers and retailers depends on foreign product (witness the staunch opposition to product tariffs by the Coalition of Independent Petroleum Product Marketers), the ironic result is that product tariffs to protect refiners threaten the next and final stage in the "national security" nexus. For this reason and others mentioned above, the SPR argument for refinery protection must be abandoned.

13. Refining and the Military

The national security argument for a refining floor is based not only on private sector demand but on the present and future needs of the U.S. military. A major part of the Ebinger study calculates a minimum level of refining capacity to provide the U.S. Defense Fuel Supply Center (DFSC), supplier of the Army, Navy, Air Force, and Marines—and even our NATO allies—with near-full needs. Of a more specific nature, the IRC argument asserts that small refiners are uniquely qualified to provide the military with highly specialized products necessary for national defense.

The U.S. military, as one of the world's leading oil consumers, would be hurt by higher prices resulting from protectionism. (Higher domestic prices, however, can be circumvented by buying abroad, as the military did during the MOIP.) The military must economize—in times of peace as well as in times of war.

The military lives in a world where not only oil is scarce; storage facilities, manpower, armaments, tanks, trucks, ships, and planes are also in limited supply. Fuel would not be the "weak link" in a full military mobilization, according to the head of the DFSC, John

Griffith. Jeffrey Jones, director of energy policy for the Department of Defense, has also recently stressed the point that oil "is not the most significant limitation in fighting a war."[46] In other words, the hardware of war is more scarce than petroleum, not a surprising fact given the relative costs involved and the surplus oil situation around the world.

The specialty-product argument for protecting the status quo of refining for military reasons is not persuasive. Under a least-cost purchase program, the military can meet its needs by a bid program and/or enter into a contract with any domestic refiner deemed crucial to satisfactory procurement. The field should be opened to all refiners, and if indeed a particular refinery is necessary to fill an order, a long-term contract can be finalized to the benefit of both parties. But for those small refiners who cannot successfully compete in military bid programs, there should be no guaranties.

The place of "regional refiners" in a nontariff world was recognized in a recent National Petroleum Council study:

> Approximately 15–20 percent of U.S. refining capacity is represented by regional refiners. Although many of these refineries are small, they each have their own niche in serving local and specialty markets with minimal transportation costs for both crude oil and products. As long as these conditions exist, regional refiners should remain viable.[47]

This particular market share (as of 1986), however, is not set in concrete. Only the consumer, military and nonmilitary, can determine—and continually revise—the place of small refining in the U.S. refining industry.

14. New Trends in 1986

A Pace Company study released in June 1985 by the IRC predicted that 1.4 million barrels per day of present refining capacity would be lost by 1990 with 1 million barrels per day idled by 1987. This has not turned out to be true. In fact, gasoline imports fell significantly in 1986, and the shutdown rate of U.S. refineries has been reversed. In 1985, idled capacity totaled 380,826 barrels per day, compared to an average 1.3 million barrels per day in the previous

---

[46]Barbara Sanders, "Energy and National Security: Military Implications," *Oil Daily*, March 9, 1987, p. 9.

[47]National Petroleum Council, *U.S. Petroleum Refining*, pp. 9–10.

four years. In 1986, capacity actually *increased* as reactivations out-paced shutdowns with both primary and secondary capacity.[48] Indeed, a National Petroleum Council study concluded in mid-1986 that "the U.S. refining industry restructuring is largely complete."[49] The IRC argument, in retrospect, was an exaggerated attempt to spur a reluctant audience into hasty action.

The 15 percent decrease in gasoline imports in 1986 from the record high set the year before saw OPEC's and OAPEC's share fall below the very small levels of 1985. The share of gasoline imports from Saudi Arabia, in particular, fell from 7 percent to 5 percent of imports. As a percentage of U.S. consumption, this translated into a drop from 0.4 percent to 0.2 percent.

Many other refining developments in the United States in 1986 did not square with the arguments made by the IRC the year before. Crude discounting by foreign governments to their state-owned refineries, leading to complaints of unfair subsidization by the IRC, blossomed during 1986 into "netback" crude pricing for major and independent U.S. refiners alike. As much as 8.5 million barrels per day of crude traded internationally was sold to refiners at prices tied to the product price.[50] Domestic crude postings plummeted with world oil prices to slash feedstock costs in half for refiners. Consequently, broad cross-sections of the refining industry, inde-pendents included, enjoyed healthy margins even with lower prod-uct prices. And under netback deals, profits were locked in.

As mentioned, almost as many refineries have been reactivated as have closed down since 1985. In 1985, 17 refiners shut down while 10 refiners started up, a net loss of 7 units and 68,000 barrels per day of capacity.[51] In 1986, a gain in operable capacity brought the nation's primary capacity to nearly 15.3 million barrels per day and downstream capacity to over 21 million barrels per day.[52] Another high point for U.S. refining was a 7 percent increase in product exports (to 617,000 barrels per day) led by expanded petroleum coke

[48]See Richard Corbett, "Product Demand Surge Keeps Leaner U.S. Downstream Humming," *Oil & Gas Journal*, March 30, 1987, p. 51.

[49]National Petroleum Council, *U.S. Petroleum Refining*, p. 130.

[50]See "Netbacks Have Deeply Changed International Crude Oil Pricing," *National Petroleum News*, June 1986, pp. 34–37.

[51]"U.S. Refining Capacity: How Much Is Enough?" *National Petroleum News*, July 1986, p. 14.

[52]For a listing of new or reactivated refineries, see appendix D, p. 255.

shipments to Western Europe.[53] Tariffs would have sealed off these incremental export opportunities by keeping U.S. product at home and foreign product abroad.

The future can be expected to hold the same promise of refinery expansion alongside contraction, depending on relative plant profitabilities. Increasing product demand has led one company to consider constructing a new 150,000 barrel per day refinery in the Caribbean and reactivating several other refineries in the general area.[54] A proposed new 100,000 barrel per day for-export refinery, the first in the United States, was announced by Alaska Pacific Refining, Inc. The Valdez, Alaska, high-technology project, budgeted at $750 million, intends to process heavy North Slope crude into middle distillates and some light products at the terminus of the Trans-Alaskan Pipeline System to ship to Japan and other Pacific Rim destinations.[55] This for-export proposal, while inspired in large part by regulation (to circumvent the Alaskan crude export ban, has three sobering implications for refinery protectionists. One, it is in response to eased import restrictions by Japan, which portend further liberalization of the international trade barriers that the IRC complained about.[56] Two, the project demonstrates the possibility of large new incremental capacity in U.S. territory. Three, it is a *U.S.* for-export project similar to foreign refinery projects criticized by the IRC.

Another trend in 1986 was for foreign interests to purchase U.S. refineries in part or whole. Petroleos de Venezuela purchased a 50 percent stake in a 320,000 barrels per day refinery in Lake Charles, Louisiana, owned by Citgo Petroleum and a 50 percent interest in

[53]DeVan Shumway, "Elusive 'Stability' in Petroleum Industry Key to Refiners' Future," *Oil Daily,* March 27, 1987, p. 12.

[54]*Oil & Gas Journal Newsletter,* January 19, 1987.

[55]Mark Emond, "Proposed Big, New Refinery in Alaska Raises Basic Quesions About Oil," *National Petroleum News,* October 1986, pp. 28–29. Oil-product exports have been increasing for over a decade. Stated Emma Brossard: "Almost unnoticed in the U.S. press is the entrance of the U.S. in the international market as a major exporter of oil products. American refiners are now exporting to twice as many countries as the U.S. is importing from, and oil *exports* since 1976 have gone up 300 percent! This has occurred because of new oil trading operation in the industry, as well as the availability of excess refining capacity. The world oil market is changing from the export of crude oil to the export of oil products." *Protectionism and the U.S. Refining Industry,* p. ii.

[56]*Oil & Gas Journal Newsletter,* January 19, 1987.

the 160,000 barrels per day Champlin refinery in Corpus Christi, Texas, as part of its "internationalization policy" to facilitate crude export sales. Saudi Arabia, Kuwait, Abu Dhabi, and other major oil exporters to the United States have either bid on U.S. facilities or are rumored to be doing so.[57] While George Jandacek expressed the IRC view that such entry "is the same as having a for-export refinery located on our shores," such partnerships further interdependence and foster a mutuality of interest between the investing country and the U.S. consuming market.[58] Their presence would no more be a threat to the United States than are Shell and Standard Oil with their current foreign ownership.

The resurgence of refining profitability in 1986, while benefiting the IRC in many ways (except theoretically), has not been without some negatives. Derby Refining, a subsidiary of IRC member Coastal Corporation, suspended crude distillation at its 30,000 barrel per day facility in El Dorado, Kansas. Derby, in what amounted to an IRC policy statement, blamed the closing on "a flood of imports to the U.S. resulting in excessive inventories and distressed prices."[59]

Another major event of 1986 that was not supportive of the IRC case was a major report by the National Petroleum Council, released in mid-1986, on the state of the American refining industry. The study sounded no national security alarms and even went the other way, with the following prediction:

> The indicated additions for 1988 together with the reactivation of some refineries appear to be adequate to meet the needs of this high demand [14.1 million barrels per day] scenario. Increased amount of simple distillation products could be manufactured using the slack distillation capacity, and some light products could be made through the use of slack conversion unit capacity.[60]

This prediction has been vindicated to date. Proving that refining

[57]Steve Frazier and James Tanner, "Foreign Oil Producers Buy Refineries in U.S. for Stake in Marketing," *Wall Street Journal*, April 4, 1986, pp. 1, 14.

[58]Ibid., p. 14.

[59]"Coastal Unit Suspends Refinery Operations," *Oil Daily*, February 9, 1987, p. 2. Also see *Oil & Gas Journal Newsletter*, February 9, 1987.

[60]National Petroleum Council, *U.S. Petroleum Refining*, p. 75. The study was in no way biased against the IRC or independent refiners in general. The NPC's National Committee on U.S. Petroleum Refining was chaired by John McKinley of Texaco and included well-known protectionists such as John Hall of Ashland and Fred Hartley of Unocal.

capacity was not at a "national security" minimum, a post-1980 record 2.6 percent increase in product demand was successfully met in 1986 by increased runs at existing facilities and incremental additions. Gasoline demand rose 2.7 percent, the highest gain since 1979 when over a hundred more refineries were in operation. Clearly the critics of U.S. refining have underrated the productivity of the industry.[61] The industry rationalization has left the industry stronger, not weaker.

15. U.S. Refining: A Healthy and Adaptive Industry

Today's industry, with only minimal protection from the vicissitudes of the world market, is lean and performance-capable. The 1986 *Oil & Gas Journal* Refining Report concluded as follows:

> Through restructuring and upgrades, the U.S. refining industry appears to be successfully meeting the effects of tough market circumstances and government rulings. If 1985 results continue, the industry will be well prepared for the 1990s.[62]

The 1987 *Oil & Gas Journal Refining Report* built upon the previous year's optimism by stating:

> In refining, increased demand may have signaled the end of the days of massive shut downs and capacity shedding. In fact, 1986 saw a slight increase in crude charging capacity. Perhaps more noteworthy, however, refiners added to their solid downstream strength for producing gasoline, distillate, and for processing heavy, poor-quality crude oils and resids.[63]

Many singular achievements make up the "bottom line" success of *adapting to changing market conditions*, whether by exit, entry, or modification. One recently noted advance may be mentioned: new inventory management techniques utilizing sophisticated procurement strategies such as location, time, quality, and "opportunity" oil trading and computerized information tracking systems.[64]

[61]Robert Beck and Glenda Smith, "Oil, Gas Price Collapse Cuts *OGJ* Group Profits One Third in 1986," *Oil & Gas Journal*, May 25, 1987, p. 20.

[62]Richard Corbett, "Industry Restructures, Capacity Up Slightly," *Oil & Gas Journal*, March 24, 1986, pp. 71–73.

[63]Richard Corbett, "Product Demand Surge Keeps Leaner U.S. Downstream Humming," *Oil & Gas Journal Report*, March 30, 1987, p. 51.

[64]See Michael Obel, "Refiners Meeting U.S. Demand with Less Product in Inventory," *Oil & Gas Journal*, February 17, 1986, pp. 19–22.

Hedging with futures trading is a self-help measure that refiners can use to manage the risk and change so prevalent in the industry—instead of being victimized by change and turning to political "solutions."

It is not an exaggeration to say that with the help of modern technology and the discipline of the market, the present refining industry is the most efficient in U.S. and world history.[65] This is not to say that the industry has reached its full potential. Much government regulation and taxation stand in the way of full industry efficiency and maximum consumer sovereignty, as do proposed new regulations and taxes.

The health of the industry, in fact, is in large part due to the *absence* of major tariffs and other government subsidies. Such artificial props would have preserved overcapacity, which not only would have misallocated resources but institutionalized cutthroat conditions in the domestic industry. Instead, a fewer number of market-dictated survivors allows these members greater opportunities to survive and prosper in the future. The benefits of tariffs would have been fleeting in the face of opposing political and market forces in the postimplementation period. The failure of the Independent Refiners Coalition to obtain protection, certainly not a loss for consumers and the economy, may have prevented a weakening of the small-refiner industry itself.

16. Politics Has the Last Say

Like other would-be planners, Ebinger and the other architects of the IRC position assume that their own recommendations can become public policy. Ebinger presents his contribution as an enlightened balance between the failings of both laissez-faire and government planning. In words reminiscent of the heyday of Keynesian economics, which also sought a "middle way," he states:

> Ideological rhetoric advocating an energy "free market" (which has never existed) or government management (which has never worked) must be rejected in favor of basic policy goals which can be fine-tuned over time. One critical policy goal must be to ensure the continuation of adequate petroleum refining capacity.[66]

Setting aside the problem of *what* adequate refining capacity is,

---

[65]For some recent efficiencies, see ibid.

[66]Ebinger, *Oil Product Imports: A Threat to U.S. National Security*, p. 54.

there remains the political problem. Our system of government is manned by elected representatives who are more interested in serving their constituents than implementing any expert's idea of the public interest. What guaranty is there that what may begin in the name of national security will continue to be true to its vision? If the past is any guide—and quota regulation under the Mandatory Oil Import Program comes to mind—political considerations will be prominent if not dominant. Even if the planners' blueprint gets the first say, politics always has the last say. This is implicit in Ebinger's statement that government management "has never worked," although he refuses to renounce his policy goal of "fine-tun[ing]. . . adequate petroleum refining capacity."

C. Summary and Conclusions

The refiners' case for product tariffs to limit imports and raise domestic refined prices of gasoline is not convincing. Politically, the national security argument has been used since at least 1979 without any manifestation of shortages or breakdown of industry performance. The national security threat concerns a *specific* product (imported gasoline) in a specific area of the United States (the East Coast) and does not justify comprehensive tariffs or partial product (gasoline) tariffs for the entire country. The increase in gasoline imports, while great in percentage terms between 1980 and 1985, is less important than conservation in the refining reconfiguration. As conservation has been forgotten in the IRC argument, so have been product exports, which, along with imports, have increased.

Dependence on foreign gasoline is small (5 to 6 percent), and dependence on Arab gasoline is minuscule (0.5 percent and falling). Prospectively, there is little reason to anticipate a flood of light product imports. Middle Eastern refiners do not specialize in gasoline compared to other products, and their primary market is Western Europe. Domestic refiners, in fact, enjoy a significant advantage over foreign refiners because of the high costs of gasoline transportation for the latter.

There has not been a "second wave" of refinery closings that, unlike earlier "first wave" shutdowns, threatens future industry performance. Both "waves" were necessary adjustments to world conditions altered by decreasing product demand, especially demand for gasoline, which revealed excess U.S. and world distillation capacity. Closer examination shows that what is called "unfair subsidized imports" merely reflects the natural incentive and ability of integrated firms to "flex," as market conditions dictate, in order to coax incremental revenues out of sunk costs.

Recognizing the characteristic of *entrepreneurial alertness* to future market conditions, refining entrepreneurs, in addition to product importers and downstream marketers, can be expected to reasonably predict future market supplies and demands (including cutoffs) to mitigate worst-case national security events hypothesized by the IRC. They may rearrange existing operating capacity, reactivate operable capacity, construct new capacity, tilt yields toward relatively scarce products, and maximize storage. Consumers, too, can alertly act in the present by anticipating future scarcity in their energy decisions and adjust to sudden product scarcity to meet budget constraints.

A look at Western Hemisphere refining and the diversity of imports demonstrates the exaggeration of national security concerns with gasoline imports. Furthermore, selective embargoes are virtually impossible.

Not only is current refining capacity reasonably congruent to feedstock capacities, but determining a national security floor of refining capacity is arbitrary and beyond science. Only the marketplace can determine what protectionists hypothesize to be the "right" capacity.

Events of 1986 contradicted the arguments of the IRC. Predictions of a major shutdown of capacity from new gasoline imports have failed to materialize, demonstrating the transient nature of the arguments protectionists use to justify the business emergencies of the moment. Incremental capacity was added, in fact, to meet a major increase in product demand brought on by lower prices. Trade barriers in other major gasoline markets show signs of being relaxed, and what were considered selected crude discounting subsidies in 1985 became par for the general refiner population in 1986. In all, new developments in the U.S. and world refining industries reinforce the abstract notion that a "spontaneous order" is at work that should be respected more than the recommendations of certain refinery executives and supportive experts for a major interventionist program.

A final word is reserved for the changing world refining market. The new refining investments of the Middle East and elsewhere are sunk costs that will benefit the world petroleum market for decades to come by increasing and diversifying product competition, rearranging world trade patterns according to transportation economies, and encouraging more congruent pricing between European markets and U.S. East and Gulf Coast markets.[67] From a utilitarian viewpoint, today's refining situation need not be cause for alarm. It is decidedly pro-consumer. To make the right investment decisions, U.S. entrepreneurs must view competition internationally, not provincially, and avoid the facile and superficial dogmas of protectionism.

---

[67]See the analysis of Philip Verleger in Patrick Crow, "U.S. in No Rush to Rescue Small Refiners Hurt by Product Imports," *Oil & Gas Journal*, May 27, 1985, pp. 27–28.

4. The Case for Wellhead Protectionism Reconsidered

If the analysis in the last chapter may be characterized as "beating a dead horse," the debate in this chapter is very much alive. Since early 1986, the tariff debate has radically shifted from protecting domestic refiners to protecting domestic producers. It is the latter debate that is the focal point of this chapter.

The chapter begins with the re-sounding of the energy alarm via major studies released by the Department of Energy, the National Petroleum Council, the American Petroleum Institute, and other groups in the spring of 1987. The multifarious statistics behind the severe depression in domestic exploration/production and subsidiary industries, and their implications for national security, are described, followed by a critical review of the debate. While it is accepted that a major reversal of economic fortunes for the domestic wellhead industry has occurred and some market-share has been transferred to areas of the world that a decade ago were unreliable suppliers, the analysis focuses on *what this means for the national economy and "national security" in both the short and long term.* Center stage is the question: Does a continuation of present trends of declining domestic output and increased crude imports mean shortages and price spikes in the future? Restated, Is increased dependence on foreign oil an inherently unstable and unwelcome event that will transform today's euphoria into tomorrow's painful price spike or gasoline line? This question is answered by (1) presenting a different view of the cause of previous U.S. oil crises, (2) reinterpreting the present state of the world oil and energy market to ascertain the ability of embargoes and production cuts to effectively raise prices, (3) studying the motivations of oil-exporting countries to try to "shock" the world market, and (4) examining the various arguments advanced for protectionism within the industry and academia.

117

A. Sounding the National Security Alarm

In the spring of 1987, a number of distinguished reports were released on the present state of the U.S. oil industry and on the policy options that might improve it. A study by the National Petroleum Council, an industry advisory group to the Department of Energy, addressed the following conclusions to Energy Secretary John Herrington:

> The National Petroleum Council strongly believes that the United States and other consuming nations face the serious threat of a repeat of the energy crises of the 1970s. We are confronted with a rapidly growing oil import dependence, which will increase our vulnerability to a supply disruption, undermine our national security, accelerate our balance of trade problems, and compromise our foreign policy. Mr. Secretary, we urge you and the Administration to join us in making every effort to alert the nation to this grave situation, and to thoroughly review all of the various options available to prevent a reoccurrence of these crises. The Council stresses the urgency of the situation and the need for prompt action.[1]

A month later, a much-awaited Department of Energy study, *Energy Security*, was released to President Reagan as a blueprint of the current energy picture and policy alternatives. In the foreword, Secretary Herrington wrote:

> The following Department of Energy review of our energy-related national security interests, "Energy Security," was conducted at the request of President Reagan in response to his concern over declining domestic oil production and rising oil imports. . . . America is at another equally critical juncture in the state of energy security. The crisis in the domestic petroleum industry, an industry that is critical to our energy security, is taking an enormous toll and is creating serious problems for the future.[2]

---

[1]*Factors Affecting U.S. Oil & Gas Outlook*, A Report of the National Petroleum Council, February 1987, front letter. The report was originally requested by Secretary Herrington on September 23, 1985. In response, the Committee on U.S. Oil & Gas Outlook was created within the NPC, with Tenneco Chairman James Ketelsen as chairman. An interim report was released October 9, 1986, because of the severe deterioration of oil prices; the final report was issued on February 24, 1987.

[2]U.S. Department of Energy, *Energy Security: A Report to the President of the United States*, March 1987, foreword. The report is also called the "Martin study" for Deputy Energy Secretary William Martin, who was instrumental in its presentation.

Another alarm was sounded by the Joint Economic Committee of Congress:

> The benefits of falling international oil prices should not blind us to our increased vulnerability to external events. . . . While the recent oil price decline has brought with it certain benefits, the long-term consequences of today's import-dependent energy policy may be more harmful to the economy than today's short-term advantages.[3]

The United States Energy Association, the U.S. member of the World Energy Conference, stated the issue in stark terms:

> The United States is drifting toward a serious national security and economic crisis. In three or four years, without corrective action starting now, U.S. economic, political, military, and foreign policy could be seriously compromised. The U.S., the most powerful economic and political force in the world, will face limits on its ability to control it own destiny. Millions of American jobs and billions of dollars in future economic growth are in jeopardy. Energy is at the root of this looming crisis.[4]

The American Petroleum Institute released its own major study, *Domestic Petroleum Production and National Security*, which concluded:

> Much concern has been expressed about what [increasing oil imports] portend for the nation's economic and military security. This paper assesses likely future trends in the nation's energy position and examines economic, military, and foreign policy implications. Its principal finding is that U.S. dependence on oil imports will increase in coming years, and that this development will adversely affect the nation's economic performance and significantly constrain its conduct of foreign/military policy.[5]

Heritage Foundation energy analyst Milton Copulos, in a report for the National Defense Council Foundation, a private foundation dedicated to military preparedness, raised the concern that today's gains from low oil prices might be unaffordable from a military perspective.

---

[3]Joint Economic Committee of Congress, *1986 Annual Report*, pp. 131, 135.

[4]USEA, *A Call for Action*, Spring 1987, p. 1.

[5]API, *Domestic Petroleum Production and National Security*, December 30, 1986, p. iv.

Although the general perception that "all is well" on the energy front persists, nothing could be further from the truth. In simple terms, the nation is facing a threat to both its military and economic security of monumental proportions. . . . Within three years, the nation may find itself simply unable to meet its fuel needs in the event it is required to bring its defense forces to a full mobilization. . . . America's defense capability could be left high and dry as far as petroleum resources are concerned.[6]

A Heritage Foundation study by Copulos also warned of dire economic consequences in the absence of a federal government commitment to the oil industry.

America once again has wandered into energy complacency. It is a complacency that could be shattered at any moment by a new Arab embargo. Only concerted and immediate action by the President can avoid the worst consequences of such an import disruption.[7]

Many industry leaders, whose intimate knowledge of their business is not to be questioned, have warned about the grave consequences of extrapolated industry trends. Noted scholars have also raised their voices to question the social beneficence of the new energy reality.[8] *Fortune* magazine titled an article, "Get Ready for the Coming Oil Crisis."[9] In short, the petroleum/national security alarm has been loudly sounded from many quarters.

B. The Wellhead National Security Argument

In chapter 1, the great price plunge of 1986 and the ensuing depression in the upstream sector were examined. This section surveys the contraction in more detail and develops the national security arguments based upon it *from a protectionist viewpoint.* Two

---

[6]Milton Copulos, "The Hidden Oil Crisis," (Alexandria, Va.: National Defense Council Foundation, 1986), pp. 5, 9. Tariff supporters from the military establishment have included former Defense Secretary Harold Brown. See *Oil Daily*, August 14, 1986, p. 1.

[7]Milton Copulos, "America's Looming Energy Crisis: The Causes," Heritage Foundation: Backgrounder, April 29, 1987, p. 8.

[8]See chapter 1, pp. 22–23, for a brief look at academic support for oil tariffs. A major academic study advocating oil tariffs is critically evaluated in appendix 4B, pp. 185–94.

[9]John Newport, "Get Ready for the Coming Oil Crisis," *Fortune*, March 16, 1987, pp. 46–53.

interrelated points are stressed: the decline in domestic activity and the heightened preeminence of Middle Eastern countries, led by Saudi Arabia, in the changing world petroleum market.

1. Contraction of the Wellhead Sector

The rapid contraction of the exploration/production sector in 1986, after its painful adjustment to the previous downturn, was the major industry story of a tumultuous year.[10] The plunge in posted oil prices from around $28 per barrel in November 1985 to $12 per barrel in March 1986, a 60 percent drop in four months, stunned the upstream industry and led to hard business and personal decisions to slash budgets and employment. Revised exploration/production budgets reduced wellhead-related employment by 150,000, or 26 percent. Active drilling plummeted, as evidenced by the Baker Hughes oil rig count. The 1986 average of 964 rotary rigs in operation was the lowest yearly average on record since World War II; the weekly average for July 14, 1986, was the lowest since February 1943. The Society of Exploration Geophysicists recorded the lowest level of activity since it began keeping records in 1974. This abrupt downturn led the National Petroleum Council to conclude that "the domestic oil and gas industry has been devastated."[11]

Not only wildcat drilling and development drilling were affected. Thousands of stripper wells, defined as producing less than 10 barrels per day, reached their economic limit as the average posted price fell from $24 per barrel in 1985 to under $13 per barrel in 1986. All totaled, producing oil wells declined by 23,200, or 3.6 percent, in 1986, the largest one-year decline in history. Leading the way were Texas with 7,768 shut-ins, California with 6,157 inactivations, and Pennsylvania with 4,000 closings.

Unlike the situation in the previous downturn of 1982–84, the offshore industry was not spared. Within several months, the largest offshore drilling fleet in history also became the most underutilized offshore drilling fleet in history. In May 1986, the *Oil & Gas Journal* reported:

> Offshore drilling worldwide is experiencing its greatest drop in

---

[10]Many statistics and events described in this section are taken from the National Petroleum Council and Department of Energy studies referred to above. Other figures are cited from Independent Petroleum Association of America publications— *IPAA News, U.S. Supply and Demand Outlook,* and *United States Petroleum Statistics.*

[11]NPC, *Factors Affecting U.S. Oil and Gas Outlook,* p. 5.

> history. . . . Pervasive uncertainties, project cancellations, and drilling postponements have resulted in the highest mobile rig unemployment in history. Over 300 rigs are stacked.[12]

Whereas the previous downturn reduced utilization rates from 100 percent to 75 percent, the depression of 1986 lowered them to nearly 50 percent.

The many faces of financial devastation were summarized by a special *Oil & Gas Journal Report* when it spoke of "bankruptcy filings, reduced capital spending, layoffs and early retirements of personnel, salary freezes, office closures, suspension or reduction of dividends on common stock and preferred stock, sales of assets, restructuring of bank debt, and missed payments on loan interest or principal."[13] In the first half of the year, 45 producers surveyed by the same trade journal alone accounted for $1.6 billion in asset writedowns. Shrinking net worths and a general erosion of financial strength and flexibility had implications far beyond the current production period.

The result of the new oil economics on the U.S. industry was a $15 billion reduction (36 percent) in exploration and development funding, a 50 percent decline in drilling activity, and *an 8 percent decline in oil production* in 1986. This last statistic, amounting to a production loss of 700,000 barrels per day, was a telling, and much-trumpeted, statistic for advocates of national security protectionism.

For the medium and longer term, further declines are expected. Not only is current exploration severely curtailed, but the projected near-term decline of Alaskan North Slope production (which now accounts for 1.8 million barrels per day, or 20 percent of U.S. production), and the postponement of high-risk, high-cost frontier wells and enhanced recovery wells—replacement sources for depleting wells—promise continuing declines in domestic production in the 1990s and beyond.

The postdecontrol (post-1980) rise and recent decline of U.S. crude oil production in relation to world crude output is shown in Table 4–1.

Within the year-to-year decline in U.S. output was a more pro-

---

[12]"Price Shock Slashes Offshore Drilling," *Oil & Gas Journal Report*, May 5, 1986, p. 91.

[13]"Crash of '86 Jolts Independents' Operations," *Oil & Gas Journal Report*, October 27, 1986, p. 48.

Table 4–1

U.S. vs. WORLD CRUDE OIL PRODUCTION: 1973–86
(thousand barrels per day)

Year	U.S. Production	World Production	U.S. % of World Production
1973	9,208	55,573	16.6
1974	8,774	55,769	15.7
1975	8,375	52,764	15.9
1976	8,132	57,193	14.2
1977	8,245	59,522	13.9
1978	8,707	59,868	14.5
1979	8,552	62,353	13.7
1980	8,597	59,225	14.5
1981	8,572	55,546	15.4
1982	8,649	52,900	16.4
1983	8,688	52,654	16.5
1984	8,879	53,834	16.5
1985	8,971	52,954	16.9
1986	8,668	55,267	15.7

SOURCE: Energy Information Administration, Department of Energy

nounced trend. Between January and December of 1986, crude production fell by 773,000 barrels per day, an 8.5 percent decline in an 11-month period.

The 1986 figure for U.S. output represents a market-share loss of 7 percent within a 4 percent rise of world output. Saudi Arabia was the major instigator, increasing its world market-share from 6.4 percent in 1985 to 9 percent in 1986.

2. The Saudi Arabia–Middle Eastern Preeminence

The United States, with a 125-year history of oil well drilling and production, is the most mature oil province in the world. Of the approximately 3.6 million oil wells drilled in the world, 80 percent or 2.9 million have been drilled in the United States. Proven reserves in the United States today represent only 23 percent of historic production, the lowest percentage in the world—approached only by Canada, on a much smaller scale. The Middle East, by contrast, led by Saudi Arabia, has reserves of 270 percent of historical production. Table 4–2 compares historic output and proven reserves of the world oil regions.

Table 4–2

OIL CONSUMPTION VS. PROVEN RESERVES
(billion barrels)

Country/ Region	Historic Production	Proven Reserves	Reserves as % of Total	Reserves as % of Production
United States	154.8	35.6	5	23
Canada	14.6	7.4	1	51
Latin America	68.4	84.3	12	123
Western Hemisphere	237.8	127.3	18	54
Western Europe	12.4	26.4	4	213
Africa	40.9	56.2	8	137
USSR/China	106.5	81.4	12	76
Middle East	147.0	397.5	56	270
Other	20.2	18.8	3	93
Eastern Hemisphere	327.0	580.3	82	178
Total:	546.8	707.6	100	129

SOURCE: *Factors Affecting U.S. Oil & Gas Outlook,* National Petroleum Council

NOTE: Proven reserves are estimates of discovered oil that is recoverable under existing technology and at existing prices.

Historically, the U.S. oil industry has been the world's leader in oil production, technology, and consumption. Prospectively, the concern is that the domestic industry will become a secondary source serving the world's largest oil-consuming market. In justification of this concern, the 5 percent ratio of U.S. reserves to world reserves is cited. Western Hemisphere reserves combined make up under one-fifth of world reserves. Conversely, potentially unstable Eastern Hemisphere sources account for over 80 percent of proven oil deposits. OPEC nations account for 76 percent of world reserves, with 63 percent located in the Persian Gulf alone. Compared to the U.S. share of 5 percent, Saudi Arabia holds 27 percent, Kuwait 15 percent, Iran 8 percent, and Iraq 8 percent of world supply. The non-OPEC leader is Mexico, with 9 percent of known world oil supplies.[14]

[14]These estimates can be revised to increase Venezuelan reserves substantially and

Compared to the average Middle Eastern field, which produces 3,100 barrels per day at an incremental cost under $1 per barrel, U.S. wells on the average produce under 14 barrels per day at a lifting cost around $7 per barrel. Finding (discovery) costs are similarly skewed—over $10 per barrel in the United States and around $1 per barrel in the Middle East. Thus finding and lifting costs are many times greater in the United States than in the Middle East, portending a shift in market-share from the former to the latter over time.[15]

3. Instability and Vulnerability

Because Saudi Arabia and other Persian Gulf suppliers are *incremental* suppliers to the U.S. and world oil market, output fluctuations of several million barrels per day can swing prices greatly. In 1973–74, a net production cut of 4 million barrels per day (7 percent of pre-embargo consumption) quadrupled prices in a several-month period. In 1979, reduced supplies of 2 to 2.5 million barrels per day doubled prices in a very short period.

It has also happened in reverse. When Saudi Arabia abandoned its role as swing supplier in late 1985, prices plummeted 60 percent on the strength of a 3–4 million barrel per day production increase, aided by netback refining agreements. The August 1986 decision by Saudi Arabia to restore prices by cutting production again demonstrated the price-setting power of incremental supply. By lowering output by several million barrels and agreeing to abide within OPEC's quota of 15.8 million barrels per day, the Saudis increased prices from around $12 per barrel to $18 per barrel, a 50 percent increase, by the spring of 1987.

The inherently unstable situation for the U.S. industry directly reflects the deliverability capacity of OPEC members, led by Saudi Arabia, relative to domestic production. While OPEC can produce as much as 25–30 million barrels per day and swing down by over one-half of this amount, the United States, with a maximum daily output of around 9 million barrels per day (exclusive of natural gas liquids), has little ability to swing because of the cash-flow needs

---

thus narrow the differential of Western Hemisphere to Eastern Hemisphere reserves. See below, pp. 153–54.

[15]NPC, *Factors Affecting U.S. Oil & Gas Outlook*, p. 8. Estimates provided by the Department of Energy in *Energy Security* (pp. 52–53) show less of a discrepancy between the United States and the Middle East, but finding and lifting costs are still twice as high for the former than the latter.

of many individual producers and the higher stripper well population. With lifting costs for most wells between $8 and $24 per barrel, many wells have been plugged or are likely to be plugged should OPEC place pressure on prices via surge production.

This discrepancy between U.S. and non-U.S. surplus capacity is dramatic. In the United States, the East Texas field, produced under a 86 percent allowable, represents the bulk of spare deliverability nationwide of 300,000 barrels per day. Led by Saudi Arabia, Iran, Iraq, and the United Arab Emirates, untapped deliverability in the Persian Gulf could well exceed 10 million barrels per day; excess capacity in Venezuela and elsewhere, within OPEC and without, would add to this total.[16] (Iran and Iraq's potential assumes a postwar return to normalcy.) This discrepancy in surplus output creates great uncertainty for the domestic industry, potentially playing havoc with even the most conservative of plans.

Excess capacity exists to a smaller extent in Canada and Mexico, but this is not necessarily good news for U.S. consumers. Not only would the contribution from these two countries be limited in a major Middle East oil disruption, but whether these neighbors would allow exports to the United States to alleviate the shortfall is questionable. Mexico, which has shown itself sympathetic to OPEC, has passed a law, with the United States in mind, limiting exports to any one country to 50 percent of the total. Canada, whose relations with the United States are better than Mexico's, has proved unreliable: They temporarily suspended their exports during the embargo and then phased out their oil exports to the United States— a process that was completed by 1980.[17]

With these inherited realities, the unstable nature of Persian Gulf supplies comes into play. Embargoes and major production cuts occurred twice in the 1970s, with well-known consequences; they can happen again. Saudi Arabia is a fair-weather supplier, and future U.S. intervention in the Persian Gulf could lead to a repeat of the Saudi-sponsored concerted production cutback that led to the first energy crisis of 1973–74. Renewed hostilities by Arab countries against Israel could be the basis for such a reoccurrence. Iran and Iraq are in the seventh year of a war that has witnessed hundreds of attacks on large oil tankers and the destruction of many oil terminals. The Strait of Hormuz and the Red Sea have been mined,

---

[16]For more discussion of surplus capacity, see below, pp. 147–48.

[17]IPAA, *Petroleum Independent*, February 1987, pp. 19–20.

and oil pipelines have been sabotaged. The civil war in Lebanon could widen to threaten oil exports from the region. The multi-directional and deep sources of instability in the region were cited by Defense Secretary Caspar Weinberger:

> Causes of instability and conflict . . . are many: ethnic and religious cleavages, irredentism and territorial disputes, rivalries for regional power and domination, and economic fluctuations and grievances. Although many of these problems are rooted deep in the past . . . they have been exacerbated by the proliferation of technologically advanced weapons systems, and by increased Soviet support.[18]

4. Ominous Parallels: Protectionism as Prevention

In 1986, the contraction of U.S. drilling and production, coupled with expanded market-share by Saudi Arabia and other OPEC members, led to a sharp reversal in the U.S. quest toward energy independence. While net imports as a percentage of product consumption declined from a high of 47 percent in 1977 to 27 percent in 1985, with Saudia Arabia falling behind Mexico, Canada, Venezuela, Indonesia, United Kingdom, Nigeria, and Algeria on the import list, imports rose sharply in 1986 to nearly 33 percent, with Saudi Arabia jumping to fourth place. Within this 20 percent import increase were some ominous trends. OPEC imports increased over 50 percent, and Arab OPEC imports surged 144 percent to account for over 40 percent of all U.S. imports.

The import-to-consumption "peril point" of 30 percent, approaching U.S. foreign oil dependence at the time of the Arab embargo, was reached in May 1986 and has continued to increase. With continued replacement of domestic production with foreign supplies, it is estimated that imports could reach and exceed the 1977 high of 8.5 million barrels per day, to equal 50 percent or more of consumption in the early 1990s. With this dependence, and the prospect of OPEC operating at near-full (80 percent) capacity to service expanding demand (which in 1986 increased nearly 3 percent in the United States), the stage is set for another major energy crisis, with many tens of billions of dollars of macroeconomic costs to the U.S. economy.

---

[18]*Report of the Secretary of Defense to the Congress on the FY 1985 Budget, FY 1986 Authorization Request and FY 1985–1989 Defense Programs,* February 1, 1984, p. 19. Quoted in Charles Ebinger, *Oil Product Imports: A Threat to U.S. National Security* (Washington, D.C.: Ebinger International, October 9, 1985), p. 56.

The rise, decline, and recent resurgence of net oil imports (imports minus exports) as a percentage of domestic consumption are shown in Table 4–3 below.

The case for protectionism is a case for prevention. By maintaining U.S. production at a higher level (e.g., 1 or 2 million barrels per day), the domestic industry can better control the nation's consumption destiny and not be held hostage, politically and economically, by alien powers that through a quirk of nature control the bulk of oil deliverability and reserves. In fact, it is argued that the U.S. government *has* that responsibility. As stated by the Department of Energy in *Energy Security:*

> Politically inspired production cutbacks by major oil producers could . . . hurt the U.S. economy or at least limit its geopolitical options. If dependence on certain oil producers carries with it these dangers, the government has a responsibility to take defensive action of some sort.[19]

Table 4–3
NET IMPORT DEPENDENCE: 1973–86
(thousand barrels per day)

Year	Net Imports	Total Consumption	Imports as % of Consumption
1973	6,025	17,308	34.8
1974	5,892	16,653	35.4
1975	5,846	16,322	35.8
1976	7,090	17,461	40.6
1977	8,565	18,431	46.5
1978	8,002	18,847	42.5
1979	7,985	18,513	43.1
1980	6,365	17,056	37.3
1981	5,401	16,058	33.6
1982	4,298	15,296	28.1
1983	4,312	15,231	28.3
1984	4,715	15,726	30.0
1985	4,286	15,726	27.3
1986	5,289	16,142	32.8

SOURCE: Energy Information Administration, Department of Energy

[19]*Energy Security*, p. 10.

An optimal tariff, free of encumbering exemptions and special features that would limit its equity or effectiveness, is such a defensive measure, argue its advocates. Such a measure, they feel, would benefit domestic consumers, the general economy, and national defense.

C. The Case for Producer Protectionism Reconsidered

Wirt Franklin's case for a protective tariff in the early 1930s was based not only on major-versus-independent rhetoric but on statistical information about the negative effect of imports on domestic production, especially stripper wells, and forecasts of national output to consumption. It was hailed by its sponsor as a pioneering attempt to raise the level of debate.

A half-century later, not only has the case for protectionism been expanded on empirical foundations (from an elaborate set of industry statistics unavailable in earlier periods), but an academic turn has decidedly complicated the debate. The case for protective tariffs has gone beyond simple factual trends and correlations to sophisticated applications of economic theory. Concepts of "market failure," "externality," and "optimality," developed within mathematical equations and econometric testing, have buttressed the argument.[20]

The remainder of the chapter offers an alternative to the world view of the energy picture painted by industry parties and academicians favoring protectionism. The previous section's case for tariffs is scrutinized in all its parts. In addition, the assumptions and methodology behind the economists' case for a "socially optimal" tariff are critically examined in an appendix to this chapter.

1. U.S. Oil Shortages Historically Contemplated

The inspiration behind current calls for protectionism stems from previous periods of shortage and crisis. The traumas of the 1970s are commonly cited as prima facie proof of the need for a well-sized domestic industry and relative import independence. Statistical analogies of the level of imports and domestic production are drawn to compare present and anticipated conditions with crisis periods. Some analysts have reached back to World War I and World War II to emphasize the need for oil domesticity for military preparedness and the national interest. Upon close examination, however, these

[20]See appendix 4B, pp. 185–94.

historical references do not make a case for protectionism. In fact, they have implications that militate against government involvement in the oil industry for the purpose of ensuring sufficient supply for whatever civilian or military needs may arise.

Pre-1970 Shortages

The first significant oil crisis occurred near the close of World War I.[21] From a combination of de facto price regulation and allocation restriction, administered by the U.S. Fuel Administration, gasoline supplies became tight in the summer of 1918. Upon the suggestion of Walter Teagel, president of Jersey Standard, the nation's first oil czar, Mark Requa, implemented a "gasless Sunday" plan for motorists, motorcyclists, and motorboats east of the Mississippi to conserve gasoline as part of the war effort. Beginning Sunday, September 1, and extending six Sundays through October 15, moral suasion and regulatory "incentives" curtailed the aforementioned transportation. Mass shortages were never experienced, but for most drivers in the eastern United States, Sundays amounted to gasoline shortages. The end of hostilities and the armistice of November 11, 1918, prevented the institution of gasoline rationing (a measure that was being favorably considered as an alternative to the Sunday ban), and price and allocation regulations were repealed by the end of the year. The first oil shortage was over.

With the discovery of major oil fields in the Southwest during the 1920s and 1930s, the nation was awash in oil. In an effort to support sagging domestic prices, state and federal authorities—not to mention many oil producers—worked hard to find ways to curtail domestic production and reduce imports. During World War II, however, the supply/consumption situation would be reversed.

Just as it had been in World War I, but in more formal fashion, the U.S. petroleum industry was placed under price and allocation controls and under the authority of several bureaucracies. In May 1941, the Office of Price Administration reached a price control agreement with major companies, and a month later a major "voluntary" conservation effort was introduced for PAD District I by oil czar Harold Ickes of the Petroleum Administration for War. The fuel situation temporarily improved, but a growing inability of gasoline prices to clear the market led to restrictions on service

---

[21]The discussion of pre-1970s oil crises is taken from chapters 24 and 25 of my forthcoming book, *Oil, Gas, and Government: The U.S. Experience.*

station hours and gasoline purchases. With unrelenting price regulation, supply became more precarious, and coupon rationing was resorted to by the War Production Board in May 1942 for 17 eastern states. Fuel oil deliveries were also rationed to most of the country in the spring of 1942. Rampant problems with partial rationing led to national gasoline rationing in November of the same year.

Despite the intention to limit coupons to available supply to avoid physical shortages, an inability to buy gasoline with both coupons and money occurred numerous times in 1943 and 1944. The black market and bureaucratic error were increasingly frustrating the planning effort. Fuel oil rationing, soon expanded to a 33-state area representing 95 percent of national consumption, was less chaotic than its gasoline counterpart, but inequities, inefficiencies, and supply problems were prevalent.

In the second half of 1945 and first half of 1946, major regulations controlling the pricing and distribution of the two major industry products (as lesser products) were terminated or relaxed, and the coordinating forces of the market began to take hold. The "oil crisis" experienced on the home front with gasoline and fuel oil was over for the time being. But oil supply problems and regulation were not quite extinct.

The third oil crisis in U.S. history occurred in the winters of 1946–47 and 1947–48. Price controls were belatedly rescinded in June 1946, freeing prices for the first time since early 1941, but authorization to reimpose ceilings remained, should prices be deemed "unreasonable" by federal authorities.

Fuel oil was tight in the winter of 1945–46 owing to lingering price maximums and refiner regulations. The industry advisory group, the Petroleum Industry War Council, complained that "the price straight-jacket prevents . . . prices from fluctuating . . . to readjust product yields and meet seasonal and other fluctuations in consumer demand."[22] Spot fuel oil shortages were reported, but major problems were averted, partly because of a mild winter.

Paradoxically, it was after fuel oil prices were decontrolled in mid-1946 that supply became the most troublesome. Gasoline, previously deregulated, also encountered problems. A number of industry and government initiatives were undertaken to avoid the first peacetime oil shortage in history, but both fuels experienced a

---

[22]Quoted in William Laudeman, "Hits OPA Price Policies for Causing Prospective Middle Oil Distillate Shortage," *National Petroleum News*, December 19, 1945, p. 7.

number of spot shortages and very tense predicaments. The problem peaked in the winter of 1947–48, but by the summer of 1948 supplies became ample. In fact, by year's end, surplus supply and weakening prices would replace shortages as the prime industry fear.

Behind the postwar supply predicaments was a "hold the line" pricing policy practiced by Jersey Standard (Exxon), with the acquiescence of other majors and independents. The failure of "scarcity pricing," however, was not a private-sector failing. It was the cumulative result of government anti-inflation jawboning, congressional and Justice Department industry investigations, and threatened state regulations that, in the words of Monroe Rathbone, president of Jersey Standard, were making it "increasingly hard to conduct our business as we would like to do it and as we feel it should be conducted."[23] De facto regulation in this case achieved what in other instances formal regulation accomplished—threatened and experienced shortages.

The Energy Crisis of 1972–74

The next oil shortage did not begin in the wake of the October 1973 announcement of an embargo against the United States by Saudi Arabia and the concerted production cuts that followed. It had begun on two fronts several years before. Damaging shortages of natural gas occurred in the winter of 1971–72 from the cumulative effects of longstanding regulation of natural gas destined for interstate commerce. Shortages of selected oil products and concerns about other product supplies, the result of President Richard Nixon's wage and price control program, were evident more than a year before the embargo had its effect. Oil problems predating the embargo are discussed in more detail below.

In late 1972, a major gasoline trade group reported that "over half of our membership is suffering acute shortages."[24] Fuel oil,

[23]Henrietta Larson, et al., *New Horizons: History of Standard Oil Company (New Jersey) 1927–1950* (New York: Harper & Row, 1971), p. 684. Upon hearing that Jersey Standard had complied with the administration's "anti-inflation" request, a Truman administration official wired: "Since the wholesale commodity price index went to a new high last week, your announcement of a "hold-the-line" policy for crude and products is a patriotic action that will be appreciated by all. Price increases, unless absolutely unavoidable, are selfish and foolhardy. To hold down the price of oil is good for the country and good for business." Ibid., p. 676.

[24]Quoted in "A Gas Pinch Hurts the Independents," *Business Week*, November 18, 1972, p. 21.

despite liberalized import quotas under the dying Mandatory Oil Import Program, encountered spot shortages in the winter of 1972–73; these problems led to selected allocation by the cabinet-level Office of Emergency Preparedness, supplier meetings by the Office of Oil and Gas (Department of Interior), and congressional investigations into supply availability. Propane and butane joined natural gas as supply-short fuels. States readied, and in some cases implemented, fuel allocation programs. President Nixon created the Office of Energy Conservation within the Interior Department and announced energy-saving recommendations. "By early 1973," one major study of the period concluded, "public, congressional, and administrative priorities had switched from fighting inflation to dealing with energy shortages."[25]

In August 1973, the newly created Office of Energy Policy unveiled an allocation plan in the event of fuel oil shortages the next winter. The Voluntary Petroleum Allocation Plan and new bureaucracies, such as the Energy Policy Office and the President's Energy Policy Council, were testimony to the unique problems that oil was experiencing. On October 2, Nixon announced the first mandatory allocation plan—for propane. Two weeks later, still before the embargo announcement, a mandatory program was introduced for home heating oil.

Congress was not diverted from its interest in mandatory allocation despite the administration's moves from voluntary to mandatory allocation. A bill sponsored by Senator Henry Jackson (D-Wash.) and Congressman Torbert MacDonald (D-Mass.) for mandatory allocation of all major oil products was well toward passage at the time of Nixon's initiatives. The supply problems experienced by downstream independents from rigid price ceilings, *not the import situation*, was the driving factor. Summarized Neil de Marchi:

> The impetus behind allocation schemes was the complaints, channeled very effectively through congressmen, of independent marketers and terminal operators. Protecting these independents (and the independent refiners) was *the* energy issue of 1973, not the Arab embargo.[26]

[25]Neil de Marchi, "Energy Policy Under Nixon: Mainly Putting Out Fires," in *Energy Policy in Perspective*, ed. Craufurd Goodwin (Washington, D.C.: Brookings Institution, 1981), p. 425.

[26]Ibid., p. 429.

In a sense, the events following the embargo announcement were anticlimactic. President Nixon's mandatory allocation programs for propane, heating oil, diesel fuel, jet fuel, and kerosene under the newly created Office of Petroleum Allocation in the Interior Department were designed to score political points in the Watergate period. This was stealing Congress's thunder, however. The day before the embargo was announced, the House approved a comprehensive allocation law, and after Senate approval, the Emergency Petroleum Allocation Act was signed by Nixon into law.[27] While this sweeping legislation may have solved political problems for some, that it did not solve shortages was demonstrated by the most visible shortage of all—the gasoline lines of early 1974.[28]

The physical and psychological effects of the Arab embargo worsened a precarious supply situation, but they did not create it. The embargo, as one observer phrased it, "was merely the straw that showed that the camel's back was broken."[29] The initial loss of around 5 million barrels per day of Persian Gulf supply was cushioned by increased production in Venezuela and other non-Arab OPEC nations of 1 million barrels per day for most of the five-month interruption. Rearranged world oil trading patterns leveled out the embargo against the United States with other import-dependent areas. But because gasoline lines and diesel fuel shortages occurred in the first quarter of 1974, precisely at the height of the embargo, the "energy crisis" has been associated almost exclusively with the Persian Gulf situation.

Not only price controls but *bureaucratic allocation decisions* were instrumental in preventing gasoline ceiling prices from clearing the market to prevent shortages. Supply allocations based on historic demand led to surpluses in low-growth areas and shortages in high-growth areas. A 5 percent oil product set-aside for state allocation to hardship cases went unused, creating a *product* supply loss comparable to the crude oil import reduction. A "refinery tilt" program that ordered refiners to maximize fuel oil output at the expense of gasoline backfired, with the latter in surplus and the former in shortage. Other factors such as the buy-sell program, which reallocated crude oil from gasoline-producing refineries to less sophis-

[27]Public Law 93–159, 87 Stat. 627 (1973).

[28]A chronology of oil problems prior to the Arab embargo is contained in Lester Sobel, ed., *Energy Crisis: Vol. 1* (New York: Facts on File, 1974), pp. 131–65.

[29]Ayn Rand, "The Energy Crisis," *The Ayn Rand Letter*, November 5, 1973, p. 258.

ticated refineries, unintendedly reduced supply of the most needed oil product. These causal factors in the shortage were not import-related but self-inflicted. It is quite possible, even likely, that gasoline shortages would have occurred without any import inter-ruption, as was the case with other major oil products and natural gas.

The Energy Crisis of 1979

From November 1978 until June 1979, between 2 and 2.5 million barrels per day in Iranian exports were halted because of the Iranian revolution. Much of this quantity, however, was replaced by increased production elsewhere. Despite this substitution, prices soared, just as they had in the aftermath of the Arab embargo. From November 1978 to November 1979, prices nearly doubled, reaching $26 per barrel. This "overreaction" has been attributed to the cumulative effects of pervasive price and allocation controls that discouraged domestic production and efficient distribution of supply while encouraging oil imports and consumption. Expectations of the worst kind were fostered. Regulation also precluded entrepreneurial actions such as crude and product stockpiling in anticipation of supply problems and price spikes.

The gasoline lines in the summer of 1979, which coincided with the Iranian cutoff, were also self-inflicted. Diesel fuel and home heating oil proved adequate because of their previous deregulation, but heavily regulated gasoline suffered a different fate. As was the case with the Arab embargo, supply problems fostered by binding price ceilings *preceded* the Iranian export cutback. On December 1 of the previous year, Shell announced a quota plan for gasoline wholesalers based on 75 percent of previous purchases, and by early 1979, the other major refiners had followed suit. What occurred in California in May, and in many parts of the country from June through August of 1979, was predestined, the Iranian situation notwithstanding.

In academic and political circles, the blame for the gasoline and diesel fuel debacle of 1979 has been pinned on domestic regulation rather than on foreign events. M. A. Adelman in congressional testimony in the fall of 1979 stated:

> The gasoline shortage was very small, perhaps 3 percent. Absent price control, there would have been a price increase, less than what actually occurred. But given price control, there had to be allocation: product by product, week by week, place by place. There was pressure on refiners to turn out more heating oil, then

more gasoline, then more heating oil again. . . . Scattered shortages led to hoarding and panic buying and worse shortages yet—
and those gasoline lines. No other consuming country cooked up
this kind of purgatory for itself. The cure is simple: decontrol of
oil product prices.[30]

Representative Jack Kemp (R-NY) expressed the suspicion, shared
by others, that regulations administered by the Department of
Energy—not foreign countries—were the primary cause of what
the *Washington Post* called the "Great Gas Mystery":

> What puzzles everyone is very basic. Because of the Iranian rev-
> olution, world oil supplies dropped by a net of only about 4
> percent. So why do we have shortages of 20 and 25 percent at the
> gas pump? Why in New York, Los Angeles, and Washington,
> D.C., but not in Detroit, Cleveland, or Buffalo? And why do we
> have gas lines only in the United States, but nowhere else in the
> world? If all the oil must go somewhere, people reason, then the
> gas crisis is only one part shortage, and about four or five parts
> misallocation.[31]

Indeed, many of the ill-fated price and allocation programs seen
in 1974 did their damage again in 1979. Price rigidities, a refiner tilt
toward fuel oil and away from gasoline, state set-asides that left
much-needed product idle, obsolete base-period allocation formu-
las, and crude oil misallocations between refineries were notable
examples. In a history of 1970s oil regulation, William Lane concluded:

> The most striking conclusion to emerge from this analysis is the
> fact that most of the "mistakes" made by the government in
> handling the Arab embargo were repeated during the Iranian
> disruption six years later. This result cannot be attributed merely
> to the change of administrations or the turnover of administrative
> personnel. If the Federal government chooses to apply price and
> allocation controls during any future disruption, it is unlikely that
> they could be applied with any greater degree of overall success.[32]

---

[30]M. A. Adelman, *Limiting Oil Imports*, Hearing before the Subcommittee on Energy
Regulation, U.S. Senate, 96th Cong., 1st Sess. (Washington, D.C.: Government
Printing Office, 1980), p. 95.

[31]Lester Sobel, ed., *Energy Crisis: Vol. 4* (New York: Facts on File, 1980), p. 63.

[32]William Lane, *The Mandatory Petroleum Price and Allocation Regulations: A History
and Analysis* (Washington, D.C.: American Petroleum Institute, 1981), pp. 100–101.

Between late 1979 and mid-1980, the landed price of U.S. oil imports increased 25 percent, to $32 per barrel. This increase was caused by (1) continued reductions, not offset elsewhere, in Persian Gulf supplies as a result of the Iran-Iraq war and (2) the "hangover" effect of U.S. oil price and allocation regulation, which, after two disastrous applications during imported oil reductions, was just beginning to be dismantled.

Iran-Iraq War: The Crisis That Wasn't

The third and last "shock" of the energy crisis period was a war-related export reduction: Beginning in late 1980, Iran cut its exports by 2 million barrels per day; Iraq by 1 million. Together these cuts represented 7 percent of non-Communist world supply. Further export cuts of 1 to 2 million barrels per day followed in 1981. Total OPEC production, which dropped 4 million barrels per day, or 13 percent, in 1980, declined another 4 million barrels per day in 1981. Non-OPEC output, on the other hand, increased less than 2 million barrels per day.

This drop in world output from late 1980 through 1981, comparable to the other "shocks" of the 1970s, was relatively uneventful. After a price surge from approximately $34 per barrel in October 1980 to $39 per barrel in early 1981, crude prices began to sag (a decline that would continue over the next 5 years). Because of price and allocation deregulation, which was underway in 1980 and completed in January 1981, there were no shortages. Prices performed their market-clearing function, and supply went to where it was most urgently needed. Conservation by consumers was also at work. The market was back to its old self after a decade of government interference.

Lessons to Be Drawn from Past Crises

The five case studies of oil shortages have one element in common. Each experience was preceded by effective price regulation, de jure regulation in three cases and de facto regulation in two cases, which restrained prices from performing their market-clearing function.

The same point can be illustrated in another way. Other than during the (approximate) periods 1917–19, 1941–49, 1950–51 (Korean conflict), and 1971–81, entrepreneurs were free to consult their own interests in pricing their products. For these unregulated periods, totaling over a hundred years, no shortages or crises occurred, despite a variety of endogenous and exogenous challenges. Several examples may be mentioned. In the dawn of the automobile age, with surging gasoline demand joining fuel oil and kerosene demand from the 1910s on, demand was successfully met year after year. The "Model T" scare, a name given to widespread predictions about gasoline shortages because of 2 million cars on the road and 1 million cars rolling off the assembly lines every year, never came true. Supply continually met record demand; by the outbreak of World War I, the shortage scare was forgotten. The 1920–23 period witnessed the "John Bull" scare—a fear that the United States had depleted its reserves and that the bulk of new reserves lay abroad.[33] Chapter 2 examined some of the exaggerated concerns, primarily of government scientists, and showed how, by 1926, the shortage fear was replaced by concerns over overproduction and price deterioration.[34]

Unfortunately, later scares were associated with regulation and thus had basis in fact. This was true during and after World War II and during the 1970s "energy crisis." Ironically, policy reform was directed at the market and not at the real culprit—regulation. Such programs as allocation regulation and mandatory conservation, not price deregulation, became the front line of defense to narrow the supply-demand gap.

The record is clear that shortages and crises have been associated with heavily regulated periods; in a free-market environment, the industry has performed reliably in a variety of situations. The conclusion from the historical record, with support in economic theory, is that the "worst case" scenario of dependence on foreign supplies is not shortages but *increased prices*. Yet even the increased prices have been primarily due to regulation. In the history of the U.S. oil industry throughout this century, major price increases have occurred during and after pervasive regulation that discouraged domestic supply and artificially increased demand. This occurred when real oil prices jumped in the aftermath of World War I planning by one-third and World War II regulation by 50 percent. It also happened with a vengeance during the 1973–81 era when nominal crude prices increased sevenfold. Declines in Persian Gulf production undoubtedly augmented the damage that price and allocation regulation

---

[33]A history of oil scares is provided in Leonard Fanning, "They Always Find the Oil," *National Petroleum News*, February 15, 1950, pp. 25–39.

[34]See pp. 33–37.

did to the domestic demand-supply balance, but the question must be asked whether without regulation (1) U.S. demand would have been so inelastic as to permit import prices to accelerate as greatly, (2) inventory buildups and a more mature spot market could have smoothed the "shocks" in the transition to decreased world output, and (3) more ongoing output and "surge" capacity within the United States could have mitigated the decline of foreign output and imports.

An unregulated oil market in the 1970s is one of the great "what ifs" of modern U.S. economic history (even with the ARAMCO nationalization). Its results would have been much closer to the periods before and after oil's decade of infamy than what actually occurred.

In conclusion, the legacy of oil scares, shortages, and energy crises do not give credence to protectionism as a means of constructing an optimal relationship between imports and domestic output. The way to "protect" against such occurrences is to *avoid formal or informal price regulation and accompanying allocation intervention.* Domestic self-sufficiency (with or without tariffs) is not a barrier to shortages and crises. The shortage experiences with natural gas, not to mention oil products prior to the Arab embargo, proved as much. Price and allocation regulation of natural gas and oil products, not import levels, has been the controlling factor in the regrettable periods of the U.S. energy industry.

2. The Foreign Oil Threat Reconsidered

The case for protectionism is built on the assumption that Saudi Arabia, the Persian Gulf producers, or OPEC will cut production steeply at some foreseeable date (with or without a specific embargo to the United States) to severely hurt our petroleum-driven economy.[35] As argued above, there is no historical precedent for this view. Pervasive regulation, not import cutoffs, has been responsible for past shortages. In this section, a case is made that this hypothesized predicament is highly unlikely to happen *given predominantly free-market conditions within the United States.* Two major points are developed: (1) the inability of selective embargoes to affect the United States without an accompanying major production decrease

---

[35]While the discussion to follow is primarily applicable to *voluntary* embargoes or cutbacks, many arguments apply as well to *involuntary* export interruptions owing to a major Persian Gulf conflict.

and (2) the unlikelihood of an OPEC-related production cut to occur—or to be successful if tried.

A division of arguments supporting the second, and more important, point is somewhat arbitrary, given the interdependence between them. The argument does not turn on a single theory or set of statistics but on numerous reinforcing observations incorporating historical experience, theoretical insights from economics, and institutional changes in the world oil market.

Embargoes versus the World Oil Market

A widely shared conclusion of the oil embargo of 1973–74 is that the concerted Arab OPEC production cutback was more important than the export embargo on the United States and the Netherlands. The "shock," in other words, was the approximate 6 percent reduction in world output in late 1973, sharply reversing decades of increasing supply to meet expanding demand, and not the pattern of world oil trade. M. A. Adelman has called the Arab embargo "a sham" by reiterating the fact that the world's oil "is one big pot and all that matters is the total."[36] In contrast to ineffectual quotas, the Arab countries' "oil weapon" of export reductions sounded around the globe. Adelman made these points clearly:

> The danger is of a production cutback, not an "embargo." The world oil market is one big ocean, connected to every bay and inlet. For that reason the "embargo" of 1973–74 was a sham. Diversion was not even necessary, it was simply a swap of customers and suppliers between Arab and non-Arab sources. The production cutback hurt all consumers. The United States, as simple economic theory would predict, lost about as much oil supply as the non-embargoed countries. . . . We did better than the "preferred" and "friendly" French and British though not as well as the "odiously neutral" Japanese. The good news is that the United States cannot be embargoed, leaving other countries undisturbed. The bad news is that any cutback hurting other consumers hurts this country. Therefore energy independence is literally impossible.[37]

What was true in 1973–74 is even more true today. The world oil

---

[36]Adelman, *Limiting Oil Imports*, Senate Hearings, p. 86. This discussion parallels the oil product/refining discussion above, pp. 100–101.

[37]Ibid., p. 99. Also see "Harvard Professor Destroys Embargo Myths," *Oil & Gas Journal*, August 5, 1974, p. 103.

market grid, as discussed in more detail below, has become more diversified, more decentralized, and better able to anticipate and handle "national security" events. Non-Persian Gulf and non-OPEC supply sources play a much greater role today than they did during the 1970s in reducing any particular country's dependence on another. Spot-market oil has gone from a fringe component of international oil trade to the equal of contract oil, facilitating any redirection to supply-short areas or countries. Oil trading, which thrives on the "chaos" of trade pattern interruptions, proliferated in the 1970s and remains very important today. Pricing on the petroleum futures market has demoted the "official" prices set by OPEC oil ministers. Given these institutional developments, and understanding why the only embargo to date was ineffectual, any threat or attempt to impose a selective embargo unaccompanied by a production reduction is naive. Such a threat cannot be used to support tariffs or quotas, nor is it even a part of the sophisticated case for national security protectionism.

Internal Constraints on OPEC

Are effective production cuts likely and sustainable? The crucial assumption in the protectionist case, that a concerted reduction in for-export world production will take place in the foreseeable future, is highly debatable. Just because it happened in the past does not mean it must happen again. There are persuasive reasons why sharp output reductions will be very difficult to implement and, more important, to sustain. Reasons include weaknesses and incentives within the OPEC "cartel" and fundamental changes in supply and demand outside of OPEC. The world petroleum market, and in particular the U.S. petroleum market, is vastly different from that of the early 1970s *because* of the traumatic experiences of the last decade and the remaining uncertainties.

To characterize OPEC as a cartel overstates its success. OPEC has often been little more than a confederation—and a fairly loose one at that. Since its 1960 beginning, the alliance has had only brief periods of quasi-concerted cartel behavior. OPEC's high points have been few and far between, and even during these moments, cracks have been evident.

The checkered past of quotas. The tumultuous history of OPEC quotas, an important new chapter of which is currently being written, may be briefly reviewed. From inception in 1960 until recently,

OPEC did not have a quota. The nations in the confederacy were reluctant to taint their autonomy with external restrictions. It was not until March 1983, in conjunction with an unprecedented price reduction from $34 per barrel to $29 per barrel, that quotas were ratified. Attempts had previously been made by Saudi Arabia to set uniform prices, but each effort had been thwarted by price "hawks" such as Algeria, Iran, and Libya.

The quota of 1983, set at 17.5 million barrels per day, did not even enjoy a honeymoon period. Although officially ratified by unanimous vote, the quota was discreetly contradicted by the production policies of many members. Barter deals by oil exporting nations and secret discounting flouted both the quantity and price agreements. For-export refineries began to turn quota-regulated crude into unregulated products ranging from slop oil to gasoline. Production underreporting and a corollary, "orphan" supply (supply of unknown origin), became commonplace. For most of their history, the OPEC quotas have served as floors rather than ceilings.[38]

Faced with declining demand and cheating among its members, the 1983 cartelization effort faced certain demise. This did not occur because of the actions of its preeminent member. Saudi Arabia, choosing to continue its role of swing producer, dropped its output (which peaked at nearly 10 million barrels per day in the early 1980s), from 5 million barrels per day in 1983 to 4.7 million in 1984 and 3.4 million the next year. In the summer of 1985, production hovered at a scant 2.5 million barrels per day. This propped prices in the mid-$20s per barrel, but clearly there was a limit to how far the Saudis could continue, given conservation and growing OPEC and non-OPEC supply. In two years, the Saudis had reduced output by one-third (with revenue falling proportionally) only to see the rest of OPEC and non-OPEC output hold steady.[39] Growing impatience was evident throughout Saudi Arabia's swing period, and the breaking point came in December 1985, when the Saudis and other OPEC members, with an eye toward disciplining non-OPEC producers such as Russia, Britain, Norway, Mexico, and Egypt (who

[38]For a discussion of some of the problems plaguing quota assignments, see Samuel Van Vactor and Arlon Tussing, "Not With a Bang but a Whimper: Why OPEC Hardly Matters," ARTA Energy Insights, December 1985.

[39]American Petroleum Institute, Domestic Petroleum Production and National Security, December 30, 1986, pp. 8–11 of Section I.

cumulatively were producing 70 percent of world supply compared to 55 percent five years before), announced intention to regain market share. The stubborn truth was that the world oil market did not need Saudi oil at $29 per barrel. An analyst's quip that Saudi Arabia would have to *import* oil by 1987 to continue to maintain price was the ironic truth.[40]

While the cartel has been driven by the market throughout most of its 27 years, there have been several high points when OPEC (or a fraction therein) arguably drove the market. But these successes were aided by exogenous factors (such as U.S. regulation) and were marred by disunity within the cartel.[41]

In late 1973, when the Saudis persuaded Kuwait, Abu Dhabi, Libya, Qatar, and Algeria to join them in a 5–10 percent production cut and to institute an embargo against the United States and Holland, not all OPEC members participated. In the Persian Gulf area, Iran, second only to Saudi Arabia with exports of nearly 6 million barrels per day, did not participate in either the production cuts or embargoes. Neither did Nigeria and Indonesia, with 3.4 million barrels per day of output between them. And importantly for the United States, not only did Venezuela stay independent, the founding OPEC member *increased* liftings by 6 percent, to 3.3 million barrels per day, to cancel some of the effect of its fellow-members' actions. Taken together, some 40 percent of daily OPEC supply did not participate with the Arab contingent in the heyday of the embargo.[42]

The second high point of the cartel has come most recently. In August 1986, after strenuous negotiation, OPEC resurrected a December 1983 quota of 15.8 million barrels per day. The accord, a cutback from 20 million barrels per day, was prompted by the severe price erosion that reduced OPEC's income by approximately $50 billion in 1986. By mid-1987, the accord, aided by a declining dollar and the Iran-Iraq war, succeeded in raising prices almost to OPEC's goal of $18 per barrel. But it required that Saudi Arabia return to its

[40]Adam Sieminski, *Natural Gas Week*, May 26, 1986, p. 1.

[41]A third OPEC high point, in 1979 and 1980 when the Saudi price hikes were followed by other OPEC producers, was a case of the market driving the cartel, or more specifically, U.S. regulation making demand inelastic and expectations elastic to allow prices and demand to simultaneously increase.

[42]"World Shaken by Arab Oil-Export Cuts, Price Hikes," *Oil & Gas Journal*, October 29, 1973, pp. 49–52.

former role of swing supplier, although whether the oil kingdom will continue to play this role is questionable.

According to the International Energy Administration, OPEC production of 16.3 million barrels per day in the first half of 1987 was only 3 percent over its 15.8 million barrel quota.[43] Saudi Arabia produced 8 percent less than its 4.133 million barrel per day assignment, while the rest of OPEC produced at or above their respective quotas. Iran produced its quota, an accomplishment under war conditions. The other 10 members, however, violated the quota to one degree or another. Iraq, which was excluded from the agreement, produced full-out and increased output in the period. "Acceptable" leakage, defined as production reasonably above assignments, was recorded by Venezuela, Kuwait, Indonesia, Algeria, Libya, and Qatar. "Unacceptable" leakage came from Abu Dhabi and Dubai, habitual quota breakers, as well as Ecuador and Gabon.

The worst could be yet to come for the tender OPEC quota. Responding to increased incentives to cheat, given higher prices, surplus production is estimated to be running several million barrels above the revised quota of 16.6 million barrels per day ratified in July 1987.[44] Continuing problems, if not greater problems resulting from a slowdown of hostilities between Iran and Iraq, will present Saudi Arabia with difficult choices in the future, not unlike those in the past.

Sources of disunity. Among the many characteristics of the world oil market that work against the unbridled power of Saudi Arabia, Arab OPEC, or OPEC proper to drive world oil prices, one of the most significant is disunity within OPEC. Competition and autonomy within the alliance have benefited consumers in the past and will continue to do so in the future.

The harmony of interests among the Persian Gulf members is far less today than when Saudi Arabia rounded up its neighbors in October 1973 to curtail output and boycott the United States. Many members have become habitual "cheaters" in the quota era, encouraged by the Saudi habit of curtailing output to prop up prices. It is an unstable cartel reeling from widespread excess capacity; any

---

[43]The following discussion comes from Roger Vielvoye, "OPEC Oil Production Jumps, But Crude Prices Remain Firm," *Oil & Gas Journal*, July 27, 1987, pp. 15–18.

[44]James Tanner, "OPEC Calls Meetings on Overproduction Amid New Signs That Pact Is Weakening," *Wall Street Journal*, August 26, 1987, p. 3.

unilateral cut by one, or some, is likely to lead to profitable production increases by other members to fill the gap. The moderate success of the August 1986 accord, immeasurably helped by the neighboring war and Saudi resolve, should not mask the cracks and strains within the alliance.

OPEC has never been unified, and there is no reason to believe it will become unified in the future. Self-interest is too divergent. There are price "hawks," with short-run revenue requirements and less reserves (Algeria, Libya, and Ecuador), and high-reserve "doves," sensitive to maximum long-run oil demand (Saudi Arabia and Kuwait). There are differing ideas of how to determine quotas. Persian Gulf producers want quotas based on reserves, while poorer members such as Indonesia and Nigeria desire the formula to be tilted toward population and the size of foreign debt. Iran has only reluctantly given agreement to OPEC pacts, and Iraq, which has refused to participate in the recent accord, has been given a formal exemption. Douglas Bohi and William Quandt have pointed to the "triangular politics" between Saudi Arabia, Iran, and Iraq, the major OPEC members, that will likely depress prices in the future.[45]

The organized factions within OPEC are noteworthy. Venezuela, which defied the Arab embargo in 1973–74, is a member of Olade, a Latin American producer group that works within OPEC to express its own views on pricing and production. Within the United Arab Emirates, Abu Dhabi and Dubai have pressed for their own agenda, and Abu Dhabi has been particularly insistent on a higher quota assignment. In fact, these two neighbors have not agreed on how to divide their quota. Four OPEC members, Algeria, Libya, Gabon, and Nigeria, recently formed the African Hydrocarbons Association with five non-OPEC nations, Angola, Benin, Cameroon, Congo, and Egypt. The Gulf Cooperation Council (Saudi Arabia, Kuwait, UAE, Qatar, and Oman) and the Organization of Arab Petroleum Exporting Countries (OAPEC) are other suborganizations that exist within the cartel but at a moment's notice could act outside it.[46] In

---

[45]They state: "What will this triangular rivalry among Iran, Iraq, and Saudi Arabia mean for OPEC in the second half of the 1980s? First, genuine cooperation on oil policy among the three giants is unlikely, and thus OPEC is unlikely to be in a strong position to raise prices." Douglas Bohi and William Quandt, *Energy Security in the 1980s: Economic and Political Perspectives* (Washington, D.C.: Brookings Institution, 1984), p. 32.

[46]Roger Vielvoye, "A New African Alliance," *Oil & Gas Journal*, Janury 19, 1987, p. 23.

all, there are 13 countries and five subgroups within the OPEC orbit; since all have separate agendas and political autonomy, OPEC is indeed a fragile cartel—or, rather, a confederation.

Whether OPEC can be considered a cartel is open to question. Even the leading proponent of the cartel interpretation, M. A. Adelman, has characterized OPEC as "clumsy" and "loose."[47] Undoubtedly, Saudi Arabia has acted as a "dominant" firm within the organization, with consequences not only for fellow OPEC members but for every oil producer in the world. Other than during the brief periods examined above, OPEC has not been an effective cartel; production and price developments can be attributed to factors such as the ARAMCO nationalization, dominant firm production/price leadership by Saudi Arabia, and unintended consequences of U.S. petroleum regulation. The leading adherents of this view are Ali Johany and Walter Mead, who have characterized OPEC's problem, in the terminology of economics, as the *cartel problem*. Explained Mead:

> First, any cartel member quickly learns that agreement on price and output is cheap; the gains come from cheating on the agreement. Second, as Britain, Norway, and the U.S.S.R. know well, it is more profitable to be outside of a cartel than to be a member and be pressured to restrict output. Outsiders are free to produce as they wish and sell at prices established by the cartel as a result of its supply curtailments.[48]

The fact that no outside producer has seriously entertained the prospect of joining the cartel gives credence to the Mead/Johany view. The last member joined OPEC over a decade ago, and no important member has joined since the 1960s.[49] Such oil powers as Great Britain, Mexico, and Norway have decided that their autonomy is more important than an alliance, and "free riding" on cartel-like practices is the best of both worlds. Oman and Egypt, two very

---

[47]M. A. Adelman, "The Clumsy Cartel," *Energy Journal*, January 1980, p. 47.

[48]Walter Mead, "The OPEC Cartel Thesis Reexamined: Price Constraints from Oil Substitutes," *The Journal of Energy and Development*, Spring 1986, p. 222. For an explanation of the cartel problem, see Murray Rothbard, *Man, Economy, and State* (Los Angeles: Nash Publishing, 1970), pp. 579–80.

[49]The five founding members of OPEC in 1960 were Venezuela, Saudi Arabia, Kuwait, Iran, and Iraq. Joining later were Qatar (1961), Libya (1962), Indonesia (1962), Abu Dhabi (1967), Algeria (1969), Nigeria (1971), Ecuador (1973), and Gabon (1975).

eligible prospects, have never joined. The cartel, stagnant in number, has also lost significant market share since 1980.

OPEC is plagued in its efforts to be an effective cartel because its member governments are ultimately independent. States Mead:

> Control over production by cartel leadership, including an effective enforcement mechanism, is an absolute requirement for long-term success of a cartel. Market-demand prorationing in the United States was enforced by the federal government. OPEC has no federal government, no court system, no police force, and no army. In its January 30, 1985, Geneva meeting, OPEC established a system to audit oil production by most member countries. However, this audit was intended to provide information only. OPEC was unable to introduce the essential enforcement system and even the audit system has been disregarded.[50]

"The only effective cartel," Mead concludes, "turns out to be one that is enforced by the power of government."[51] In OPEC's case, it would be a government of governments—a superstate that does not exist.

The curse of excess capacity. In 1977, OPEC production peaked at over 31 million barrels per day. In 1986, after stepping up output 14 percent from the year before, OPEC produced 18.4 million barrels per day. Other things being equal, these statistics would suggest surplus capacity of between 12 and 13 million barrels per day. Many things have changed, but this figure could remain reasonable today.

In Saudi Arabia, the difference between 1980 and 1986 output, around 5 or 6 million barrels per day, is a respected estimate of surplus capacity. The same comparison with Iran and Iraq reveals between 2 and 6 million barrels of spare output, although postwar repairs and a period of general stability would be necessary to approach the upper bound. The United Arab Emirates has pleaded for a higher quota, claiming to have over 3 million barrels per day of excess capacity. Venezuela claims to have a million excess daily barrels. No one (not even the OPEC leaders) knows what total capacity versus current deliverability is, but it could be as little as 8 million barrels per day or as much as 15 million barrels, or more. Widespread excess capacity within the cartel implies an ever-pres-

[50]Mead, "The OPEC Cartel Thesis Reexamined," p. 221.
[51]Ibid., p. 222.

ent competition and the ability of certain groups to cushion the reduction of others. These factors act both as an incentive against output reductions and as a buffer should it occur.

It is a mistake to believe that OPEC reserves and deliverability will remain dormant while world demand catches up to it. A pillar of the protectionist case is that increasing demand and falling U.S. supply will combine to steadily reduce excess capacity within OPEC and thus put the cartel back in the driver's seat. Putting aside the argument that oil conservation is still alive and well, this view severely underrates the incentive of countries to develop new reserves as existing reserves are depleted. M. A. Adelman and others have emphasized that *quota assignments within OPEC depend as much on reserves and deliverability as anything else.*[52] OPEC members will replenish surplus capacity if for no other reason than to enhance their position at the OPEC bargaining table. Exploration for new reserves in the Persian Gulf and elsewhere in OPEC has been neglected because of surplus deliverability, but there is every reason to believe that, as demand increases, the shelves will be restocked. Excess capacity is not a short-term aberration but can be expected to be an ongoing feature of the world petroleum market as long as finding costs are sufficiently below the anticipated selling price. And even if OPEC exploration is nil, it will take many years, if not decades, to work off the millions of barrels a day of unused deliverability to reach the 80 percent "threshold" of OPEC capacity that was a factor in the cartel's 1970s pricing latitude. The August 1986 accord has moved the timetable back by adding several million barrels per day to surplus capacity and raising prices to reduce consumption, although quota cheating will reduce this.

OPEC incentives: Market share and price. The OPEC members need revenue and singularly cannot afford to cut production. Concluded a recent study published by the Washington Institute for Near East Policy:

> The strongest force depressing oil prices will be the revenue need of oil-exporting countries and the increasing competition for market shares. Spending patterns of most oil exporters have showed

---

[52]"Venezuela needs plenty of excess capacity, hence excess reserves, because without it, it gets no respect from its fellow cartelists, and a smaller quota." M. A. Adelman, "Venezuela: Plenty of Oil on the Shelf," *Wall Street Journal*, May 21, 1987, p. 25.

them to be "large absorbers" of oil revenues. In fact, many OPEC countries have come to rely on continued production and export of oil to satiate their large appetite for revenues. Saudi Arabia, for example, needs oil revenues to maintain the high level of expenditure to which it grew accustomed in the 1970s and to cope with its growing budget deficit. If current trends continue, Saudi Arabia will completely exhaust its once-huge financial reserves in about four years.[53]

The surplus deliverability situation described above makes singular and even multination production cuts financially counterproductive. The absence of surplus capacity, on the other hand, could provide the opportunity to maximize short-term profit by restricting output and raising prices. Yet not only is this prospect many years away, but Saudi Arabia, key to such a strategy, is very much opposed to this action because it would sow the seeds for another conservation crisis for the cartel.

OPEC (and Saudi Arabia, in particular) continues to fight the consequences of the price "shocks" of the 1970s, which encouraged conservation, development of non-OPEC reserves, major alternative-fuel investments, and fuel-switching capability. As Adelman has observed, the cartel "overreached."[54] Just as consumers learned important lessons from the 1970s' energy crisis, Saudi Arabia and other oil-exporting powers have learned a lesson from their "energy crisis" of the 1980s. They have learned that price increases have short-run effects and magnified longer-run effects. Modest price increases can give the residual oil market to natural gas and coal almost immediately, as the recent OPEC accord has shown. Larger increases could accelerate heavy oil investments from Kern County, California, to the Orinoco belt in Venezuela and incite new interest in coal, hydropower, and, perhaps in time, nuclear power capacity. New energy-efficient technologies and habitual reductions in energy use as a result of higher prices could also trigger another round of conservation. With gasoline, a fuel once thought to be immune from substitution, increasing interest in methane (compressed natural gas) as a motor fuel could be accelerated. Methanol (gasohol) is also a competitor, and diesel fuel could increase market-share to

[53]Eliyahu Kanovsky, *Another Oil Shock in the 1990s: A Dissenting View* (Washington, D.C.: Washington Institute for Near East Policy, 1987), p. v.

[54]M. A. Adelman, "The Competitive Floor to World Oil Prices," *Energy Journal*, October 1986, p. 9.

reduce dependence on light products. Lost gasoline demand would not only hurt crude oil demand but, directly or indirectly, gasoline demand from OPEC for-export refineries. In short, let the seller beware.

Many scholars believe that maximum price increases for short-run gains are not in OPEC's interest. Bohi and Quandt have stated:

> It will not be in the oil cartel's interest to initiate or sustain an increase in oil prices, and individual countries will be disinclined to follow a cooperative strategy that sacrifices their market share. Unlike in the 1970s, when the interests of exporting and importing countries seemed to be diametrically opposed, it now appears that OPEC and the importing countries will both lose if prices rise. Similarly, in the event that a supply disturbance occurs for non-economic reasons, it is not in OPEC's interest to capitalize on the price shock and try to establish a new price floor as they did in the 1970s.[55]

Price stability has other advantages for the cartel. Bohi and Quandt continue:

> Apart from their damaging effect on long-run demand for OPEC oil, price fluctuations increase the difficulty of maintaining cooperation in production and pricing agreements, particularly in the downward phase of the price cycle. In addition, price fluctuations and their attendant revenue fluctuations make internal budget planning difficult, cause turmoil in planning domestic development projects, and create political tension. Consequently, it is reasonable to imagine that most OPEC members will recognize their self-interest in stable prices in coming years.[56]

The recent move by Kuwait into downstream operations, expected to be followed by other oil-export powers, is yet another reason that cartel members can be expected to favor price moderation and stability.[57] Another area of interdependence between oil exporting and oil importing countries is the hundreds of billions of dollars invested by Arab oil powers in the United States. Price shocks would have a negative impact on many of these investments, as it would on much of the U.S. economy.

[55]Bohi and Quandt, *Energy Security in the 1980s*, p. 18.

[56]Ibid.

[57]"Kuwait Now Refines and Markets Oil Too, in High-Powered Shift," *Wall Street Journal*, June 25, 1987, p. 1.

Tangible support for the above thesis is the well-known position of Saudi Arabia and Kuwait as price doves. Their position was recently supported by OPEC chairman Rilwanu Lukman of Nigeria, who admonished the United States for increasing uncertainty in the Persian Gulf by reflagging Kuwaiti tankers and thereby undermining price stability essential to the long-run interests of the cartel.[58]

Until excess capacity and fundamental incentives radically change, worst-case scenarios that underlie the argument for protectionism are improbable.

External Constraints on OPEC

Reinforcing the internal constraints on OPEC is the external discipline of the world petroleum market. Substantial evidence indicates that the non-OPEC world has a say in OPEC decisions and that outside producers and consumers constrain the pricing and production policies of Persian Gulf producers and possible allies—and will continue to do so for the indefinite future.

The reasons for this are not difficult to comprehend. Energy supply and prices in the last decade caused hardship for millions of U.S. consumers, and government rhetoric, particularly during the Carter era, exaggerated the predicament by blaming the niggardliness of nature instead of misguided policy. Consumers reacted with resolve and ingenuity, and producers responded resoundingly to the same incentives created by OPEC. Government demand-side responses such as mandatory conservation accelerated the conservation process, although supply-side responses have been muted by tax disincentives.

Diversification of production. OPEC's share of world oil production has decreased from 56 percent in 1973 to 33 percent in 1986, and the market-share of Arab OPEC has fallen from 32 percent to 21 percent in the same period. Much of this decrease occurred after 1980. The significant transfer of market-share reflected not only the yearly OPEC production cuts shouldered by Saudi Arabia but a significant rise in non-OPEC production. Table 4-4 compares OPEC, Arab OPEC, and non-OPEC crude output between 1973 and 1986.

In the above period, OPEC output declined by 41 percent, with

Table 4–4

OPEC vs. NON-OPEC CRUDE PRODUCTION: 1973–86
(thousand barrels per day)

Year	OPEC Production	Arab OPEC* Production	Non-OPEC Production	World Production
1973	30,989	18,009	24,584	55,573
1974	30,729	17,724	25,040	55,769
1975	27,155	15,986	25,609	52,764
1976	30,738	18,578	26,455	57,193
1977	31,298	19,221	28,224	59,522
1978	29,805	18,457	30,063	59,868
1979	30,928	21,094	31,425	62,353
1980	26,891	19,050	32,334	59,225
1981	22,646	15,764	32,900	55,546
1982	18,868	11,758	34,032	52,900
1983	17,583	10,364	35,071	52,654
1984	17,481	10,294	36,353	53,834
1985	16,068	9,033	36,886	52,954
1986	18,386	11,513	36,881	55,267

*Includes Algeria, Iraq, Kuwait, Libya, Qatar, Saudi Arabia, and the United Arab Emirates.
SOURCE: Energy Information Administration, Department of Energy

Arab OPEC dropping nearly as much. Non-OPEC output, meanwhile, rose 50 percent, keeping world output relatively constant.

Table 4–5 identifies the major new players in world oil production that responded to the price escalations of the last decade. Production in 1973 is contrasted with 1986 production to calculate the increase.

In the future, other non-OPEC countries will expand production and increase exports. This is evident even in OPEC's backyard. New discoveries in the western desert and new pipeline capacity promise to increase Egypt's exports. North and South Yemen "are on course to join the ranks of oil exporters."[59] Syria and even Jordan are expanding exploration and production activities, with exports expected to follow.

[59]Roger Vielvoye, "Middle East Report," *Oil & Gas Journal Report*, August 24, 1987, p. 38.

Table 4–5
MAJOR NEW NON-OPEC PRODUCERS
(thousand barrels per day)

Country	1973 Production	1986 Production	Increase
United Kingdom	2	2,548	2,546
Mexico	465	2,418	1,953
China	1,090	2,520	1,430
USSR	8,329	11,651	3,322
Other*	3,690	7,816	4,126
Total	13,576	26,953	13,377

*Includes Norway, Brazil, Peru, Argentina, India, and several dozen other producing nations.
SOURCE: Energy Information Administration, Department of Energy

Production did not increase in *all* non-OPEC countries during the period under study—nor are these figures meant to suggest that non-OPEC production will only increase in the future. Canadian output slumped from 1.8 million barrels to 1.5 million barrels per day in the above period, while U.S. output dropped a half million barrels per day, or 6 percent—despite the Prudhoe Bay field that came on stream and reached full production during the above 14 years. If prices fall to 1986 levels and are anticipated to stay depressed, these countries and other relatively high-cost regions can be expected to lose more market-share of the world oil market.

Diversification of reserves. Behind the diversification of non-OPEC production has been a diversification of reserves and reserve growth in the non-OPEC world, particularly in Mexico, Great Britain, China, and Norway. In percentage terms, however, non-OPEC reserve growth is not as significant as non-OPEC production growth. But neither are reserves as important a gauge of OPEC "power" as production and deliverability, given the ability of 70 percent of free-world deliverability to meet current free-world demand.

The reserve estimates presented previously, which calculated only 12 percent of world reserves in the Western Hemisphere and 5 percent in the United States, should be substantially revised to paint a truer picture of the relative size of Western Hemisphere reserves. Venezuelan reserves, currently estimated at under 30 billion barrels, have recently been reestimated at between 55 and 325 billion barrels. This revised estimate places Venezuela in the upper echelons of world oil powers and could even vault the South American country past Saudi Arabia as the world's most endowed oil nation.

The implications of this reassessment are noteworthy. For over 70 years, Venezuela has been the most prolific and reliable oil supplier to the United States. When the Arab OPEC members embargoed the United States in 1973–74, Venezuela expanded its output and exports to the United States to cushion the loss. Three decades before, tankers of Venezuelan crude evaded Nazi Germany submarine attacks to be a major wartime supplier of the United States. In 1986, Venezuela was the leading exporter of crude oil, gasoline, and residual fuel oil to the United States. This record of performance (setting aside the many problems, culminating in nationalization, that U.S. oil firms had in Venezuela), coupled with excess deliverability of 1 million barrels per day under their current OPEC quota, make Venezuela an "ace in the hole" for the United States. But with its prolific heavy oil reserves, Venezuela is more— *a check on Persian Gulf producers to moderate price increases for long-run considerations.* Any incentive the Persian Gulf producers give to Venezuela to put these vast reserves into play would be a major blunder. The incentive for Saudi Arabia and neighboring producers, contrarily, is to moderate change in the world petroleum market to let the sleeping dog of Venezuelan reserves lie. High prices could make even Venezuela's high-cost production competitive.

Oil conservation. A major legacy of the energy crisis is oil conservation. Oil conservation is demand that is not diverted to another energy source but lost (temporarily or permanently) because of technological change, new investments, or changed habits. Conservation has occurred from *market* responses to higher prices and perceived supply problems and *government-mandated* conservation standards for automobiles, buildings, appliances, and industrial and powerplant boilers. Subsidies for conservation research and energy audits also represent government discouragement of oil demand and energy demand in general.

The overall result of market and nonmarket conservation was a major decline in oil demand beginning in 1979—a decline that was not reversed until 1986 with the 50 percent fall in oil prices. The table below shows a 15 percent drop in U.S. oil consumption between

Table 4–6

U.S. vs. World Petroleum Consumption: 1973–86
(thousand barrels per day)

Year	U.S. Consumption	World Consumption	U.S. % of World Consumption
1973	17,308	56,530	30.6
1974	16,653	56,120	29.7
1975	16,322	55,280	29.5
1976	17,461	58,310	29.9
1977	18,431	62,020	29.7
1978	18,847	62,840	30.0
1979	18,513	65,110	28.4
1980	17,056	63,030	27.1
1981	16,058	60,710	26.5
1982	15,296	59,740	25.6
1983	15,231	58,950	25.8
1984	15,726	59,702	26.3
1985	15,726	59,745	26.3
1986	16,142	N/A	N/A

Source: Energy Information Administration, Department of Energy

1979 and 1985 and an 8 percent decline in world demand between 1979 and 1985, the last year for which data is presently available.

In the OECD countries, comprising Canada, Japan, and the bulk of Western Europe in addition to the United States, consumption fell 11 percent in the above period. Between its peak in 1979 and nadir in 1985, consumption fell by over 7 million barrels per day, nearly 18 percent. In 1986, consumption marginally increased as a result of falling prices, but this increase was hardly a threat to the conservation gains of the last decade. In fact, much of the demand increase in 1986 was not for immediate consumption but inventory build-ups that will *weaken* future oil demand. In short, what has been a decade in the making will not be reversed overnight, pointing toward a long period of OPEC overcapacity and constraint.

Diversification of energy consumption. A second factor related to lower oil demand in the 1980s is competing fuels, which have increased their share of the energy pie at the expense of oil and natural gas. Table 4-7 compares U.S. consumption of primary fuels from 1973 to the present.

As seen above, the major inroads in the electric generation market have been made by coal and nuclear power, at the expense of oil and gas, while hydroelectric power modestly increased its market-share. Between 1973 and 1986, coal consumption increased nearly 40 percent, and nuclear-generated electricity increased fourfold. Oil and gas production fell 6 percent and 26 percent respectively from a combination of higher prices and supply problems. Coal and nuclear power steadily increased their combined market-share from 24 percent in 1973 to 37 percent in 1986. Conversely, the combined share of oil and gas steadily fell from 67 percent in 1973 to 54 percent in 1986. Clearly the role of oil and gas in the energy picture is less dominant today than in the 1970s, with negative ramifications for the oil national-security argument.

Table 4–7

U.S. ENERGY PRODUCTION BY SOURCE: 1973–86
(quadrillion Btu)

Year	Coal	Crude Oil	Nat. Gas	NGL	Hydro	Nuclear	Total*
1973	14.0	19.5	22.2	2.6	2.9	.9	62.1
1974	14.1	18.6	21.2	2.5	3.2	1.3	60.8
1975	15.0	17.7	19.6	2.4	3.2	1.9	59.9
1976	15.7	17.3	19.5	2.3	3.0	2.1	59.9
1977	15.8	17.5	19.6	2.3	2.3	2.7	60.2
1978	14.9	18.4	19.5	2.2	2.9	3.0	61.1
1979	17.5	18.1	20.1	2.3	2.9	2.8	63.8
1980	18.6	18.2	19.9	2.3	2.9	2.7	64.8
1981	18.4	18.1	19.7	2.3	2.8	3.0	64.4
1982	18.6	18.3	18.3	2.2	3.3	3.1	63.9
1983	17.3	18.4	16.5	2.2	3.5	3.2	61.2
1984	19.7	18.8	17.9	2.3	3.3	3.6	65.8
1985	19.3	19.0	16.9	2.2	2.9	4.1	64.8
1986	19.5	18.4	16.5	2.2	3.0	4.5	64.3

*The total also includes electricity generated from wood, waste, geothermal, wind, photovoltaic, and solar sources. These fringe energies totaled 0.2 quadrillion Btu in 1986.
SOURCE: Energy Information Administration, Department of Energy

The growth of alternate fuel supply and fuel switching among oil, gas, and coal in major industrial and boiler fuel markets profoundly limits the ability of OPEC or any other oil-producing contingent to increase prices above certain ranges. Given the interdependence among the three fuels, each price determines, and in turn is determined by, the other two. In the United States, *an estimated 5 Tcf per year, or around 30 percent of the end-user market for natural gas, is fuel-switchable, and this percentage is still growing.*[60] The pervasiveness and implications of the relatively new phenomenon of fuel interdependence has been emphasized by Arlon Tussing:

> About half of the world's primary energy consumption is of the B-fuels [boiler fuels] variety, and a substantial and growing fraction of this market has the installed capacity to switch fuels. The fact that such uses are "marginal" (in the economic sense) for each of the primary fuels means that *the prices of all fuels will tend to converge toward the cost of the fuel whose supply is most elastic. . . .* [This] means that *disruption in the supply or a longer-term decline in producing capacity of any one of the three primary fossil fuels will not bring about an absolute scarcity in B-fuels nor a catastrophic price flyup.*[61]

Tussing estimates that oil prices above $20 per barrel would price oil out of the B-fuels market, depressing demand and thus increasing an already substantial surplus capacity, not only within OPEC and its Persian Gulf core but outside OPEC as well.

Given the importance of the primary fuels in the oil national security debate, appendix A to this chapter discusses the interfuel situation with natural gas, coal, nuclear, hydroelectricity, and purchased power, and the prospects of synthetic fuels and renewable energies.[62]

3. Entrepreneurship versus a New Energy Crisis

To cope with a possible energy crisis in the future, both the public and private sectors have made major investments and created new

[60]In the trade press, estimates have run as high as 40 percent. See, for example, *Natural Gas Week*, December 29, 1986, p. 2.

[61]Arlon Tussing, "Fundamentals of Gas Supply and Price," *ARTA Energy Insights*, October 1986, p. 3. He adds: "The exceptionally high prices between 1979 and 1985 were possible only because of an unprecedented heavy dependence of the world's B-fuels markets on oil, which in turn stemmed from the exceptionally low oil prices that prevailed in the 1950s and 1960s."

[62]See pp. 173–83.

institutions. Not only can a case be made that the United States is prepared for the worst—thus substantially mitigating the impact of a crisis—but it might be asked whether the country is *too prepared*.

Private Sector Entrepreneurship

In chapter 3 a major defect of the refiner protectionist position was identified—the neglect of market entrepreneurship.[63] The entrepreneur is the alert businessman who continually seeks profit opportunities in the marketplace. In the petroleum market, anticipating events that surprise or "shock" consumption is a major entrepreneurial function. The case for oil protectionism, consequently, must square its worst-case scenario with the incentive and ability of entrepreneurs to anticipate and mitigate sudden shocks to the system.

Free-market environment. The U.S. oil industry is more able to respond to sudden challenges in the world market in the 1980s than it was in the 1970s because of a *changed regulatory environment encouraging entrepreneurial alertness*. In the 1970s, the industry labored under a variety of regulations that severely hampered firms in dealing with uncertainty in ways that would benefit themselves and, unintentionally, the general economy. Profiting from anticipated price changes was not possible because prices were fixed, and accumulating and de-accumulating supply according to market opportunities was prevented by pervasive allocation requirements. Not only were these regulations repealed in 1981, but price and allocation regulation was rejected on a standby basis by President Reagan in 1982.[64] With special-interest support for standby regulation dissipated, market allocation and pricing can be expected in the future. Consequently, the susceptibility of the United States to a future embargo cannot be inferred from statistical analogies between present/predicted situations and past import interruptions. The fundamental variable of entrepreneurship has changed for the better.

Inventory versus OPEC. A very important entrepreneurial action, given uncertain oil imports, is *inventory speculation*. Whether inventories are built up or drawn down depends on the supply and price

[63]See chapter 3, pp. 98–100, for a parallel discussion of entrepreneurship on the refining side.

[64]The "national security" implications of this and other free-market policies are discussed in chapter 5, pp. 234–41.

expectations of entrepreneurs. In this regard, OPEC not only competes against the consumer and non-OPEC suppliers but also against profit seeking entrepreneurs, who *in effect make OPEC compete against itself.* This occurs when cartel output is perceived to be abnormal. When production is considered high during a market-share/price war, inventories are built up; when production is considered tight, stock drawdowns replace purchases. The expectation of a crisis will trigger massive stockpiling so that stocks can be profitably unloaded when the expected event occurs. Both actions equilibrate prices, the first by increasing prices and the second by decreasing prices, to ease the transition to increased scarcity.

OPEC's drive to restore oil prices after nine months of a price war in 1986 encountered this entrepreneurial phenomenon. Anticipating that prices would rise, firms around the world—particularly the majors—stockpiled oil during the summer of 1986. Thus, OPEC's decision to discontinue netback agreements and cut output had to be prolonged enough for bulging inventories, estimated to be as much as 200 to 300 million barrels worldwide, to be drawn down. This situation led one OPEC minister to complain about "the monstrous use of inventories to weaken prices."[65]

Any concerted production cut to raise prices must outlast inventory drawdowns (and survive the cartel problem in the process). Furthermore, it must "fool" the market—the market must be unable to anticipate that such a production cut would have a good chance of outlasting inventory. To assume total entrepreneurial surprise, as has been implicitly done in several protariff studies by Harvard economists, is untenable.[66]

The verdict of entrepreneurship. Given the predominantly free-market environment, entrepreneurs can be expected to follow their instincts and take actions to profit from any market change to the extent they really believe it will occur in the foreseeable future. Oilmen who advocate tariffs on a theme of impending crisis are

---

[65]Youssef Ibrahim, "Saudis' Return to Swing-Producer Role in OPEC Is Seen Sustaining Oil Price," *Wall Street Journal*, February 11, 1987, p. 2. OPEC's own inventory is another stabilizing force. Saudi Arabia's Norbec, in particular, has an estimated 60 billion barrels of oil stored onshore and in floating inventory in the Caribbean, West Africa, Southeast Asia, Europe, and elsewhere. This inventory could be profitably sold during a non-Arab supply crisis or substituted if Saudi output or transportation was involuntarily disrupted.

[66]See appendix 4B.

invited to "put their money where their mouth is." To the extent that they are *not* gearing up to drill and otherwise position themselves to profit from a tight supply situation, they undermine the case they are making. To the extent that they believe what they say, they will take actions that will— as if by an "invisible hand"— mitigate the object of their concerns. An example of the latter is the action of Transco chairman Jack Bowen, a prominent tariff advocate, who in May 1987 announced a major offshore drilling program predicated on shortages and $40 per barrel oil by 1995.[67] But only the future can vindicate this expectation—other oilmen are acting more cautiously.

Even if the underlying conditions for an energy crisis exist, its severity will be mitigated to the extent it is anticipated by the market. If tariff advocates are able to convince their industry brethren that there is a storm on the horizon, self-interested actions would make present prices and (higher) future prices converge to defuse the price shock. If the tariff advocate is a contrarian, however, his legislative pleas become a conviction of superior foresight that has been previously criticized as a "pretense of knowledge."

Public Sector "Entrepreneurship"

Two major public-sector responses to the threat of disrupted Arab OPEC cargoes are the Strategic Petroleum Reserve in the United States and the construction of major oil pipelines in the Middle East. These projects can be seen differently: the SPR as a malinvestment that could have been avoided completely, and the pipeline network as a rational response to unstable shipping lanes that private firms, if still in control, would have seriously considered.

The Strategic Petroleum Reserve. A major political response to the energy crisis of the 1970s was the federal government's creation of the Strategic Petroleum Reserve. The existence of this crude stockpile, currently containing over 525 million barrels of crude oil with a present drawdown capability of 3 million barrels per day, is a thorn in the side of the protectionist case. (So are foreign government crude stockpiles that cumulatively hold another 225 million barrels). Protectionists have been forced to assume that any cutoff

---

[67]J. Michael Douglas, "Transco Chief Sees $40 Oil, Shortage," *Houston Post*, May 21, 1987, p. C-1. For some other examples of aggressive drilling programs, see Gene Smith, "Bullish Attitude at National Gas Seminar Tempered by Jabs at FERC, Congress," *Oil Daily*, June 1, 1987, p. 4.

would be severe and prolonged given the potential contribution of the SPR in addition to private inventory. At present import rates, the SPR represents approximately a 125-day supply; at full inventory, it represents a 175-day supply. With the most likely scenario of a partial crude import loss, the public stockpile could easily augment a year or more of reduced imports. In this amount of time, long-run adjustments could join short-run adjustments to render the worst interruption impotent.

As an insurance policy, the reserve is an embarrassment of riches, reflecting its over $20 billion premium. Not only does this expenditure equate to a total storage cost of $38 per barrel, its "opportunity cost" is the purchase of a major oil field (such as the Yates field in West Texas), which normally sells for a 75 percent discount compared to aboveground supply.[68]

While the government reserve represents another nail in the oil protectionist coffin, a more subtle implication arises from a free-market perspective. Given that the SPR is *nonmarket* crude inventory, that it is not the result of profit-maximizing action but a political response to a (politically produced) crisis, a case can be made that the federal stockpile represents an *overinvestment* in crude inventory, and therefore the United States is *too* prepared for the emergency the SPR is intended to mitigate.[69] The government, in other words, has uneconomically allocated resources away from other areas of the economy and overbuilt the crude storage sector. Continued progress toward its goal of 750 million barrels will only add to the malinvestment.

Private inventory positions, which reflect future supply availability and any uncertainty therein, are the first line of defense against supply interruptions. The SPR, on the other hand, is a political good with an undefined role to play in a future "emergency." Its use, as in past decisions not to withdraw supply, depends on government expectations that the emergency is worse now than it will be in the future—a risky assumption. These problems notwithstanding, it is still a huge accumulation of raw oil that influences the market. Chapter 5 will explore policy options for turning the SPR from a *political good* into an *entrepreneurial asset*, so that it

---

[68]James Griffin and Henry Steele, *Energy Economics and Policy* (New York: Academic Press, 1986), p. 234.

[69]See the criticism of the SPR in chapter 3, pp. 106–7.

may be better positioned for a positive contribution whatever the future may bring.[70]

Middle Eastern oil pipelines. Supply interruptions are of concern not only to consumers in import-dependent areas but to oil exporting countries as well. Persian Gulf producers are very dependent on oil revenue, and lost market access means lost revenue to meet the ongoing military and social obligations upon which their political stability depend.

To reduce the risk of disruption, a strategy of Persian Gulf producers has been to diversify transportation away from tanker shipments through the Strait of Hormuz. In response to the Iran-Iraq war, an oil pipeline network has sprung up to reduce dependence on tanker carriage through this relatively narrow strait, which is situated in the war area. Saudi Arabia and Iraq have each constructed several million barrels per day of pipeline capacity to bring oil to alternate tanker receipt points on the Red Sea and Mediterranean Sea. Iran has begun a major pipeline project that may eventually allow the warring nation also to bypass the potential bottleneck at the 17-mile tip of the Arabian/Persian Gulf. Kuwait is considering its own major pipeline as an "insurance policy" and as an alternative to paying tanker rates inflated by high insurance costs. All told, pipeline capacity in the region has grown from 2.5 million barrels per day in 1980 to over 5 million barrels today, and potential additions (including new pumping stations on existing lines) could bring this total to 7 million barrels per day and more.[71] The lesson of the "market" response to wartime dangers was summarized by a *Wall Street Journal* report in early 1986:

> The new pipelines are like a giant safety value, spreading around strategic risks and dangers that were concentrated solely on the Persian Gulf. . . . Indeed, the broadest lesson to be drawn from the changes in the gulf's strategic position may be that oil markets can find solutions to dangerous situations more easily than once predicted. Nobody would have dared to forecast in the 1970s that there could be a war in the Persian Gulf, a shutdown of Iraq's gulf oil terminals and attacks on oil tankers and facilities—and that oil

[70]See pp. 234–35.

[71]See Murray Gart, "Who Needs the Gulf, Anyway," *Time*, August 24, 1987, p. 27; and "Oil Importers Seen Surviving Closure of Strait," *Oil & Gas Journal*, August 31, 1987, pp. 20–22.

prices and the gulf's strategic importance would decline in spite of it all. Yet this is exactly what has happened.[72]

Diversification of transportation does not spell an end to uncertainty in the region. But because oil pipelines are relatively easy to repair when sabotaged, and because the option of tanker transport through the Persian Gulf remains, this development mitigates the national security threat of present and increased dependence on Persian Gulf oil.

4. The New World Petroleum Market

The differences between the 1970s and 1980s world petroleum market cannot be overemphasized. Major differences in supply, demand, and the entrepreneurial environment have already been discussed. Several other major fundamental changes have occurred, all of which bode well for the ability of the market to anticipate and mitigate worst-case situations in the future. These *entrepreneurial responses to the market's need to reduce uncertainty* were made not for altruistic reasons—to avert a national security crisis—but for self-interested reasons—to make a profit.

Spot Market Oil and Oil Trading

The growth of the oil spot market was a consequence of the nationalization of ARAMCO and subsequent OPEC actions, particularly the 1979 Iranian revolution. In the early 1970s, spot oil composed less than 5 percent of total international oil sales. Long-term contracts and relatively few transactions characterized the oil trade, and so did stability. Today, an estimated 50 percent of oil transactions are short-term, high-turnover deals. The popularity of these contracts has mirrored the instability of the oil market.[73]

The results of the changeover from long-term to short-term contracting have included (1) an increase in market-sensitive provisions to accurately reflect market realities and anticipations (including impending uncertainties), (2) inventory reductions from improved access to spot supplies, (3) a decrease in panic buying, (4) better distribution to areas of highest demand, and (5) less political assign-

---

[72]Gerald Seib, "Persian Gulf Declines as a Vital Highway for Mideastern Oil," *Wall Street Journal*, January 24, 1986, p. 1.

[73]Noted Bohi and Quandt, "The market has come to rely less on long-term contracts, because these instruments have proved to be unreliable at precisely the time they are most needed." *Energy Security in the 1980s*, p. 14.

ability between parties.[74] Each of these unintended consequences combats uncertainty, discourages underlying conditions breeding supply and price instability, and engenders economic efficiency.[75]

Changed contracting involves hundreds of independent oil traders who thrive on specialized knowledge, secrecy, and the ability to act when profitable opportunities strike. Any disruption of normal trading patterns presents profitable opportunities for traders and others "in the know," and by overcoming the supply hurdles, their actions help consumers and thus contribute to "national security." With the challenges and experience of the last decade under its belt, this oil industry community is well poised for the future.

Futures Market and Energy Asset Insurance

The explosive growth of futures trading on the New York Mercantile Exchange (NYMEX) in crude oil, home heating oil, and gasoline has shifted pricing from the cartel to the electronic screen. Rumors, leaks, insights, opinions, as well as interpretations of hard statistics, are quickly integrated into the market's knowledge to continually price oil quite independently of the OPEC official line. OPEC, and even some U.S. oilmen, "kill the messenger" by decrying the verdicts of futures trading as speculation and games of chance, but the positive contributions of such trading, like those of the spot market itself, cannot be denied. Firms most vulnerable to the vicissitudes of the market can now lock in prices to eliminate uncertainty and let risk-seekers satisfy their opposite desires. Resulting prices from the bulls and bears, whether speculators or hedgers, create a *transparent* market signal that has been seized upon not only by the financial community but by the industry itself for negotiating contracts.

The market has pronounced futures trading an overwhelming success. Annualized volume on the NYMEX today is 20 billion barrels of oil, an amount approximately equal to the world's annual crude output.

Although it is too early to judge a market institution, a variation on NYMEX trading to manage risk has made a successful debut. The Energy Asset Insurance program, recently introduced by Had-

---

[74]Ibid., pp. 14–15, 19.

[75]New characteristics of oil as a commodity are described in Philip Verleger, "The Evolution of Oil as a Commodity," in *Energy: Markets and Regulation*, ed. Richard Gordon et al. (Cambridge: MIT Press, 1987), pp. 161–86.

son Energy Risk Management in partnership with Mount Lucas Associates, puts together price hedgers from opposite market positions to lock in a base price for each for up to five years. The oil producer and oil consumer (anonymously through Hadson) reach a mutually acceptable price by agreeing to pay the other the difference between the market price and the base price (with a portion of the upside to each going to the matchmakers). If the market price is above the base price, the producer pays the consumer; if the market price is below the base price, the consumer pays the producer. By eliminating uncertainty for *both* parties, this strategy facilitates capital procurement and allows drilling programs to be undertaken amid severe price fluctuations. If the early response to the "perfect hedge" between Production Value Insurance for producers and Energy Cost Insurance for consumers is indicative, this program could be an important supplement to oil futures trading and can be expected to attract imitators.

A case study of spot oil and the futures market during a period of high uncertainty occurred in the summer and fall of 1987 when the United States embarked on its reflagging mission with Kuwaiti tankers. With brinkmanship in the air and a reflagged tanker hit by Iran, the possibility of a widespread disruption of tanker travel through the Strait of Hormuz chilled the market. Oil pierced the $20 threshold and reached $22 per barrel on the NYMEX. What was behind the run-up was precautionary buying by refiners and speculators in anticipation of a worst-case event—*evidence that the market was preparing for the worst to keep the worst from happening.* The worst would not come to pass, but the spot market and futures pricing had done its job.

Refining Flexibility

Another major change in today's world oil market is the ability of domestic and foreign refiners to process a variety of heavier crudes and convert residual fuel oil into light products. This has made refineries, according to William Johnson, "more immune to an interruption in crude supplies, especially light supplies from the Middle East."[76] Charles Ebinger has made the same point by estimating that as much as 1.5 million barrels a day of imported residual fuel oil from Western Hemisphere suppliers could be transferred

---

[76]Patrick Crow, "Rising U.S. Oil Imports Get Attention but No Action," *Oil & Gas Journal*, July 6, 1987, p. 17.

from boiler fuel markets to refiners for middle distillate and gasoline production, thereby backing out an equivalent amount of disrupted Eastern Hemisphere crude or product.[77]

5. Other Protectionist Arguments Reconsidered

A critical review of the case for protectionism must consider four other arguments. Protectionists claim that oil tariffs would (1) reduce the negative trade balance to help the general economy, (2) stabilize the industry by preventing temporary price fluctuations, (3) conserve stripper wells for national security, and (4) prevent predatory pricing. Each of these claims is considered in turn.

Balance of Trade

Tariff proponents cite a favorable balance of trade as an advantage of their position. It is not. The trade balance argument assumes what cannot be assumed and rests on a fallacy of economics—that imports are inherently bad and exports are inherently good.

In 1986, the surge in crude imports did not contribute to a negative trade balance. Because crude prices fell by 50 percent, the foreign oil "bill" actually decreased 25 percent in 1986 from a year before, an estimated savings of $42 billion.[78] With the reversal of price and higher imports thus far in 1987, the balance of trade will go the other way, but probably not enough to reverse the result in 1986.

Because of the inverse relationship of price and quantity demanded, the effect of a change in import prices or quantity on the balance of payments is ambiguous. The assumption made by protectionists is that the United States, by becoming "hooked" on foreign oil, will simultaneously increase imports and pay higher prices in so doing. This assumption, however, is highly uncertain, even unlikely except in the short run, given the present and foreseeable state of OPEC versus the world market.

While it is speculative to predict the configuration of price and quantity under open trade, it is certain that a tariff will *encourage general imports* and *discourage general exports* by making U.S. firms less competitive internationally and foreign firms more competitive in the United States. An oil tariff increases domestic prices for the home industry while *lowering* world oil prices by decreasing the marketability of non-U.S. oil. (Because Japan, Western Europe,

[77]Charles Ebinger, *The Critical Link: Energy and National Security* (Cambridge: Ballinger Publishing Company, 1982), p. 62.

[78]*Wall Street Journal*, January 21, 1987, p. 6.

Taiwan, and other staunch U.S. competitors in the world market do not have much or any domestic oil industry to protect, it is assumed that they will not follow suit with a tariff to neutralize the U.S. tariff.) This double effect *subsidizes* imports by making them cheaper and *taxes* exports of U.S. goods by making them more expensive. The interrelated effects skew the trade balance away from the United States.

If it could be demonstrated that increased oil imports overwhelm the price effect to increase the total outlay on foreign oil, it does not follow that this is inherently detrimental. The opportunity cost to purchased foreign oil is the production and consumption of more expensive domestic oil. By buying the cheaper supply, U.S. consumers save money and stimulate the economy by residual purchases elsewhere. Moreover, U.S. dollars abroad are used either to *export* U.S. goods (to negate the trade imbalance) or to invest in the United States. Regarding the latter, petro-dollars from the Middle East have been an important source of investment capital in this country. They contribute to economic investment and capital formation just as much as the savings of U.S. citizens do. In short, it is erroneous to depreciate the value of cheap supply because it is imported and not home product.

Temporary Stability

One of the earliest protectionist arguments in the current debate is the case for a variable import fee (VIF). Since at least 1984, S. Fred Singer has advocated a VIF to neutralize the ability and incentive of OPEC nations to selectively flood the market.[79] Upon closer examination, however, the superficial appeal of this policy proposal, which purports to protect the U.S. industry from sudden decimation by setting a floor oil price, loses its plausibility.

Singer's proposal is appealing because the argument assumes that the future can be correctly predicted. But how can the "temporary" price and "real" price really be known *ex ante*? If the market could recognize the difference, then the imperfect price would converge toward its "true" level, and the tariff floor would not take effect. Contrarily, it is only *ex post* that a price can be recognized as temporary or lasting. If Singer really knows the future state of

[79]S. Fred Singer, "Restrictions on Oil Imports?"in *Free Market Energy*, ed. S. Fred Singer (New York: Universe Books, 1984), pp. 99—117; idem, "If Oil Price Drops, Leap in with Fee,"*Wall Street Journal*, January 18, 1985, p. 16.

prices, differentiating between transient and fundamental price movements, he can amass incalculable wealth in the petroleum futures market and subsidiary markets. But short of this litmus test, modesty about his ability to outpredict the market should prevail.

If there is uncertainty, and there is, the question becomes whether the market or the government has better forecasting ability. On theoretical and empirical grounds, there is reason to believe that entrepreneurs with profit and loss at stake, and with the 18-month futures market and the 5-year Energy Asset Insurance program to aid their vision, are better prognosticators of future market conditions and resulting prices than are academic theoreticians or government planners.

Stripper Well Conservation

Stripper wells, defined as producing less than 10 barrels per day, account for approximately 1.3 million barrels per day, or 15 percent of national production. It is argued that a sufficient tariff would prevent "premature" abandonment of these properties, thus preserving their output both for normal times and for any emergency that would make their contribution even more important.

This argument, used to justify not only tariffs but oil-state market-demand proration since the 1930s, is not persuasive. The stripper wells at issue are marginal assets, often in the twilight of long careers. All productive assets depreciate or deplete, oil wells included, and face the time when marginal revenue can no longer exceed marginal cost. At this point retirement becomes economic, so that nonspecific resources may be transferred to higher-value uses. When stripper wells are abandoned, lifting costs (pumper, storage, and transport costs) are avoided, and these resources are available for properties that are more productive and have lower unit costs. The history of the oil industry is the history of old wells leaving the scene and flush wells entering production. To create artificial price incentives for submarginal assets distorts the exit/entry process at the expense of consumers and economywide efficiency.

With a sudden price plunge, many owners of stripper wells must decide whether to abandon the wells or not. This is a function not only of present prices but of anticipated prices as well. If the price decline is expected to be temporary, then the entrepreneur will postpone his decision to plug the well permanently. If the outlook shows no promise, then a decision to cement the well will be made. There are three implications from this emphasis on *expectations*.

First, tariffs to save stripper wells cannot be based on "temporary" price declines, because entrepreneurs, not outsiders, judge what is temporary and what is not, and they act accordingly with regard to their portfolio of stripper wells. Second, not all stripper wells— just the least-productive, highest-cost ones—are at risk at a given level of prices. Tariffs, in other words, do not save stripper wells per se but only the most marginal stripper wells. Third, state and federal plugging regulations, which require nonproducing wells to be cemented shut (permanently so, for practical purposes), interfere with entrepreneurial decisions (and the nation's active oil base) and should be repealed, with environmental matters settled on a tort basis. (In fact, plugging regulations have been relaxed as an industry relief measure.[80]) Counterproductive regulation, artificially reducing the stripper well population in distressed periods, does not make a case for federal intervention (such as protectionism) but a case for regulatory reform.

Predatory Pricing

The charge of predatory pricing has had particular application in the petroleum industry. It was a major complaint against the Standard Oil Trust in the last century. More recently, independent gasoline service station dealers have trumpeted the charge against integrated rivals. It is also part of the protectionist argument, although it has been limited by its lack of persuasiveness.

The protectionist predatory-pricing argument proceeds as follows. The Saudi strategy unveiled in December 1985 was designed to do more than regain market share and strong-arm fellow OPEC members into disciplined production. Its true design was, in the words of *World Oil* editor R. W. Scott, "to eliminate all competition from any high-cost production anywhere, especially from the United States [by] . . . driving prices below production cost."[81] Then, with the market secured, the Saudis could, almost at will, increase prices in the competitive vacuum left by the retired higher-cost production.

Predatory pricing is a very risky profit-maximizing strategy, and it has been soundly refuted by the historical record. Any dominant firm is wary about getting into a price war because short-term profits are forgone for an open-ended period, and present-period profits

[80]See chapter 5, pp. 198–200.

[81]R. W. Scott, "We Must Have an Import Fee," *Houston Chronicle*, April 27, 1986, p. 6-4.

are preferred over later returns. If the market believes that the dominant firm is following a price-cutting policy to charge higher prices later, then besieged firms will linger rather than exit, and buyers will stockpile supply in anticipation of arbitrage gains. Indeed, in Scott's example several hundred million barrels of "cheap" oil found their way into inventory during the Saudis' price war, and many stripper wells inactivated (rather than plugged) in 1986 were reactivated with the price improvement in 1987.

The Saudi strategy change in December 1985 was not a sinister plot. It was a logical response to a predicament that could not continue. Continued production cuts by the Saudis, already over 7 million barrels per day from its peak, would have led to an end to oil exports. The August 1986 accord, whereby the market-share/ price-war strategy was abandoned by Saudi Arabia, affirmed not only the other intentions of the program but the impotence of predatory pricing itself, should it have been followed.

6. Politics Has the Last Say

In chapter 3, the point was made that while the academicians, planners, and industry experts get the first shot at designing an "optimal" policy program, with all its hypothesized advantages over the unfettered market, politics gets the last say. The history of oil (and gas) intervention is replete with programs that began on high-sounding premises but degenerated into special-interest tug-of-wars. For an outstanding example, the Mandatory Oil Import Program from 1959 to 1973 can be cited. This program began with a singular vision of national security through restricted oil imports but disintegrated into a macroeconomic management, public-works, environmental, and foreign-policy program. As the Cabinet Task Force on Oil Import Control concluded in its study of the MOIP in 1970:

> The fixed quota limitations that have been in effect for the past ten years, and the system of implementation that has grown up around them, bear no reasonable relation to current requirements for protection either of the national economy or of essential oil consumption. The level of restriction is arbitrary and the treatment of secure foreign sources internally inconsistent. The present system has spawned a host of special arrangements and exceptions for purposes essentially unrelated to the national security.[82]

[82]Cabinet Task Force on Oil Import Control, *The Oil Import Question* (Washington, D.C.: Government Printing Office, 1970), p. 128.

The desire, no matter how strong, of protectionists to keep the program free of competing and contradictory goals is no impenetrable shield against political realities. Once the fundamental business decision of whether to buy or sell oil according to relative cost is taken from the market and placed into the political arena, there are no guarantees of focused purpose—or, indeed, even of what that purpose (or purposes) might be. It becomes an agenda item of temporary political majorities who are not mesmerized by visions of the common good but, rather, of furthering their own interests.

With the prize of cheaper oil at stake, it is particularly naive to believe that consumer forces, industry constituencies, and friendly neighboring countries will not tilt the tariff or quota their way. The interest of motorists in cheaper gasoline and homeowners in lower heating bills will dovetail with both the interest of industry members who can profitably deliver it to them and countries that are secure providers. Their voices will be heard and will prevail, probably sooner than later. And once a few cracks appear in the dike, economic forces and self-interest will widen the openings and demand further "equities" to continue the process. There may be "regrouping" and backsliding along the way, again the inevitable result of the shifting sands of politics, but the dynamics of the process cannot be denied.

D. Conclusion

The struggle of OPEC to achieve $18 per barrel oil under very favorable conditions (the Iran-Iraq war), an effort necessitating that Saudi Arabia resume its familiar role as swing producer in OPEC, is indicative of how far the world oil and energy markets have tamed the cartel. Consumer demand, while increased, has not exploded from the 50 percent price decline. Demand is relatively inelastic with lower prices as it is relatively elastic with higher prices, a troublesome combination for world production mired in excess capacity.

The present world oil market is much more diverse, complex, and "intelligent" than in decades past. The OPEC cartel, despite occasional high points, has been an unstable alliance and faces serious challenges in the future, as it has in the recent past. Surplus deliverability is not a short-term market aberration but is characteristic of a market with selling prices well above finding costs. The entrepreneurial environment, complete with new market institutions such as futures trading and energy asset insurance, is conducive to anticipating and mitigating supply disruptions—processes that were severely hampered in the highly regulated 1970s. The overhang of the Strategic Petroleum Reserve (despite all its problems) and new oil pipelines to bypass the volatile Persian Gulf are "public sector" insurance policies that overwhelm worst-case events. Each of these points has fundamental implications for the ability of the Persian Gulf cartel to control the market now and for decades hence.

The growth of the non-OPEC oil market in diversity, deliverability, and reserves has been a major response to spiraling prices of the 1973–81 period. Increased oil conservation and the increased market-share of coal and nuclear energy are other legacies of the oil boom that have tamed the cartel for the foreseeable future. The market has "learned" not to depend on oil exclusively and not to be oil-intensive.

Douglas Bohi and William Quandt have summarized the implications of the above changes for future challenges to normal market operations.

> The international oil market has adopted to the traumas of the 1970s with a more flexible system of conducting transactions, more diversity in the distribution of oil production, and more efficiency in oil consumption. In short, the market is more resilient now and oil prices may be expected to behave differently as a consequence.[83]

The 1970s world oil market no longer exists, nor can it be expected to reappear to make a national security case for oil protectionism. The genie is not only out of the bottle, but the bottle has been firmly recorked.

---

[83]Bohi and Quandt, *Energy Security in the 1980s*, p. 20.

Appendix 4A
Interfuel Competition to Oil

The promoted role of interfuel competition with oil is a major theme of the present U.S. energy market and an important argument in the national security and oil protectionism debates. A sudden loss of oil imports does not mean as much if alternate fuels can be substituted for certain oil products to allow refineries to tilt output toward particularly scarce products.

Interfuel Competition and Substitution

Instantaneous substitution between fuels, as discussed in chapter 4, is a major characteristic of the boiler fuels (B-fuels) market and an important source of pricing restraint. Although the home heating and motor vehicle markets do not have the same flexibility in switching from oil, they are not immune from interfuel competition.

Natural gas is the preeminent fuel substitute for petroleum. As emphasized by Milton Copulos, methane's attributes of availability, fungibility, and versatility make it "the most flexible alternative to oil."[1] In industrial and powerplant boilers, gas is the most common alternative burn to residual fuel oil, with coal a distant second. With the sharp drop in residual fuel oil prices in 1986, oil took many markets from natural gas; with the rebound of oil prices in 1987, these markets have been regained by gas.[2]

The American Gas Association has estimated that natural gas in an oil crisis could immediately replace 352,000 barrels per day of imported oil, 720,000 barrels within one year, and 1.7 million barrels in five years. This would require 750 billion cubic feet, 1.5 trillion cubic feet (Tcf), and 3.6 Tcf of gas, respectively. The lion's share of

---

[1]Milton Copulos, *Natural Gas: The Vital Energy Security Link* (Alexandria, Va.: National Defense Council Foundation, 1985), p. 3.

[2]See "Crude Price Slide Lets Oil Regain Lost U.S. Bulk Fuels Market Share," *Oil & Gas Journal*, April 13, 1987, pp. 17–19.

the backout is in the B-fuels market, with the remainder in the home heating and vehicular markets examined below.[3]

In the B-fuels market, electricity generated from oil- and gas-fired plants competes on an incremental cost basis against coal-fired, nuclear, and hydroelectric power. Oil and gas also can be backed out by decisions to buy electricity from other utilities on the purchase power grid, another important—and growing—fossil fuel substitute.

In residential and commercial heating markets, gas competes against #2 fuel oil—but not at the flip of a switch, as it does in boiler markets. Initial decisions are made between home heating oil and natural gas burners, after which the users are "captive" to their initial choice. Retrofit decisions are possible, however, with up-front costs weighed against longer-run savings. Despite these constraints, competition is pronounced, as marketers for the two fossil fuels vie for incremental markets.

Electricity and natural gas compete for water heating and cooking load, but not simultaneously. In residential and commercial cooling markets, new system designs that burn natural gas are just beginning to challenge the dominant market-share of electricity.

In the motor fuel market, the preeminence of gasoline and diesel fuel could be challenged in the future by compressed natural gas (CNG) or methanol, a mix of CNG and premium unleaded gasoline. Although commercial implementations of this technology were set back by oil price developments in 1986, interest remains strong in some sectors. Natural gas vehicles, which currently number 30,000 in the United States and 375,000 worldwide, are very competitive, on an incremental cost (fill-up) basis, with gasoline and diesel fuel vehicles. CNG's competitive viability, however, is blocked by major infrastructure investments in vehicle conversion, fueling stations, and tank trucks. This has not discouraged government interest in natural gas vehicles as a strategy against a "looming" oil crisis and a strategy for helping nonattainment areas achieve compliance with the Clean Air Act.[4]

---

[3]AGA, "The Strategic Role of Natural Gas in Replacing Imported Oil," *Energy Analysis*, May 22, 1987.

[4]For an "oil crisis" perspective of CNG substitution, see Charles Ebinger et al., *Natural Gas Vehicles: A National Security Perspective* (Washington, D.C.: Center for Strategic and International Studies, 1984).

The Current Alternate Fuel Situation

Given the present and potential role of alternate fuels in the oil market, the next question is the availability and flexibility of each. The following fuels are considered in turn: natural gas, coal, nuclear power, hydro power, purchased power, and synthetic/renewable energies.

Natural Gas

The natural gas "bubble" in the United States is in its sixth year. Domestic deliverability estimated at 20 Tcf and a 24 Tcf pipeline system swamped 1986 consumption of 16 Tcf. Although reduced drilling will slow reserve replacement and decrease deliverability in the lower 48, many factors point toward continued abundance of the "ideal fuel" and a growing role in the nation's fuel mix. Canadian imports, examined in more detail below, are an important and growing supplement to lower-48 proven reserves of 160 Tcf, a 9- to 10-year supply at current consumption levels.[5] The demotion of state and federal regulation restricting pricing, transportation, and fuel use choices has opened up new market opportunities. Order 451 has freed gas from stifling contracts to seek higher regulated prices. Laborious Section 7(c) filings under the Natural Gas Act have been replaced in part by expedited transportation under Section 311 of the Natural Gas Policy Act. Effective repeal of the Powerplant and Industrial Fuel Use Act of 1978 (Fuel Use Act) has placed combined-cycle gas-fired plants at the forefront of new electric generation capacity. These changes, fostering a national natural gas spot market characterized by scarcity pricing, make shortages like those experienced in interstate markets in the 1970s a distant memory. This is not to say that federal, state, and municipal regulation will not continue to distort the market; it suggests that the industry today is more efficient and customer-responsive than ever before, thus giving natural gas unprecedented clout to compete in incremental markets against oil and other energy substitutes.[6]

[5]"Probable" lower-48 reserves have been estimated at 270 Bcf and "speculative" reserves at 200 Bcf. Alaskan gas reserves of 35 Tcf are not included in the "probable" category because of a lack of transportation to consumer markets. The 4,790-mile Alaska Natural Gas Transportation System (ANGTS), approved in 1977 by regulators, is not economically viable and is not expected to be so for the foreseeable future. A more viable alternative may be a recent proposal to ship liquefied natural gas from the North Slope to Asian markets.

[6]The new era of the natural gas market is summarized and anticipated in Arlon Tussing and Connie Barlow, "You Can't Go Home Again," *ARTA Energy Insights*, September 1985.

The Potential Gas Agency of the Colorado School of Mines has estimated that over 750 Tcf of gas remain to be discovered in the United States alone, exclusive of tight sands and coal seam gas, representing a 50-year supply.[7] Another "bullish" factor is a growing belief that natural gas not only has *biogenic* (fossil decomposition) origins but *abiogenic* (pervasive) origins, which would explain why at great depths gas has come to be unexpectedly plentiful. If this hypothesis is correct, supply would be virtually inexhaustible, and deep gas would thus be an "ace in the hole" if conventional prospects, imports, and Alaskan reserves were sufficiently depleted.

The U.S. gas market is part of the prolific North American gas market.[8] Canada, in particular the province of Alberta, is a bastion of methane, with 76 Tcf in marketable reserves alone. (Another 23 Tcf of reserves are not connected to markets for economic reasons.) At current consumption rates, Canada boasts a 25- to 35-year supply. Despite eased import regulation by the Energy Regulatory Administration (U.S.) and National Energy Board (Canada), and over 4 Bcf per day of pipeline capacity between the two countries, with incremental expansions on the horizon, imports averaged just over 2 Bcf per day in 1986. This low figure was due in part to access problems—created by Federal Energy Regulatory Commission Order 436—to U.S. pipelines. The major export destination point for Canadian gas in 1986 was California, followed by the Midwest and Northeast.

At currently authorized export volumes, surplus Canadian gas is poised to more fully utilize existing pipeline capacity into the United States and increase its historic market-share of 5 percent of U.S. consumption. In the past several years, the Canadians have shown their ability and willingness to be price leaders (or more subtly, price matchers) to capture or share incremental markets; once the remaining regulatory and transportation impediments are removed, Canadian competition can be expected to accelerate, with consequent pressure on residual fuel oil and coal in the B-fuels market.

The other part of the North American gas market is Mexico. Production from a 70 Tcf reserve base, primarily associated with oil, is currently either internally consumed or flared. Outside of one

[7]See "Natural Gas Can Play Key National Security Role," *Oil & Gas Journal,* February 2, 1987, p. 111.

[8]See Connie Barlow, "Toward a North American Gas Market," *ARTA Energy Insights,* February 1985.

brief exception, Mexico has not exported natural gas since 1975 because of a political impasse between the Department of Energy and Petroleos Mexicanos (PEMEX). The prospects for resumed exports to Texas from the Reforma field and other major basins depend on the political and economic situation of PEMEX, but it remains a lucrative opportunity that could materialize. It was estimated not long ago that daily imports from Mexico would be between 2 and 4 Bcf per day; any realization of this potential would be a significant addition to domestic production and Canadian imports, and would promote the continuation of the present buyers' market and stiff gas-to-gas and gas-to-oil rivalry.[9]

Natural gas in liquefied form has reentered the energy picture with recent flexible contract pricing between Algeria's Sonatrach and Panhandle Eastern in the United States and with Indonesia's Pertamina and Japanese electric and gas firms abroad. The Panhandle Eastern contract calls for deliveries of up to 3 Tcf over a 20-year period, representing nearly 1 percent of projected gas consumption in the United States at full contract. (The floor price, however, would need to be around $2.00 per MMBtu to begin deliveries in late 1987, as scheduled.) In Nigeria, a LNG project conceived in the 1970s is being rescaled for possible implementation. With price-sensitive contracts and a rebound of gas prices, LNG has the ability to intensify gas-to-gas competition, turn the North American gas market into an *international* market (as it was in the last decade), and back out residual fuel oil in the process, with worldwide ramifications.

Coal

The United States, with presently recoverable reserves of approximately 250 billion short tons, is the Saudi Arabia of coal—it has more than one-third of the world's total supply. On a heating value basis, these reserves equate to over a trillion barrels of oil. The United States is the world's leading producer and exporter of the product. In 1986, it exported 85.5 million short tons, while importing 2.2 million short tons. Coal's major application is in electric generation, where it enjoys a market-share greater than its competitors combined. Coal gasification and liquefication are not economically feasible.

[9]Arlon Tussing and Connie Barlow, *The Natural Gas Industry* (Cambridge: Ballinger Publishing Company, 1984), pp. 147–53.

Coal competes against oil and gas in some electric powerplants and in certain industrial burns such as steelmaking. Coal was a major beneficiary of higher oil prices in the 1970s and has enjoyed record demand since 1984. Part of this success has been artificial, however. Coal has benefited at the expense of natural gas from the Fuel Use Act, which prohibited (without a special exemption) new electric-generating capacity from burning oil or gas. Between 1978 and 1985, coal expanded its share of the electric generation market from 44 percent to 57 percent, while gas fell from 14 percent to 12 percent, and oil fell from 17 percent to 4 percent.

When nuclear power reaches its licensed maximum in the next decade (see below), and until the economic and environmental prospects of coal improve (75 coal-fired baseload plants have been canceled since 1974), oil- and gas-fired combined cycle will be the most likely source of new capacity to meet electric demand growth. The Edison Electric Institute has estimated that as much as 100,000 megawatts of new capacity will be needed by the year 2000 to meet demand, led by the Northeast. Technological developments may solve some of the challenges presented by sulfur emissions and the acid rain problem, but the capital-intensive nature of the solutions will remain a disincentive. Historic labor problems and political opposition to strip mining and coal slurry pipelines also are obstacles. In the short run at least, expanded coal use lies with incremental expansion of "coal by wire" (purchased power) interties to increase utilization of existing coal facilities.

Nuclear Power

In the last two decades, nuclear power has gone from a fringe energy source to the second leading generator, next to coal, of electricity in the United States. Uranium overtook oil in 1980, natural gas in 1983, and hydro in 1984 to reach this position.

In 1973, 39 nuclear plants supplied less than 5 percent of domestic electric generation; today, over a hundred plants, with a generating capacity of nearly 94 million kilowatts, supply approximately 17 percent of this market. Nuclear plants not only generate power for their native utilities but sell surplus power to areas without nuclear power. (The purchased power market is examined below.) The growth of nuclear capacity has reflected not only higher energy prices and government subsidization through Price-Anderson Act liability maximums but, in retrospect, incentives under public-utility regulation to pad the rate base.

With major cost overruns and falling alternate-fuel prices, nuclear projects have encountered market and political resistance at full cost passthrough. Partial cost disallowances by state Public Utility Commissions have become commonplace to break the once sacrosanct "regulatory covenant." Over 80 nuclear plants have been canceled since 1973, a testament to the lagging growth of electric demand, the competitive viability of more traditional fuels, and the "at risk" disincentive—in addition to other problems.

Twenty-eight remaining licensed nuclear plants are under construction, and no new licenses are pending. (The last announced project was in 1979.) With no new applications foreseen, nuclear capacity will level out with a design capacity around 119 million kilowatts. Market and regulatory (safety) reasons have combined to make new projects too expensive, time-consuming, and potentially unrecoverable in the rate base. Short of improved capacity utilization, which slipped slightly in 1986 to 57 percent, future electric-demand growth will go to fossil fuel-fired combined cycle plants and other efficient, relatively low-cost options, after remaining nuclear plants come on stream.

Hydroelectric Power

Hydropower, comprising 5 percent of U.S. energy production, is concentrated in the electric-generation sector, where it has a 13 percent market-share. The hydro industry is centered in the Northeast and Northwest, where rainfall, rivers, streams, and elevated snowpack are abundant. Hydro imports from Canada, which flow south to satisfy the U.S. summer peak, supply 2 percent of U.S. demand. As with other energy sources, the energy crisis inspired many hydro investments that have come on stream to find a more competitive environment than anticipated. The surplus has gone to the thriving purchased-power market.

Hydro projects certified as qualifying facilities (QFs) under the Public Utility Regulatory Policies Act (PURPA) have added incremental capacity to the electric grid. (Utilities are required to buy QF power at a determined avoided cost under PURPA.) For environmental reasons, however, a moratorium has recently been enacted in the Electric Consumers Protection Act (ECPA) against hydro QFs.[10]

In addition to the loss of PURPA benefits for smaller projects,

---

[10]Public Law 99-495, 100 Stat. 1243 (1987).

high up-front costs and a recent reduction in the investment tax credit will limit new hydro investments. Existing facilities are not imperiled, however. QFs have assured markets and "avoided cost" rates exceeding variable costs. Non-PURPA hydro projects are substantially cheaper than fossil fuel electric generation on a variable cost basis under average year conditions. Hydro imports presently benefit from an open trade environment between Canada and the United States. With continued improved access to the purchase power grid and intertie additions, hydro can be expected to maintain, if not increase, its market-share to displace fossil fuels.

Purchased Power

Overinvestment in energy resources in the last decade, reflecting overestimated prices and demand, has prominently included electric generation. Many projects conceived under expectations of high growth in energy demand and rising energy prices, and encouraged by the rate-base mentality of public-utility regulation, are now on stream and compete on the basis of variable cost. It has been estimated that excess power in North America is currently between 30 and 40 percent, an amount that could double if remaining scheduled nuclear, coal, and hydro projects are completed.[11] This thriving purchased-power pool originates from baseload coal, nuclear, and hydro facilities whose output is surplus to the demand of home utilities. The promoted role of purchased power is evident: between 1981 and 1986, the share of electricity purchased from another utility has increased from 7 percent to 20 percent.

Electric current purchased on the grid is a major competitive force in the boiler fuels market. If it is cheaper for a utility to purchase power than burn residual fuel oil or gas at a utilities' own plants, purchased power will back out these fuels. Oil and gas powerplants, once the mainstay of a utilities' portfolio, have been relegated to a secondary position as swing or "peaking" load in electric generation.

The purchased power boom has been partly the result of government intervention in the marketplace. Utilities under PURPA are required to buy power produced from QFs at a predetermined avoided cost. Gas-fired cogeneration, the central qualifying facility, has benefited the fossil fuel at the expense of cheaper purchased power produced from other sources. Instead of discretionary power

[11]Arlon Tussing, "Natural-Gas Markets in an Era of Universal Competition," (Executive Enterprises, October 1984, mimeo.), p. 2.

purchases backing out conventional powerplants fired by gas, QF gas has backed out cheaper purchased power. This has resulted in higher electric rates among other distortions, inspiring PURPA reforms on the federal and state level to slow the rush of projects.[12]

Undergirding the purchased power market is a well-developed transmission system. The current North American electric transmission grid is trifurcated; on the western side, a grid exists between Canada and the Pacific Northwest, California, the Southwest, and Mexico. On the eastern side, Canada is linked to the Northeast, the Southeast, and portions of the Midwest and Southwest. Texas has its own interconnected transmission grid. The North American Electric Reliability Council, established in 1968 in response to Northeast blackout, consists of nine regional power pools whose primary purpose is to ensure the *adequacy* of member utilities to meet peak demand and the *security* of supply against unanticipated disturbances.

The full potential of surplus power has been blocked by (1) a lack of transportation access ("wheeling") across franchise areas, (2) regulated pricing based on embedded cost rather than market rates, and (3) inefficient marketing practices by federal power marketing agencies (such as the Bonneville Power Administration). New industry practices and regulatory attitudes, however, are loosening up what was once a rigid, utility-specific grid. Over a dozen utilities and power agencies in the western United States recently formed a power pool to buy or sell purchased power over a seven-state area via computerized postings. The two-year experiment was approved by the Federal Energy Regulatory Commission, which has been traditionally opposed to such market-oriented arrangements. Another recent strategy to break the gridlock is utility mergers between firms with surplus power and firms with excess transmission capacity. New investments in transmission lines between utilities are also being undertaken to improve system reliability and back out relatively expensive electric generation from conventional oil- and gas-fired powerplants.

Power imports from Canadian hydro projects and Mexican geothermal projects have become increasingly important in the U.S. energy market. Although imports presently constitute less than 2 percent of U.S. consumption, Canadian supply has increasingly penetrated markets in the Northeast, Midwest, Pacific Northwest,

[12]Policy reform for the electric industry is discussed in chapter 5, pp. 238–40.

and California since 1970; such penetration is expected to continue for the rest of the century.[13] A recent 10-year contract between Comisión Federal de Electricidad, the national electric utility of Mexico, and San Diego Gas & Electric could be the forerunner of greater imports from the south.

Synthetic Fuels and Renewable Energy

The reversal of energy prices in the 1980s has killed or indefinitely postponed a host of alternative fuel projects that were born of the energy crisis and government subsidization a decade ago. The federally funded Synthetic Fuels Corporation is out of business, and new projects in the private sector are not being contemplated. *Coal gasification* has so far proven uneconomical even on a variable cost basis, as shown by the Great Plains Coal Gasification Project and the Cool Water Coal Gasification Project. Symbolic of the economic problems confronting coal gasification is the absence of new capital commitments, despite the variety of available competing technologies.

Coal liquefication (coal oil) is uneconomic compared to conventional crude oil recovery and imports. The competitive prospects for wind, solar, and biomass against the primary fuels are dim. Without the PURPA "avoided cost" subsidy, far fewer projects of these types would exist; with revamped PURPA subsidies on the state and federal level, many fewer such projects can be anticipated.

In summary, with sunk costs and preferential regulatory treatment, some synthetic fuel applications and renewable energy technologies cling to life. Start-up projects, on the other hand, have faded with the energy crisis.[14]

Conclusion

The supply of alternative energies to oil is encouraging and not a point in favor of the protectionist case. Excess capacity in the world oil market is joined by excess gas deliverability and excess electric-generation capacity in the United States and, indeed, in North America. The maturation of the purchased power market is a major development that has increasingly demoted conventional power plants.

---

[13]U.S. Department of Energy, *Energy Security: A Report to the President of the United States*, March 1987, p. 146.

[14]A review of energy substitutes and their viability vis-à-vis oil is contained in Walter Mead, "The OPEC Cartel Thesis Reexamined: Price Constraints from Oil Substitutes," *The Journal of Energy and Development*, Fall 1986, pp. 223–38.

The natural gas surplus will persist as new baseload capacity comes on stream to crowd out the fossil fuel from the electric generation market. In particular, the approximately 15 nuclear plants under construction will enter saturated markets and add to the surplus power pool.

Coal will never be anything but abundant to power existing coal plants. New capacity faces environmental hurdles in need of technological advances. To the extent "clean coal" capacity can be economically built, fossil fuels can be redirected away from electric generation and toward the home heating and vehicular markets.

The evolving energy transmission network with alternate fuels is a major development with broad ramifications for the domestic energy picture. The United States is approaching a *national energy grid system*. Oil has long enjoyed flexible transportation and congruent pricing between diverse geographical regions; natural gas and surplus power from coal, hydro, and nuclear generation is approaching the same exalted state.

The above alternative-fuel situation led the Department of Energy to conclude in *Energy Security* that "the United States is better prepared than ever to deter, as well as respond to, any energy supply emergency arising from foreign oil disruptions or from domestic incidents involving our basic energy industries."[15]

---

[15]DOE, *Energy Security*, p. 212.

Appendix 4B
Quest for an Optimal Tariff:
The Harvard Study

In November 1986, two economists associated with Harvard University's Energy & Environmental Policy Center (EEPC) released a major study justifying an oil tariff between $10 and $11 per barrel. *Oil Tariff Policy in an Uncertain Market*, by Harry Broadman and William Hogan, is a recent contribution to a technical economic literature attempting to estimate the "optimal" size of an oil tariff.[1]

This appendix does not attempt to summarize and evaluate the literature on imported oil externalities.[2] The Harvard paper is focused upon because it is a leading article in the field and one of the most recent. It has also become part of the political debate. It was commissioned for this purpose and unveiled on Capitol Hill by tariff advocate Raymond Plank of Apache Petroleum and Energy Security Policy, Inc.

Like virtually the entire literature on the subject, this study sees OPEC as an effective cartel creating a major market imperfection. The negative externality has an *economic* component and a *security* component. The economic component reflects the fact that because the United States is the world's major oil importer, higher incremental U.S. demand (moving along an upward sloped supply curve) increases oil import prices that pre-existing (U.S.) importers must also pay. To use their example, if 4 million barrels per day is purchased at $18 per barrel and higher demand increases this to 5 million barrels daily at $20 per barrel, then the *incremental* million

---

[1]After this review was completed, a "popularized" version of the above essay was published by Hogan and Bijan Mossavar-Rahmani, entitled *Energy Security Revisited*. Sponsored by Energy Security, Inc., and Mitchell Energy, the EEPC booklet received wide press attention and was predicted by the *Wall Street Journal*, September 21, 1987, p. 1, to be "likely to revive national debate over the import-fee issue."

[2]For a review of oil import externality estimates, see Harry Broadman, "The Social Cost of Imported Oil," *Energy Policy*, June 1986, pp. 242–52.

barrels do not cost $20 per barrel (the private cost). It costs $28 per barrel (the social cost). This divergence is created by the incremental barrels, which raised the cost of the base users by $2 each or $8 million, making the fifth million barrels responsible for $28 million of expenditure—$20 million internally and $8 million externally for other buyers. A truly competitive situation, by contrast, would find the market as a price taker of oil imports without the externality of higher prices from higher demand. Private and social costs would be synonymous.

The second negative externality is the *security* component, based on the familiar argument of oil import insecurity and the macroeconomic problems therein. Because import interruptions have a probability of occurrence, associated inflation, unemployment, trade deficits, and lost Gross National Product do also, and all of these must be factored into the social equation. Consequently, the oil price in tranquil times must be increased to cover these social costs, thus eradicating the negative externality and inducing efficient economic behavior.

The "oil import premium" is estimated in the Broadman-Hogan model to be between $10 and $11 per barrel, comprising approximately $4.50 per barrel for the economic component and $6.00 per barrel for the security component. The efficient solution is to enact a tariff of this amount to equate private costs (the unregulated price increased by the tariff) with social costs (the free trade price plus the oil import premium).

The oil import externality/tariff argument is open to complete review. The criticisms below center upon the abstraction from historical and institutional complexity, the assumption that the social cost of imported oil can be accurately estimated, the reasoning behind the two externality components, the macroeconomic assumptions that drive the estimation model, and the neglect to derive the "social cost" of a major tariff.

The Abstraction from Complexity

In addition to the specific assumptions that drive the empirical estimates of the Harvard study, surveyed below, one general assumption can be emphasized—*the abstraction from complexity*. Regulatory circumstances surrounding past oil crises are not considered as causally related. The simplistic "it happened, it will happen again" (in their words, "The 'energy crisis' is . . . intrinsic to the nature of oil"[3]) neglects the crucial link between price and allocation controls in creating and exacerbating shortages and price escalations in the last decade. The fact that the energy crisis for many oil products occurred *before* foreign oil interruptions in the 1970s—and, indeed, the way in which imports of oil and gas in this period *alleviated* crises created by domestic supply-demand imbalances—contradicts the world view behind the assumptions and estimates.[4]

Similarly, the authors fail to appreciate, much less discuss, the fundamental *institutional* changes of the world petroleum and North American energy markets, examined in chapter 4 and the previous appendix, that make simple analogies between the 1970s and today's energy market misleading. A variety of "shock-proofing" investments and business practices, contrary to the opinion of the authors, have been made by the world market in production, transportation, trading, refining, and consumption. These changes were not made to reduce "social costs" but to reduce private costs. Such market responses to the very real oil "shocks" of the 1970s limit the ability of oil to drive the energy market and the ability of OPEC to drive the oil market away from the consumer.

Homogenized history and institutional neglect are characteristic of the study under review. Inherent in this type of approach to the subject is the need to simplify and assume away many causal variables, in order to set up the mathematical equations.

The Estimation of Social Cost

The Harvard study, like the other contributions to this literature, confidently calculates the social cost of unregulated oil imports as the basis for public policy. However, such an estimate has a large range of error, precluding a rational policy decision.

A fundamental insight of economics is the subjectivity of cost. Value is subjective, and so is *cost*, which is the highest *value* placed on the opportunity forgone by the act of choice. Subjective costs can be estimated, however imperfectly, by referring to monetary outlays; indeed, transactions are made by individuals and firms by weighing benefits against cost. But the ephemeral, subjective qual-

---

[3]Harry Broadman and William Hogan, *Oil Tariff Policy in an Uncertain Market* (Cambridge: Harvard University, Energy & Environmental Policy Center, 1986), p. 7.

[4]In a different context, the authors state (p. 41) that "price controls subsidized oil imports" in the last decade but fail to consider its implications for their argument.

ity of cost on the disaggregated level becomes magnified when aggregated to the national level (the United States) and when no transactions take place to hint at demonstrated preference. With weighty questions of public policy hanging in the balance, the myriad uncertainties surrounding the "optimal" oil tariff calculation should be heavily discounted and certainly not presented as scientific.

The winner of the 1986 Nobel Memorial Prize in Economic Science, James Buchanan, has referred to social cost measurement as "the source of pervasive error in applied economics."[5] Even assuming that there is a "social cost" of imported oil apart from its "private cost" (which is disputed below), *quantifying* the external effect of the "market failure" to arrive at a "corrective" tariff-tax is an arbitrary exercise. Explains Buchanan:

> The analyst has no benchmark from which plausible estimates can be made. Since the persons who bear these "costs"—those who are externally affected—do not participate in the choice that generates the "costs," there is simply no means of determining, even indirectly, the value that they place on the utility loss that might be avoided.[6]

If certainty existed about the magnitude and timing of an oil price shock from an import interruption and if the effect of higher oil prices on inflation, employment, and national output were known, a "social cost" of oil imports could be surmised. But then if this knowledge existed, *the market could be expected to seek and exploit it* because of its detrimental effects on individual situations. The resulting adjustments in prices, inventories, and consumption would internalize the externality and remove the rationale for a tariff.

In the real world, the chasm of uncertainty surrounding the "optimal" tariff calculation makes the issue ripe for special-interest tainting. The "public choice" problem of government intervention is that politicians, or more precisely the special interests driving the political process, are concerned far less about what is "Pareto optimal" for society than what is good for their specific situations. The

---

[5]James Buchanan, *Cost and Choice* (Chicago: University of Chicago Press, 1969), p. 38.

[6]Ibid., p. 72. Broadman and Hogan (p. 42) admit that "these imperfections are invisible to the individual consumer" but do not consider what this means for quantifying the externality.

juxtaposition of quantitative economics and politics as a solution to the oil import "problem" is a problematic alliance.

The Security Externality Reconsidered

Previous sections of chapter 4 have reconsidered the likelihood of an oil import disruption occurring and the ability of such a disruption to effectively interfere with consumption and significantly increase prices. All of these arguments suggest that the "security" externality of Broadman and Hogan is overestimated. Furthermore, the authors fail to consider that oil prices today reflect the market's perception of future conditions (discounted for time-preference). To the extent that oil entrepreneurs anticipate disruptions in their planning horizon, and it is in their pecuniary interest to do so, an "oil import premium" is already built into prices to negate any externality. This was the case in the Persian Gulf incidents of 1987, when heightened uncertainty induced precautionary stock additions that added a premium to spot oil prices, which reached nearly $23 per barrel. Indeed the oil futures market, working within an enlarged spot market because of uncertainty itself, has become respected (or notorious) for reacting to the slightest provocation concerning perceived supply-and-demand conditions. To say that posted prices, inventory positions, contracts, and the futures market are impervious to *anticipated* conditions is untenable; to concede that the market is anticipatory but that expectations are wrong is a pretense of knowledge. Academicians who are convinced that they know the future state of the market better than the prevailing wisdom are invited to put their own expectations into play. To the extent that their expectations prove superior to those of the market, not only are private profits gained but the externality is narrowed. For such academicians to use their armchair expectations to advocate a major tariff program, with the well-being of the world's largest economy at stake, is unjustified.

The holistic externality argument and "one size fits all" tariff neglects the heterogeneity of energy consumption within the U.S. economy. Some consumers, whether households with the latest in energy-efficient insulation and appliances or firms with dual-fuel-efficient burners, have internalized the "externality" compared to oppositely positioned users. "Pareto optimality" in the microeconomic sense (and therefore the macroeconomic sense) must somehow compensate relatively prepared consumers, yet this would necessitate another layer of bureaucracy and introduce another set of calculational problems to the protectionist program.

The Economic Externality Reconsidered

The other half of the perceived externality, the "economic" component, is as faulty as it is obtuse. It hinges on a definitional trick. By postulating the United States as the buyer, a monopsony situation is created whereby increased prices from incremental demand create a divergence between social and private costs. By postulating an individual company as buyer instead, prices become virtually given and the externality unrecognizable. To make the same point another way, the Texas-Oklahoma-Louisiana Southwest could equally as well be defined as the seller with PAD District I (the East Coast) as buyer, to create an analogous monopsony situation. Under the reasoning of Broadman and Hogan's argument, a consumption tax should be levied on the East Coast to increase private costs toward social costs. Such a tax, in fact, would apply in any (nonoil) situation where demand increases to increase price—hurting the "base" buyers by raising prices.

Another *reductio ad absurdum* is that if demand *decreases* to lower prices, then a *positive* externality is created for remaining buyers who by themselves would pay higher prices. With private costs above social costs, the policy implication is to *subsidize* demand to decrease private costs and eradicate the divergence.

The unacceptable implication of the pecuniary externality is that *any* price change, by defining the buyer in broad enough terms, posits market failure and the need for government intervention to tax price on the way up and subsidize price on the way down. The only "correct" price is the *same* price, yet since all prices changed in the past, any current price is presumably also inefficient and also provides a role for government intervention.

In a game of assumptions, one could just as well make the opposite argument: that imported oil per se is a *positive* externality and should be *subsidized* by the government. Not only is foreign production lower cost and more plentiful, it allows U.S. supply to remain in the ground (discovered and undiscovered) to better negate the foreign oil advantage in the future. As will be seen in the next chapter, a thoughtful, patriotic argument held in government, and outside of government, has been that domestic supply conservation is akin to national security, that U.S. reserves should not be depleted when foreign oil would suffice.

One final error of the economic externality argument should be noted. The authors assume that "the greater the volume imported, the higher the price, and vice versa."[7] This static assumption of a frozen upwardly sloped supply curve conveniently allows the authors to conclude that any increase in U.S. demand *ipso facto* creates the economic externality explained above. However, recent experience suggests that imports and price are *inversely* related, as economic theory suggests. U.S. demand for imports fell by 50 percent between 1979 and 1983, in response to prices that were 50 percent higher over most of this period. In 1986, the inverse relationship held in the opposite direction. Imports surged 28 percent precisely because import prices fell from a weighted average cost of $25.83 per barrel in 1985 to $12.37 per barrel in 1986. The Saudis and OPEC know that to sell more they must discount more—hence the emphasis on quotas to achieve their target prices. If the authors are making an unstated assumption—that there is or will be no excess capacity in the world oil market—they are obligated to make explicit the heroic postulates about demand and supply that give them the results they seem to long for.[8] The fact is that surplus capacity is many years ahead of demand growth, and in the longer term OPEC nations can be expected to expand their reserve and deliverability base as demand increases and pricing prospects improve.

Problematic Quantification Assumptions

"Although any operational estimate of the tariff will depend upon an array of assumptions and judgments," Broadman and Hogan state, "it is possible to make these judgments and organize them in an internally consistent set of calculations."[9] Internal consistency, however, cannot right the wrong of false assumptions and the neglect of historical and institutional factors. Nor can it undo the inherent ambiguity of social cost measurement.

The striking conclusion that social efficiency requires a tariff between $10 and $11 per barrel reflects extreme assumptions about

---

[7]Broadman and Hogan, *Oil Tariff Policy*, p. iii.

[8]This argument also refutes the authors' argument (p. 12) that higher imports deteriorate the trade balance. The result of greater imports on the trade balance is ambiguous because of the price effect. In 1986, total expenditures on oil imports decreased, despite the surge in quantity, because of the magnitude of the price drop. See pp. 166–67 above.

[9]Broadman and Hogan, *Oil Tariff Policy*, p. 28.

the effect of interrupted oil imports on inflation, unemployment, GNP, and the trade balance. Inflation is cavalierly assumed to be caused by relative price movements (an oil price increase). However, while higher oil prices *increase* prices for energy substitutes, they *decrease* prices for energy complements. The net outcome of these opposite effects on the general level of prices is ambiguous. Only to the extent that higher oil prices decrease output or increase inflationary expectations are aggregate prices increased. Yet the authors fail to spell out why general prices are driven by a relative price change, and they overestimate the relationship.[10]

From the base assumption of inflation, several rigid macroeconomic relationships are introduced that drive the negative externality and social cost estimates upward. A Phillips Curve estimate of two percentage points of unemployment for one year to "cure" every percent of inflation (created by the oil price surge) is employed. This estimate is combined with an "Okun's Law" postulate of a one-to-two relationship between unemployment and lost GNP to conclude that *every percent of inflation created by oil imports creates a social cost of $160 billion.*[11]

The two-for-one Phillips Curve and one-to-two Okun's Law postulates are not exceptions to the rule that there are not fixed, functional relationships in economics. Empirically, as new evidence has falsified old evidence, both "laws" have taken their lumps. Any specific estimate of this relationship is therefore speculative. Both "laws," furthermore, are based on the premise that cyclical disturbances occur on the real side of an economy, ignoring the monetary side. While an oil price "shock" can certainly trigger cyclical economic activity in Houston, Texas, and other oil-dependent economies, the diversity and complexity of the U.S. economy as a whole mitigates the macroeconomic effects of such a relative price change.[12] On the other hand, monetary disturbances, which systematically falsify relative prices, can simultaneously affect a variety of industries in complementary ways to engender a true macroeconomic boom and bust.

A recent "case study" suggests a much weaker relationship than the Broadman-Hogan study postulates between oil price changes

---

[10]For further discussion of the effect of higher oil prices on the general price level, see chapter 5, pp. 208–9.

[11]Broadman and Hogan, *Oil Tariff Policy*, p. A-4.

[12]Also see chapter 5, p. 209.

and economic aggregates. Between 1986 and 1987, oil prices rose over 50 percent. The macroeconomic effects, however, were far different from what the above model would predict. This price "shock" did not add points to the inflation rate or double points to the unemployment rate. It did not result in a GNP loss of hundreds of billions of dollars. Market expectations, offsetting changes in other relative prices, and economic diversification "localized" its effects far short of rocking the U.S. economy. The Broadman-Hogan model has been contradicted by the most recent oil price "shock."

The above model, in summary, is a pyramid of questionable assumptions and false relationships, one level leading to the next. The base assumptions can be disputed to dismantle the structure, and the upper level (modeling) postulates can also be denied to further discredit the conclusions. As the structure is imploded, the oil-import externality disappears and the rationale for tariffs falls to the ground.

"Tariff Shock": The Missing Analysis

A blatant inconsistency of the model is its failure to apply the same reasoning to itself. A $10 per barrel (or more) tariff is certainly a "shock" to the economy, as admitted by Broadman and Hogan,[13] yet the authors do not derive its costs under the same Phillips Curve and Okun's Law assumptions. *It is simply assumed away as a "transition cost."*[14] Yet the aggregate cost of "tariff shock," to coin a phrase, must be subtracted from the "social costs" derived by a future price shock *at a minimum*. A truer cost tradeoff must incorporate *time preference* to correctly assess the tradeoff between higher *immediate* prices (from a tariff) and higher prices *later* from a hypothesized foreign oil interruption. The most common "D-Day" for such an interruption, judging by what tariff proponents have said, is the 1990s. Using a 5 percent discount rate, it would take an inflation-adjusted price spike of over $15 per barrel in 1995 and $20 per barrel in 2001 to justify what the authors currently propose. And even then, years of compounded GNP growth without the tariff would be a net benefit of "shock waiting" to require even higher future price spikes.

---

[13]Broadman and Hogan, *Oil Tariff Policy*, p. 51.

[14]Ibid., p. 52. In *Energy Security Revised* (p. 17), Hogan and Mossavar-Rahmani correct this omission by estimating the cost of a $10 per barrel tariff at $25 billion.

Other Problems

More problems should be cited. The emphasis on macroeconomic costs fails to incorporate the effect of declining world income on U.S. income from a major tariff. For example, the extent to which a tariff hampers the will or ability of heavily indebted oil-exporting countries to repay U.S. banks has macroeconomic effects that must be incorporated. There are major equity questions of "tariff shock" that deserve a look even by economists.[15] Administrative and other "deadweight" costs of a major political/regulatory program are not weighted in the analysis. The Broadman-Hogan assumption of constant long-term elasticity of demand totally denies the ability of entrepreneurs and consumers to find new ways to economize in the face of high prices and thus overestimates the "social cost" of interruptions. Oil conservation in the last decade has shown that the market, over time, increasingly adjusts to price. Another assumption, that the real cost of energy will rise 3 percent per year, is contradicted by the history of recorded oil prices.[16] Complexities within a tariff program, such as establishing light oil and heavy oil differentials, setting an array of oil product tariffs, and assigning blendstocks to tariff tiers, are ignored.

Finally, political modification away from the "optimal" tariff is mentioned, as if simple acknowledgment makes the problem go away. The authors, so candid about market imperfections, fail to apply the same rigor to political imperfections, which so prominently have had the "last say" in oil and gas regulation. The insights of the Public Choice school of economics, which factors the self-interest of lawmakers and bureaucrats into the equation, are relevant here.

The Harvard study authors admit that "any argument for a U.S. oil tariff must bear a heavy burden of proof."[17] This burden of proof has not been satisfied to justify a tariff of any size, much less one of the magnitude proposed.

[15]See chapter 5, pp. 213–14.
[16]See appendix A, pp. 245–47.
[17]Broadman and Hogan, *Oil Tariff Policy*, p. 34.

Part III

An Energy Policy for Consumers and Producers

5. The Free-Market Alternative

The case for protectionism has misinterpreted history, neglected institutional factors, misused and violated economic theory, and resorted to claims of superior knowledge to conclude that an oil tariff program is in the national interest. The grain of truth in the protectionist argument is that there *is* an industry crisis that government can alleviate by policy reform. Such reform is not predicated on averting a national security threat but on advancing consumer and industry welfare through cost minimization, expanded market entrepreneurship, and greater energy choices.

Policy reform must not disadvantage consumers and the national economy—and thus the national interest. Neither should reform leave vulnerable industry segments with jerry-built relief. Consumer sovereignty must be respected, oil industry relief must be sustainable, and the nation's energy assets must be fully utilized through market entrepreneurship.

To achieve these ends, three sets of policy objectives are stressed in this chapter.

1. Rejection of higher oil tariffs and removal of existing intervention that stand in the way of open international trade, at least from the U.S. side. While this is not strictly an industry relief measure, it is a necessary step for achieving (a) the economic-interest objective for consumers and the economy as a whole, and (b) consistency with the second policy objective.

2. Maximization of market conditions in the domestic industry to provide immediate and lasting relief. This step entails (a) removing regulation that narrows industry opportunities and unnecessarily adds costs to industry performance, and (b) repealing—or at least relaxing—local, state, and federal taxes to increase industry profitability within any given price structure.

3. Privatization of oil assets now in the public sector, which are concentrated in crude oil production and storage, to ensure their timely role in America's energy future.

A. Policy Reform to Date

The silver lining of the oil price crash of 1986 for the oil industry has been a long overdue reconsideration of burdensome tax and regulatory policies. Whereas in better times the propensity to regulate and tax escaped this scrutiny, now there is a realization that neither the industry nor consumers can afford the heavy hand of government. The bad habits and propensities of legislatures during the oil boom, in short, have run aground on the shoals of a new reality.

1. State Reform

Most, but not all, oil states have enacted policies to arrest depressed wellhead conditions. Although these measures are no panacea, they have provided timely relief for many operators and point the way toward greater reform on the political strength of home-state sympathy.

In *Texas*, a requirement that stripper wells be plugged with cement within 90 days of inactivation to protect fresh water from contamination was amended to extend the time limit to one year, unless the well was deemed a pollution hazard. (Stripper wells are generally defined as wells producing a maximum of 10 barrels per day.) The March 1986 emergency ruling, applicable to wells abandoned after January 1, 1986, immediately resulted in a 25 percent drop in plugged wells.[1] The Texas Railroad Commission also initiated a paperwork reduction effort estimated to save producers millions of dollars annually. The regulatory agency's call for tax breaks to revitalize the industry, however, has fallen on deaf ears because of state budgetary problems. One minor exception was a new appeals procedure by the Texas Property Tax Board that allowed inflated oil and gas asset valuations to be reappraised. Texas's General Land Office and the University Lands Office, finally, eased royalty-payment conditions to postpone abandonments and reestablish incentives for future drilling and production.

Oklahoma followed Texas's lead by extending the grace period before a well had to be permanently plugged. On the tax side, production increases from enhanced oil recovery projects were exempted from the state gross production tax, but more substantive

---

[1]Stated Texas Railroad Commission chairman Jim Nugent: "The policy appears to be saving hundreds of wells in the state from premature abandonment." "Texas Eases Well Plug Deadline," *Natural Gas Week*, September 8, 1986, p. 6.

tax reform was blocked by state budgetary problems. Another reform, interventionist rather than market-oriented, was to "redistribute the wealth" by transferring gas well allowables from flush wells to smaller producers.[2]

Louisiana enacted statewide tax holidays and royalty holidays for certain production on state lands. The Severance Tax Exemption Plan suspended levies for three years for wells drilled between July 1986 and July 1987 for up to 10,000 barrels per year if prices remained elow $21 per barrel. The Louisiana Economic Acceleration Program excused wildcat and subsequent development wells drilled between 1986 and 1989 from severance tax payments until the end of 1989. Independents drilling wildcat wells on state land were also exempted from the 12.5 percent oil and 7 cents per Mcf gas royalty through 1990. With companies in Louisiana paying nearly one-fourth of the value of their production to the state, amounting to over $4 barrel of oil in most cases, these reforms have significantly improved the economics of marginal wells.

New Mexico's fixed tax was replaced with an *ad valorem* percentage (variable) tax, a tax cut under present industry conditions. Another market-oriented reform has been to extend state leases for currently shut-in wells. But, along with market liberalization have come non-market measures—the New Mexico Energy and Minerals Department's marketing of shut-in gas and a ban on gas utility brokering in the state.[3]

Another idea inspired by the current industry environment has been to exempt producers from state antitrust law. New Mexico and California have legalized gas producer cooperatives. Assuming that traditionally independent producers can unify themselves to "levelize" the playing field against purchasers, some opportunity may exist to increase their economic rent relative to downstream parties.

Kansas reduced both its *ad valorem* tax on oil production and severance tax on marginal wells, reductions that are estimated to save operators over $6 million per year. The Kansas Corporation Commission made major staff reductions to avoid increasing the conservation tax on oil and gas output. Another market-oriented

[2]"Most Producing States Move to Give the U.S. Industry a Boost," *Oil & Gas Journal*, June 22, 1987, pp. 14–15.

[3]"New Mexico Mobilizing to Reverse Continuing Slump in Gas Industry," *Inside F.E.R.C.'s Gas Marketing Report*, May 29, 1987, pp. 11–12.

reform was to relax the state's minimum spacing requirement to allow in-fill drilling in the Hugoton gas field, thus adding hundreds of wells to the state.

In *Mississippi*, severance tax exemptions were made for new wells drilled between March 15, 1987, and June 30, 1988, if prices are below $25 per barrel. *Alabama*, with the highest severance tax in the nation, has considered a similar tax incentive package; to date, however, the measure has not been passed. *Alaska*, like Alabama, has been unable to legislate industry relief because of fiscal concerns.

In the West, *Montana* has relaxed environmental requirements for new wells and enacted tax breaks for stripper wells and new production. *North Dakota* legislated tax breaks for stripper, secondary, and tertiary wells and relaxed royalty payments on certain state lands. *Wyoming* also reduced severance taxes and redefined stripper wells to allow more properties to qualify for tax breaks.

In *California*, forced abandonments were restricted to oil wells where future production would not be lost. Although relief would not be forthcoming on the tax, public land, and regulatory fronts, this change was good news for one-half of the state's oil wells that had stripper production.

2. Federal Reform

While Congress so far has rejected industry pressure for a major increase in oil tariffs, it has enacted policies to ease financial stress at the wellhead. Free-market initiatives have taken place with public-land leasing, oil-equipment exports, and natural gas production and end-use. One interventionist relief measure has been for the Department of Energy to begin buying domestic oil for the Strategic Petroleum Reserve.[4]

As the Texas Railroad Commission had done a month before, the Department of Interior extended the plugging deadline from 60 days to one year for stripper wells on a case-by-case basis. The waiver, applying to some 21,000 wells on federal land, ran through May 31, 1987, before being extended another year. The Interior Department's Mineral Management Service also lowered royalty rates on selected onshore and offshore tracts to prolong production where abandonment at the old rate was imminent. As of January 1, 1987, over 600 wells participated by paying the yearly $1 per acre

---

[4]"DOE to Start Buying Domestic Oil for SPR," *National Petroleum News*, October 1986, p. 41.

royalty. The minimum bid on selected deepwater tracts was relaxed from $150 per acre to $25 per acre to increase leasing and development. A new bid program, biased toward exploration expenditure rather than up-front money, has been proposed to stimulate activity on federal and Indian lands for oil, gas, and coal extractions.[5]

Another market-oriented reform, unilaterally taken by President Reagan in early 1987, directly benefited the most depressed sector of the oil business. By executive order, Reagan revoked a ban, first implemented by President Carter in 1978, on exports to the Soviet Union of drilling rigs, bits, mud systems, and blowout prevention devices.[6] The ban had hurt the U.S. oil field service industry more than it had the Soviets, who turned to Western European and Japanese suppliers. Its revocation returns U.S. firms to the world's largest market for their products. If U.S. suppliers can regain a fraction of their pre-ban market share of 25 percent, billions of dollars can flow into this depressed sector, with thousands of jobs saved or regained.

Several major policy changes in the natural gas industry have been facilitated by industry conditions. Order 451 of June 6, 1986, by the Federal Energy Regulatory Commission (FERC) authorized producers of regulated gas (gas discovered prior to 1978) to request renegotiation with first purchasers (interstate pipelines) to reprice their gas to the highest price category under Section 104 of the Natural Gas Policy Act.[7] (This amount is $2.57 per MMBtu for June 1986, adjusted for inflation.) This administrative attempt at quasi-deregulation falls short of true wellhead deregulation for several reasons. Because a producer's high-priced contracts are also subject to renegotiation with old-gas contracts, some old gas will remain nonnegotiated. Second, should market conditions significantly change, what is now a ceiling price could become a floor price to make regulation effective again. Producer relief, in any case, will be limited, since present market conditions are holding spot prices well below the ceiling.

Revision of the Powerplant and Industrial Fuel Use Act of 1978,

[5]*Oil & Gas Newsletter,* April 21, 1986; "MMS Cuts Minimum OCS Bid, Considers Alternative Systems," *Natural Gas Week,* November 3, 1986, p. 10. "U.S. Proposes Changes in Gas Royalties; Producers Would Get Up to $100 Million," *Wall Street Journal,* January 14, 1987, p. 8.

[6]43 *Federal Register* 33,699, August 1, 1987.

[7]Order 451, 51 *Federal Register* 22,168, June 18, 1986.

signed into law by President Reagan on May 7, 1987, has been a second major policy change wrought by industry conditions.[8] The change allows existing and new electric powerplants and industrial boilers to install burners that burn oil and gas so long as they are "coal capable" with system modifications. Under the Fuel Use Act, only coal-fired units, short of expensive and time-consuming exemptions, were permitted for new capacity. The same law repealed the incremental pricing provisions of the Natural Gas Policy Act, which forced industrial rates to subsidize residential rates within the revenue requirement of utilities. With these changes, the demand for oil and gas, relative to coal and other substitutes in electric generation and industrial markets, will increase to bring wellhead benefits over time.

Depressed upstream industry conditions affected federal tax policy. The result was to *keep* special tax provisions scheduled for elimination. Indeed, Reagan has emphasized, as one of the highlights of his administration, that "several important energy tax incentives were retained."[9]

The Tax Reform Act of 1986 had a general theme of reducing special provisions in return for lower tax rates.[10] The corporate tax was reduced from 46 percent to 34 percent beginning July 1, 1987. The depletion allowance and intangible drilling cost expensing, the two major provisions specific to the oil industry, had been scaled back in a series of tax revisions beginning in 1969 and were ripe for extinction—as first proposed in "Treasury I" by Secretary Donald Regan in 1984. However, with the industry's full lobbying effort focused against repeal and a depressed industry climate to buttress their case, the 15 percent depletion allowance for independents (it had previously been repealed for majors) and full expensing of intangible costs in the year incurred for independents (and 80 percent expensing for majors) remained unchanged.

The benefits of the corporate tax reduction to 34 percent were mitigated by certain provisions of the law. The *passive loss rule* limited loss deductions from limited partnerships to certain offsets; the *minimum tax* negated some of the depletion allowance and intangible drilling cost writeoff for independents. Certain expenses incurred prior to actual production, such as lease bonuses, were

[8]Public Law 100-42, 101 Stat. 310 (1987).
[9]Office of the Press Secretary, White House Release of May 6, 1987, p. 1.
[10]Public Law 99-514, 100 Stat. 2085 (1986).

excluded from percentage depletion. Compared to what could have been—complete elimination of deductions—the Tax Reform Act of 1986 represented a tax decrease; compared to the status quo ante, it was a tax increase, because of generic tax-code changes whose negative effects on the oil and gas industry outweighed the lower tax rate.[11]

3. Conclusion

State and federal efforts to relieve the industry pale in comparison to what could have been done—and what remains to be done—without compromising consumer sovereignty and the national interest. The patience of the industry, understandably, has worn thin. In Canada, in contrast, the provincial and national governments have aggressively made concessions to bolster drilling, although nonmarket programs like the $350 million per year in drilling subsidies, passed as an alternative to expanding the depletion allowance, promise economic distortion and bureaucratic problems in addition to short-term industry aid.[12]

The U.S. government's reaction to the exploration/production depression has been typical. "There is a growing feeling in the industry," commented industry journalist Roger Vielvoye, "that governments around the world are not responding positively enough to suggested innovative tax treatment to match developments in low cost technology."[13]

What could have been done by state and federal authorities or *what remains to be done* will be summarized below. But first the policy alternative of higher tariffs for national security must be criticized and current tariffs reconsidered.

---

[11]The American Petroleum Institute has estimated that the new tax bill will cost the oil and gas industry $2 billion annually over the first five years. API, *Response*, February 13, 1987, p. 1.

[12]The Canadian Exploration and Development Incentive Program provides cash subsidies of one-third of exploration/production budgets, up to $10 million per year, for any firm drilling in Canada. The major market-oriented government concession to the industry consisted in eliminating the Petroleum and Gas Revenue Tax 27 months ahead of schedule, saving the industry an estimated $1 billion. See "Study of Canadian Tax Relief Measure Demonstrates Proceeds Aimed Toward Exploration, Development," *Oil Daily*, June 2, 1987, p. 5.

[13]"Taxes and Incentives," *Oil & Gas Journal*, April 6, 1987, p. 22.

B. Trade Policy

Previous chapters have demonstrated the failure of tariffs and quotas in practice and the unsatisfactory case for protectionism in theory. The first policy implication of these conclusions is that neither crude nor product tariffs should be increased. The second policy implication is that *existing* fees (tariffs by another name) should be repealed to lower prices for consumers, encourage international trade by promoting imports and exports, and terminate associated paperwork and bureaucracy.

1. Rejecting Higher Tariffs

Chapters 3 and 4 focused upon empirical and theoretical arguments against protectionism. Some specific disadvantages of oil tariffs for consumers, the economy, and the oil industry itself can now be considered.

Conservation and the National Interest

The classical national-security argument against oil tariffs, which from the turn of the century to the 1940s was official U.S. policy, is that America should husband its petroleum reserves and maximize consumption of foreign reserves as dictated by market incentives. Clarence Randall, chairman of the Council on Foreign Economic Development, criticized the Mandatory Oil Import Program several decades ago with the following argument:

> I think that the placing of any restrictions on oil imports is wrong. . . . Ostensibly, the program is based on national security, but if domestic petroleum reserves are required for our defense in war, or our recovery after war, I do not see how we advance toward that objective by using up our reserves. It seems to me that our policy should be to conserve that which we have, rather than to take measures which would cause our supplies to be exhausted more rapidly.[14]

A recent version of this argument was presented in a letter published by the *Oil & Gas Journal*. Taking some of his colleagues' national security rhetoric to task, an oil company executive stated:

> The proponents [of tariffs] ignore our dangerously small amount of reserves and appeal to the threat to our national security arising

---

[14]Quoted in William Barber, "The Eisenhower Energy Policy: Reluctant Intervention," in *Energy Policy in Perspective*, ed. Craufurd Goodwin (Washington, D.C.: Brookings Institution, 1981), p. 247.

out of a possible reduction in the capacity of our domestic industry to find and produce those few reserves. . . . We have made little progress in conserving our resources while simultaneously importing as much oil as possible.[15]

The important point of the "classical" national-security argument is that to the extent a tariff stimulates production beyond what an open trade policy would, U.S. oil, relatively high cost to begin with, is substituted for cheaper foreign oil, thus *exacerbating the competitive disadvantage of the United States compared to the lower-cost regions from which the oil was not imported.* The emphasis admittedly is not on short-term competitive parity or relief; it is an argument about the counterproductive longer-term consequences of short-term government subsidization.

Charles DiBona, president of the American Petroleum Institute, has launched a counterattack on this national security argument. Despite its superficial appeal, he argues, the position fails to recognize the future-is-now basis of true national security and that the nation can get more oil today *and* tomorrow from government initiatives because today's drilling advances knowledge and technology.[16]

The first point, emphasizing immediate relief over long-run considerations for national security, has been dealt with in chapter 4. The need for an *artificially* large industry to counter an oil shock that lies around the corner simply does not square with history, theory, or the present institutions composing the world petroleum market. The second argument turns an arguably valid observation into a non sequitur. It is true that experience is knowledge and knowledge in drilling can reduce costs, but this is not an argument for government subsidization. First, DiBona neglects the *opportunity cost* of expanded drilling, whatever its future results. More resources dedicated to wellhead activities mean fewer resources deployed elsewhere in the economy. While the benefits of drilling are imagined, would-be benefits elsewhere in the economy without incremental drilling are not imagined. Only in a world without scarcity and without choice between alternatives would such extra drilling be costless. Second, to the extent individual firms factor in the

[15]"No to the Import Tax," *Oil & Gas Journal*, January 12, 1987, pp. 9–10.

[16]Charles DiBona, " 'Drain America Last' Policy's Appeal Doesn't Consider Negative Results," *Oil Daily*, April 13, 1987, p. A-12.

synergy of current drilling on future exploration, they will increase current activity to exhaust the benefit without government favor. Quantifying the "optimal" exploration rate today to lower finding costs tomorrow, furthermore, is far more difficult than establishing a qualitative relationship. As soon as DiBona steps into the policy arena with a specific recommendation about what tariff is necessary to achieve the "right" amount of drilling, he encounters the "economists' problem"—the inability to solve for "optimalities" outside the marketplace.

The classical national-security argument, domestic resource preservation as market incentives dictate, is an important and valid perspective. It is difficult to treat this argument with less patriotic respect than the most revered arguments for protectionism that would have the industry perpetually at full throttle.[17]

Economic Consequences

The debate over oil tariffs has produced numerous estimates of the effect of tariffs on oil prices and the impact of these prices on macroeconomic variables in the domestic economy. This section deviates from this common approach. The analysis begins by qualitatively describing the *potential* macroeconomic effects of an oil tariff and the problem of quantification. In place of aggregation, the *microeconomic* costs of tariffs are highlighted by identifying particular groups that are unambiguously disadvanted by oil tariffs. These groups can then be compared to the beneficiaries of protectionist policy. A final section raises the issue of resource adjustments that a tariff would necessitate to achieve its desired ends, a neglected "social cost" of protectionism.

Macroeconomic effects: A qualitative analysis. Economists have measured the effects of a major tariff on inflation, unemployment, and the gross national product (GNP). For a $10 per barrel tariff, such estimates have placed the annual economic loss between $35 billion

---

[17]DiBona's "the future is now" argument is identical to Wirt Franklin's argument for tariffs in the early 1930s, which makes the short-run emphasis of the argument wear thin. Franklin stated in 1931: "Gentlemen, our only safety as a nation lies in providing that the oil industry shall at all times be kept up to the highest pitch of efficiency." Quoted in Samuel Pettengill, *Hot Oil: The Problem of Petroleum* (New York: Economic Forum, 1936), p. 52.

and $189 billion.[18] Adherents of a looming energy crisis have similarly estimated the cost of a major price spike from *not* enacting a tariff (see appendix 4B).

The analysis of tariff proponents, finding the social cost of a tariff negative, and that of tariff opponents, calculating positive net economic costs, share a common problem. The quantification process is subjective and necessarily imprecise, making all such endeavors tentative. The argument for and against tariffs thus cannot hinge on probability distributions, correlation coefficients, confidence intervals, and "bottom line" GNP estimates. The protectionist debate turns on a much broader understanding of the issues from theoretical, historical, political, and institutional perspectives. Measurement and prediction in the social world, unlike that in the laboratory sciences, is necessarily tentative and thus must be relegated to secondary consideration in the debate.[19]

The theoretical conditions behind a full price pass-through and no price pass-through of an oil tariff can be described short of "estimating" or "predicting" real world effects. If there were no change in demand as a result of higher prices, a tariff would be fully passed through, and domestic oil prices would rise by approximately the same amount. A $5 per barrel levy, for example, would increase gasoline prices by nearly $0.12 per gallon, and a $10 per barrel tax would double this premium. The consumer, in this scenario, would bear the full incidence of the tax.[20] On the other hand, if demand were perfectly elastic, with any increase in price totally eliminating demand, and producers were making sufficient profits

[18]The low estimate was made by William Hogan and Bijan Mossavar-Rahmani, *Energy Security Revisited* (Cambridge: Harvard University, Energy & Environmental Policy Center, 1987), p. 87; the high estimate is that of the U.S. Department of Energy, *Energy Security: A Report to the President of the United States*, March 1987, p. D-10.

[19]Economics as a science of qualitative laws of human action instead of a quantitative science of estimation and prediction is a major tenet of the 'Austrian' school of economics. For a comprehensive defense and application of this methodological approach, see Ludwig von Mises, *Human Action: A Treatise on Economics* (Chicago: Contemporary Books, 1966).

[20]A problem with the full pass-through condition, however, is that if demand were really insensitive to price, then prices would *already* be at the higher level. The full pass-through assumption must assume (1) it was not known that higher prices were sustainable, (2) entrepreneurs knew demand would support higher prices but chose not to exercise their discretion, or (3) the inelasticity condition began when the tariff took effect.

to supply the market as before, the tariff would not be passed through at all. The *incidence* of the tax in this case would fall entirely upon the exporting country. In reality, however, it is very likely that both demand and supply will be changed by a tariff, and the result will be a partial pass-through, with consumers absorbing a larger proportion than exporters.

The instigator of economic costs from an oil tariff is the higher oil, and consequently energy, price level. A major question is the extent to which nonenergy prices are affected. It is true that energy is a pervasive cost in an advanced economy, and thus a change in its price has broad repercussions. Only when certain conditions are met, however, can such relative price changes drive the *general* price level or create cyclical effects on employment and output to significantly affect GNP.

To support a higher level of energy prices, consumers, *ceteris paribus*, must decrease purchases elsewhere, creating opposite price effects. The "inflation" of some prices, e.g., higher energy prices, creates a "deflation" of other prices, as long as other variables are unchanged. For example, higher gasoline prices effectively increase the cost of driving, thus reducing the demand for and prices of automobiles (the complement effect). The same thing is true for many other energy-using items that now become less affordable to utilize.

Inflation of general prices as measured by a price index can occur from an oil price rise. The specific height of the price rise depends on three factors: the output effect, the expectations effect, and the index-weighing effect. The *output effect* is the degree to which higher energy costs lower output in an economy. Less output means that money "chases" fewer goods and services, with the result that prices are pushed up. The *expectations effect* is the degree to which individuals believe inflation will increase from rising energy prices.[21] To the extent that inflationary expectations come into play, the demand to hold money decreases; the effective quantity of money relative to goods and services is thus increased, causing prices to increase. The *weighing effect* is the extent to which the consumer

---

[21]The investment community *does* hold inflationary expectations with rising oil prices (and vice versa). For example, one financial reporter recently stated: "U.S. oil prices, which many investment managers view as a symbol of inflation pressure, jumped above $21 a barrel." Tom Herman, "Big Rise in U.S. Oil Prices Sends Bonds to Fifth Decline in Past Seven Sessions," *Wall Street Journal*, July 29, 1987, p. 25.

price index (CPI) is unrepresentative of "true" inflation because of an improper weighing of oil prices. If energy prices are overstated in the CPI, then an oil price increase will overstate inflation (and vice versa).[22]

The effect of oil price changes on GNP and employment are also indeterminate at first glance because of opposite effects. Some economic sectors benefit from higher oil prices, while other sectors benefit from lower prices. The *mix* or *diversification* of an economy, divided between oil (net oil producing) and non-oil (net oil consuming) segments, crucially determines the cyclical effects from price changes, not an a priori standard.

The *Wall Street Journal* in a series of articles over the years has reported on the economic climate of Houston, Texas, and Detroit, Michigan, as "the tale of two cities." An oil price change has opposite price, employment, and gross product effects in the two cities. In the 1970s, Houston enjoyed a boom, while Detroit was in a recession; more recently, Detroit has fared much better than its opposite. The same is true for states (Texas, Oklahoma, and Louisiana versus Massachusetts, New York, and Nevada) and regions as a whole (Southwest versus Northeast). Still other areas such as California are so diversified between oil and non-oil industries that other factors swamp oil-price effects. As a whole, however, the United States is an oil consuming country more than an oil producing one. It has 40 net oil consuming states, including the most industrialized and populated areas of the country, compared to 10 net oil producing states. Oil imports also account for over one-third of national petroleum consumption—another way of saying that oil consumption is more important than oil production in the United States. Oil price changes, therefore, have more of an impact on consumers than on producers; hence, an oil tariff, and any other measures that generate higher energy prices, *ceteris paribus*, have net inflationary, unemployment, and recessionary effects on the U.S. economy. But far from creating "social" costs apart from private costs, these aggregative distortions are shouldered by identifiable groups, many of which are mentioned below.

---

[22]Inflation in this paragraph is defined in its popular usage as rising prices and not as an increase in the money supply, which typically precedes and creates higher prices.

Microeconomic effects. The effects of a tariff on the domestic economy can be gauged by identifying particular sectors and groups
that are "losers" from an oil tariff. These groups can be compared
to the "gainers" from oil tariffs, the upstream oil industry and
certain geographical regions of the country. The majority of sectors
vulnerable to an oil tariff have identified themselves in the tariff
debate before Congress and elsewhere.

The list of tariff losers can begin within the *petroleum* industry.
U.S. firms with foreign oil exploration and production are hurt, as
are terminal operators, jobbers, and marketers who depend on
imported petroleum for their livelihood. The *petrochemical* industry,
an adjunct to the integrated oil industry, is also unambiguously
disadvantaged by an increase in crude prices.

The *transportation* industry has been a vocal opponent of protectionism. Before Congress, an ad hoc association of trade groups
organized as the Direct Transportation Users (DTU) testified that
an import fee "discriminates against transportation compared with
other industries" because transportation composed approximately
20 percent of GNP but consumed 62 percent of all petroleum used
in the country.[23] Subgroups of the DTU were the Air Transport
Association of America, American Automobile Association, American Bus Association, Regional Airline Association, and United Bus
Owners of America.

The air-fare wars of the recent past have been attributable in part
to lower aviation fuel prices, and trucking and bus discounting
under decontrol has been sustainable because of lower gasoline and
diesel fuel prices. A reversal of these costs would reverse the process. The DTU estimated that a $10 tariff would cost airlines $3
billion (four times their annual profits in 1985) and exceed the net
income of the 2,100 trucking firms that report to the Interstate
Commerce Commission.[24]

The loss of for-hire transportation would be joined by higher fuel
costs in the not-for-hire sector as the Highway Users Federation
has also emphasized. According to the *Lundberg Letter*, in 1986
American drivers saved $25.5 billion in fuel costs, the result of a 30
percent fall in gasoline prices accompanied by a 3 percent increase

---

[23]*Taxation of Imported Oil*, Hearings before the Senate Subcommittee on Energy
and Agricultural Taxation, 99th Cong., 2d Sess., February 27–28, 1986 (Washington,
D.C.: Government Printing Office, 1986), p. 585.

[24]Ibid., p. 593.

in consumption.[25] With the recent speed limit increase on many interstate highways from 55 MPH to 65 MPH, a tariff-induced reversal of motor fuel prices would be even less affordable than before. The United Automobile Workers, concerned about lower automobile demand resulting from an increase in the cost of driving, has opposed tariffs for this reason.

Agriculture is another energy-intensive industry whose economics are directly influenced by oil prices, and agricultural interests have warned that further damage to their already depressed sector cannot be absorbed. The National Grange, representing 400,000 farmers and ranchers, identified falling oil prices as a "ray of hope" for a "wounded farm economy."[26] As one of the largest costs in agricultural production, oil prices at a market-driven minimum are a necessary but not sufficient condition for agriculture's return to profitability. In congressional testimony, the National Grange also expressed concern about the depressing effect of oil tariffs on the general economy and thus on the demand for agricultural products. For direct and indirect reasons, the farming/ranching industry has staunchly opposed this energy tax.

Consumer groups who depend on energy for transportation, heating and cooling, lighting, and cooking have rallied against oil tariff proposals. The interventionist-minded consumer group Citizen-Labor Energy Coalition and the free-market Citizens for a Sound Economy, along with the Consumer Federation of America, have wholeheartedly opposed oil tariffs as an affront to consumers who, after a decade of hardship, were having the market work their way.

By no means are the above industrial sectors or consumer classes the only victims of trade barriers raising oil prices. The domestic *tire industry*, which used an average of 7 gallons of oil in each of the 290 million tires it made in 1985, will lose market-share to foreign competitors from any action that simultaneously increases domestic oil prices and lowers foreign prices.[27] The Associated General Contractors of America, representing the *homebuilding* industry, whose material costs are directly affected by energy prices, have lobbied Congress against oil tariffs. *Road building* interests, represented by the National Asphalt Paving Association, registered their unequivocal opposition to oil fees in the same hearings. The *plastics* indus-

---

[25]*Houston Chronicle*, December 27, 1986, p. 2-2.

[26]*Taxation of Imported Oil*, pp. 709–10.

[27]Statement of the Highway Users Federation, *Taxation of Imported Oil*, p. 679.

try, which includes many of the nation's largest petroleum and chemical companies, has returned to profitability on the strength of lower oil prices and sees higher oil prices as a threat to these long-awaited gains.

The negative repercussions of oil tariffs on American business have led the broad-based U.S. Chamber of Commerce to oppose protectionism. Beneficiaries of oil tariffs, on the other hand, have had virtually no support from industries other than oil. If the self-interested calculations of American business are any guide, the "losers" far outdistance the "gainers" from oil tariffs in the U.S. economy.

Asset redeployment. A major tariff must do more than "rescue" the status quo. The great majority of vulnerable firms and subsidiary assets in the industry have already left, and few of the remaining firms are now dependent on protectionism for survival. What protectionism aims to do is to trigger a major asset redeployment to return to a bygone era of much greater industry activity. Yet to the extent resource adjustments have already been made to the new realities of the world oil market, any return to the previous state of affairs is impractical and grossly inefficient.

A tariff today would require many of the resources that left the industry—from the "roughneck" who returned to Michigan, to reservoir scientists in different occupations or back in school, to early retirees now comfortably set in different routines—to abandon these changes and return to the oil patch. Whether the artificial incentives of a tariff would inspire these changes (or in the longer run, even attract more college students to major in the petroleum sciences) is questionable. Government subsidies are transient and change with political majorities, and the market recognizes this. There is simply too much uncertainty—or simply stated, too much non-U.S. oil in the world—to inspire a return to the industry euphoria of the 1970s.

The major restructuring programs and stock buyback programs by Exxon, ARCO, Amoco, and others in the 1981–85 period, and the takeover attempts of the period, represented major asset redeployments in the face of changing market conditions. In 1986, after the initial shock of low oil prices set in, industrywide layoffs were quickly resorted to. A tariff returning prices to their 1985 level would be imposed on a radically changed industry; it would be a classic case of "wrong" market signals being substituted for the "right" market signals. The economic consequence would not only be *over-investment* in the wellhead industry but *underinvestment* elsewhere in the economy where the assets—labor, managerial, and physical—came from. With the industry restructuring largely complete, a tariff is not only "too late" to help the industry but unable to avoid major dislocations elsewhere in the economy.[28]

Oil Tariffs as an Inequitable Tax

An economic welfare perspective of oil tariff proposals fails to come to grips with the equity effects inherent in such a tax. On equity grounds too, oil tariff proposals must be countered.

Tariffs impose a regressive tax on lower-income consumers by increasing their fuel costs disproportionately. A 1981 study by the Congressional Budget Office found that low-income households (below $7,400 annual income) spent 8.2 percent of their income on gasoline, while it cost upper-income households (above $36,900) just 3.7 percent of their income.[29]

The irony of poorer persons as large consumers of oil products deserves elaboration. Less affluent Americans drive older cars, which are generally larger, not as well maintained, and get fewer miles per gallon than newer models. Consequently, older cars use more fuel, and their owners suffer disproportionately from a tariff that raises their motor fuel bills. Many of these same individuals use energy-intensive appliances that are less efficient than newer, more expensive models.

Individual situations, not only relative income, introduce inequities and thus unequal financial effects from a tariff. The Direct Transportation Users made this point before Congress:

> An import fee discriminates against individuals based on their individual location, family size, and work status. It penalizes motorists in Wyoming, for instance, who on average must drive the longest distances in the nation—more than double the distance driven by New York residents. More generally, small-town and rural residents who do not have an option of public transportation are hit harder than city dwellers. Large families, which are more likely to require larger, hence less fuel-efficient vehicles

---

[28]It will be shown below how oil tariffs also *disadvantage* the petroleum industry. See pp. 215–20.

[29]*Taxation of Imported Oil*, p. 589.

also must pay more. So do households in which the breadwinner(s) must drive to work.[30]

International Repercussions

The economic consequences of oil tariffs include international problems that have repercussions in the United States. Many countries are dependent on oil exports for revenue, and the United States is the world's leading market for oil products. Any restriction placed on the U.S. market makes world supply less marketable and lowers world oil prices. This occurred during the Mandatory Oil Import Program, and given effective import barriers, it will happen again.

U.S. banks have outstanding loans to the following major oil-exporting countries: Mexico ($97 billion), Venezuela ($25.5 billion), Indonesia ($22.9 billion), Egypt ($16.4 billion), Nigeria ($12.7 billion), and Colombia ($12.6 billion). Some individual exposures to Mexico and Venezuela alone include Citibank ($4.2 billion), Manufacturers Hanover ($3 billion), and Bank of America ($3 billion). The top five Texas bank holding companies are owed $1.1 billion by Mexico and $168 million by Venezuela. Mere talk of tariffs has incited dire remarks from the oil ministers of these countries. The most blunt warning has come from Venezuelan energy minister Arturo Hernandez Grisant, who warned that "Venezuela's possibility of economic recovery would be profoundly damaged, and the possibilities of paying the foreign debt would remain definitely cancelled" if a major U.S. oil tariff came to pass.[31] Canadian interests have warned of reciprocal protectionism should an oil import tariff materialize.[32] Given these international repercussions, in addition to the negative effects on agriculture, real estate, and other major industries, oil tariffs are not beneficial for the U.S. banking system as a whole.

Since 1983, Canada, Mexico, and Venezuela have been the leading oil exporters to the United States, ahead of Saudi Arabia and other Persian Gulf countries. Consequently, the incidence of a tariff would fall relatively more heavily on these three Western Hemisphere nations and less heavily on the others. This counterpro-

---

[30]Ibid., pp. 588–89.

[31]*Houston Chronicle*, March 3, 1987, p. 2–2.

[32]"Canadians Wary of Possible U.S. Oil Import Fee," *Oil & Gas Journal*, March 3, 1986, p. 30.

ductive result has foreign policy implications that must be included as a cost of protectionism.

Tariffs: A Trojan Horse for the U.S. Oil Industry?

A case can be made that protectionism is not in the best interest of the U.S. oil industry, broadly considered, despite the high-profile support tariffs have received in some industry quarters. Seven areas of disadvantage are identified.

U.S. firms and international oil. For over a half-century, the U.S. oil industry has actively explored for and produced oil abroad. A tariff depreciates the value of these properties, and future drilling is discouraged. Multinational majors such as Exxon, Shell, and Mobil have strongly opposed tariffs because of the effect on their foreign drilling programs and exports to the United States.

A partial listing of active exploration and production programs of U.S. companies abroad would include Exxon (Canada, United Kingdom, Malaysia, Australia, North Yemen); Shell (Canada, Malaysia, Cameroon); Chevron (Canada, Nigeria, Angola); Mobil (Canada, United Kingdom, Norway, Netherlands, Germany, Nigeria); Texaco (Canada, United Kingdom, Denmark, Ecuador, Colombia, West Africa, and Brazil); Occidental (United Kingdom, Libya, Peru, Argentina, Colombia, Pakistan); Phillips (Norway); and Tenneco (Colombia, United Kingdom, Nigeria, Norway, Gabon, Ecuador). Tariffs would reduce the value of this production and discourage further exploratory work, to the detriment of these companies, their stockholders, and the national interest in availability of diverse, low-cost non-OPEC world supplies.

A second industry segment that has staunchly opposed tariffs has been independent terminal operators, jobbers, and marketers whose competitive niche depends on imported crude oil or oil products. They have raised the valid consideration that import restrictions amount to regulatory predation that lessens competition between majors and independents in the industry.

Political price of interventionist favors. Any regulatory "fix" will have a political price for the petroleum industry. Political liabilities are incurred that can carry a heavy price in future legislative decisions. Anti-industry regulation and taxation that dogged much of the industry in the 1970s did not happen overnight with oil shortages. They were a backlash from decades of regulatory and tax policies perceived to be pro-oil and anticonsumer. As discussed in chapter

1, the Independent Petroleum Association of America refused to support tariffs as an option until tax reform was decided; a longer-run view from the same (domestic producer) perspective should recognize that the legislature is either in session or about to be, and any political body capable of helping an industry with intervention can hurt it with intervention. A major tariff could persuade Congress to extend the Windfall Profits Tax past its expiration date in the early 1990s or block earlier repeal. Another recognized possibility in an era of government deficits is an oil tariff turning into a Btu tax on all domestic forms of energy.

Tariff proponents have been emphatic about the necessity for a "clean" tariff, without any exemptions for consuming groups, exporting nations, or particular crude types or oil products. The experience of the Mandatory Oil Import Program several decades ago has not been forgotten. Yet beginning a program clean and keeping it clean is tantamount to *taking politics out of politics*. It is inconceivable that special interests will leave a major regulatory program alone, especially a program that involves one of the most pervasive commodities in the economy. The political "price" of a tariff will be amendments, whether for foreign policy, macroeconomic, welfare, equity, or environmental reasons. And once leaks are sprung in the protectionist dike, pressure is created that will produce other leaks, if not widen existing ones. An exemption for Canada (which exports most of its crude to the United States by pipeline), for example, could encourage greater imports by Canada to displace domestic supply for export to the south. A Canadian exemption could also create one for Mexico, which in turn could exempt Venezuela, historically our most reliable supplier. An exemption for home heating oil, to take another example, would de facto exempt diesel fuel, its chemical equivalent. Diesel fuel deregulation, in turn, would create political pressures for liberalizing regulation of other motor fuels.

The "political problem" is never far from the oil industry. Making it closer with an oil tariff is not in the industry's interest.

The U.S. petrochemical industry. The petrochemical industry is an integral part of the oil and gas industry. It is oil based and has been a part of major oil company operations for decades. Yet the U.S. petrochemical industry is an unambiguous loser from a tariff that increases the cost of its primary feedstock while *lowering* feedstock costs of international competitors, led by Saudi Arabia. The chairman of E. I. du Pont de Nemours, Richard Heckert, made this point by stating:

> If we cannot buy energy and feedstocks at world prices, we cannot sell at world prices. And if we cannot be cost-competitive with foreign manufacturers, we are out of business.[33]

The Petrochemical Energy Group and sister organizations, such as the Chemical Manufacturers Association and the Society of the Plastics Industry, have actively lobbied against oil tariffs for this reason.

With the recent decline in oil prices, petrochemicals have joined refining and marketing as industry bright spots, balancing the trauma of the upstream side of the business. Enacting tariffs would upset this balance and hurt the petroleum industry, broadly defined, while allegedly helping it.

Market-share. Oil is not a monopolistic energy resource. It competes directly, indirectly, or potentially with natural gas, coal, nuclear power, hydropower, geothermal power, and purchased power. The market-share of oil, consequently, depends on its relative competitiveness with these other fuels. In the 1970s, oil lost market-share to coal, natural gas liquids, hydropower, and nuclear power; a major strategy for the future must be to regain market-share by attractive pricing and political stability. Artificially increased oil prices, without corresponding tariffs on natural gas, coal, and hydropower, adversely affect oil's competitive position. Not only is current demand decreased, but future demand also shrinks, as more and more substitutions for petroleum are made. The short-run advantages of an oil tariff for the wellhead sector are thus diluted compared to a situation where consumers are wed to oil because of minimum-cost pricing and market stability.

Support for oil tariffs by the nuclear lobby group, Americans for Energy Independence, and other alternative energy lobbies is fair warning that a motivation for—and consequence of—protectionism is not only less foreign oil for domestic markets but fewer domestic oil markets as well. The demand-side consequence of oil tariffs

---

[33]Barbara Shook, "Trade Policies Worry Petrochemical Executives," *Houston Chronicle*, April 8, 1987, p. 2-4. Heckert added: "It is difficult to call to mind any U.S. manufacturing industry that would not be negatively affected by an oil import tariff."

detracts from the supply-side consequence, to the detriment of the oil industry.

Oil equipment export markets. The Petroleum Equipment Suppliers Association (PESA) has described its 218 members as "highly export-dependent."[34] Despite the export ban, discussed above, the industry exported $2.5 billion worth of equipment in 1986, amounting to 35 percent of total sales. With decontrol of export licenses in early 1987, exports can be expected to gradually rebound. Yet to the extent that a domestic tariff redirects to foreign markets oil that would have been imported by the United States, world prices are driven down. And to the extent that foreign frontier and development wells are discouraged, U.S. exports of oil equipment and technology will suffer. This negative effect could well be canceled or exceeded by increased equipment orders at home, thus explaining tariff support from the PESA and the International Association of Drilling Contractors. But the indirect export effect dilutes the net benefit that an oil tariff would bring to the most depressed sector of the oil patch. It too is an industry cost of protectionism.

Diluted benefits from oil tariffs. The situation of oil production as a highly taxed and, in a number of cases, heavily indebted sector dilutes the "bang" of an oil tariff. State, local, and federal government—not only producers—share in the higher netbacks that a tariff would bring. Help earmarked for the industry is therefore siphoned off to these public sectors. This is particularly true with the Windfall Profits Tax, which is computed by multiplying the tax rate by the difference between the current price and a base price (around $17 per barrel for pre-1980 discoveries). A tariff can bring the WPT itself into play by increasing the current price past the base level (as would have occurred in 1986 and 1987); otherwise, it would simply increase the differential to increase the tax.

The fact that a number of firms most desperate for shortsighted relief are past the state of solvency also brings into question the magnitude of help a tariff would give the industry. Increased cash flow from higher prices would go not only to producers but to bankers and other creditors, who are not apt to reinvest the proceeds into drilling. This was recognized by one drilling industry executive, who stated:

[34]"U.S. Foreign Policy Control on Exports of Oil and Gas Equipment and Technology to the Soviet Union," Comments by the PESA, December 20, 1985, p. 1.

Any "floor" under energy prices would not help the domestic industry. . . . It is my view that the vast majority of such increased domestic revenue will go immediately to financial institutions to repay debts. Thus, the voting consumer who pays the higher price for fuel will receive none of the perceived benefits. The "defrauded" voter/consumer will then initiate the political process to restore low fuel prices.[35]

A third area of diluted benefit concerns cost. A silver lining of the depression has been dramatically reduced costs throughout the upstream oil sector as excess drilling-related inventory has been marketed and leasing prospects have been pick-of-the-lot. One company with a major exploration and production affiliate reported a 27 percent decline in domestic finding costs in 1986, from a combination of "reducing costs and high-grading drilling prospects." These typical reductions included a 40 percent drop in rig costs and as much as an 80 percent cost decline in drilling mud and well logging.[36] Although the input-cost effects of the downturn did not cancel out lower output prices, it did mitigate the unfavorable economics of current period drilling and set the stage for a rebound. A tariff, to the extent that it increases drilling activity, would firm up costs to dilute the industry gains from artificially imposed higher prices. It would also reduce the incentives to pare costs and maximize efficiency that the current environment has necessitated.[37]

Short-run relief versus industry rationalization. The discipline of the market encourages long-run industry health from short-run challenges and dislocation. The oil industry has been no exception. The shakeout experienced in the exploration/production sector has eliminated less efficient firms and made surviving firms more efficient. The survivors have been able to enjoy significantly reduced costs and acquire competitors at a fraction of former values to position themselves for the future. With the price recovery in 1987, the future, while not assured, is brighter. The "survivors of 1986" are stronger and leaner because they did what the market required them to do to remain in business. Although in the aggregate they

[35]"Rowan Chief Backs Administration's Stand Against Crude Oil Import Fee," *Oil Daily*, September 17, 1986, p. 4.

[36]Pacific Lighting Corporation, Los Angeles, *1986 Annual Report*, p. 22.

[37]See, for example, "Operators Finding Ways to Boost Drilling, Production Efficiency," *Oil & Gas Journal*, March 16, 1987, pp. 20–22.

are much smaller than in better times, pound for pound they give reason for optimism.

Had a tariff allowed marginal competitors to cling to life, industry problems would not have been resolved. They would have been perpetuated. Life would have remained tenuous, not only for the underclass but for more efficient firms, because costs would not have fallen as much, consolidations would not have taken place, and more firms would be competing against each other. And to the extent that tariff protection was eliminated, piecemeal or in total, the adjustments postponed earlier would still have to be faced—most likely in magnified form, because profits made behind tariff walls would prolong the "fight to the finish" among strong-willed firms.

The state of American agriculture is a case study of subsidies begetting more subsidies and weakening the industry.[38] Had hard choices been made long ago in this sector to "rationalize" the industry, a healthier, albeit smaller, population would have emerged. On the other hand, because oil tariffs were not substantially increased, as advocated by many, the pain of contraction is behind the industry rather than ahead of it. A Reagan administration official dismissed oil tariff proposals by stating, "We're not interested in setting up a farm program for oil."[39] The analogy is a telling one, and neither should the industry desire what could become the equivalent of the federal farm program.

2. Policy Reform for Open Trade

The arguments in chapter 4 and the above section make a case not only against increasing tariffs but for repealing existing tariffs. Fixed import fees currently in place add around $0.22 per barrel to crude oil prices; variable fees, assuming a $15 per barrel price, equate to approximately $0.04 per barrel. These levies, along with the statutory authority to invoke new tariffs or quotas, require policy reform toward open trade.

---

[38]A Wall Street Journal editorial ("Sacred Farmers," March 5, 1987, p. 24) summarized the policy morass: "U.S. farm policy has careened from one misguided government invervention to another. With each new program—whether it be loan guarantees, price supports or export subsidies — the farm problem gets a little worse and the price a little more expensive. Spending on agriculture price supports—$4 billion in 1981—cost taxpayers $26 billion last year."

[39]"Murmurs in the Oil Patch," Wall Street Journal, December 18, 1986, p. 26.

Existing Tariffs and Regulation

Import barriers that currently apply to petroleum are (1) the traditional General Agreement on Tariffs and Trade (GATT) tariffs, (2) a harbor maintenance fee, (3) an oil spill fee, (4) a Customs Department fee, and (5) a Superfund fee. Quota restrictions do not exist. Other import restrictions that have been used recently are exhortation (suasion) and formal sanctions. Standby authority to enact tariffs or quotas on items important for the national security, including oil, also exists.

GATT Tariff Schedule. Traditional tariffs, a legacy from the Revenue Act of 1932 last amended in 1958 under the General Agreement on Tariffs and Trade, are currently as follows:

Table 5–1

CURRENT OIL TARIFF SCHEDULE

(dollars per barrel)

Oil Type	Most Favored Nation	Communist Nation
Crude Oil (under 25°)	$.0525	$ .1050
Crude Oil (over 25°)	.1050	.2100
Fuel Oil (under 25°)	.0525	.1050
Fuel Oil (over 25°)	.1050	.2100
Gasoline/Jet Fuel	.5250	1.0500

Natural gas and natural gas liquids are not subject to the GATT tariffs. Until late 1986, in fact, methane and its derivatives were not subject to any form of importation tax, nor were purchased power imports from Mexico or Canada.

Harbor maintenance fee. Effective April 1, 1986, a 0.04 percent fee became applicable to all oil and oil products moving from and to a U.S. harbor. An exemption was made for petroleum moving from the contiguous United States to Hawaii. This broad-based "user fee," estimated to raise $1.7 billion over three years, applied to all harbor merchandise to underwrite federal harbor expenditures.[40]

---

[40]Office of Management and Budget, *Budget of the U.S. Government, Fiscal Year 1986* (House Document No. 99-17), pp. 2–21 to 2–22.

Oil spill fee. Effective February 1, 1987, a $0.013 per barrel fee was enacted for all imported oil to underwrite the Oil Spill Liability Trust Fund, with previous payments made into Deepwater Port Liability Trust Fund and the Offshore Oil Pollution Compensation Fund credited against the new tax. The fee is scheduled to terminate on January 1, 1992, or at an earlier date if $300 million is collected.[41]

Customs fee. Effective December 1, 1986, a 0.22 percent "user fee" was placed on all imports into the United States including oil, natural gas, and their derivatives. The Bureau of Customs tax drops to 0.17 percent for fiscal 1988 and 1989 and is set to expire on September 30, 1989.[42] Exemptions were made for the 22 countries covered under the Caribbean Basin Initiative, for U.S. insular possessions, and for certain countries designated as "least developed."[43] The *ad valorem* fee of $22 per $10,000 of imports, anticipated to raise nearly $600 million in the first year alone, has drawn the ire of the General Agreement on Tariffs and Trade (GATT) council, as has the more sizable Superfund tariff (see below). Canadian and Mexican officials have also threatened to retaliate and have expressed a fear that the modest fee would set a precedent for larger levies by a protectionist U.S. Congress.

Superfund import fee. Effective January 1, 1987, imports of crude oil and oil products became subject to a $0.117 per barrel tariff. This fee contained a $0.035 per barrel differential above the $0.082 per barrel tax on domestic crude production.[44] Together, these revenues are anticipated to raise one-third of the $9 billion budgeted for toxic waste cleanup. This burden is far in excess of what the petroleum industry as a whole is responsible for, not to mention the inequities involved for individual firms. As in other areas, the petroleum industry was an easy political target for bearing the brunt of environmental restitution.

The "back-door" oil tariff (so labeled by the *National Petroleum News*) has been protested by the 12-nation European Economic

[41]Public Law 99-509, 100 Stat. 1874 at 1957–58 (1986).

[42]Public Law 99-509, 100 Stat. 1874 at 1965–67.

[43]The CBI nations are Trinidad, Netherlands, Antilles, Bahamas, Antigua/Barbuda, Barbados, Belize, Costa Rica, Dominica, Dominican Republic, El Salvador, Grenada, Haiti, Honduras, Jamaica, Montserrat, Panama, St. Christopher-Nevis, St. Lucia, St. Vincent and Grenadines, and British Virgin Islands.

[44]Public Law 99-499, 100 Stat. 1613 (1986).

Community, Mexico, Canada, Venezuela, and Great Britain. The GATT council, representing 92 nations, has launched an investigation into whether the $0.035 per barrel differential violates Article 3 of the GATT accord prohibiting discrimination against imports once they have entered a country. The differential has also been criticized for competitive reasons by the Society of Independent Gasoline Marketers of America and the Petroleum Marketers Association of America.[45]

Exhortation. A subtle form of protectionism is government-to-government suasion to limit imports or stabilize price. This occurred in April 1986 when Vice President George Bush traveled to Saudi Arabia to express administration concern over the effect of the oil price war on domestic production. The publicized visit generated a modest price rebound from a recent-year low, and oil would not again trade under $10 per barrel.[46]

In early 1987, the United States pressured Norway to rebuff OPEC's request for cooperation in production policy.[47] The next month, a visit to the oil kingdom by Treasury secretary James Baker included a request that the Saudis reduce volatility in oil pricing.[48] Baker's request was more ambiguous than Bush's masked plea for higher prices; it could be interpreted equally as a warning not to return to an oil price war or as a warning not to increase prices above present levels.

Reasoned speculation has been that while the Reagan administration has frontally opposed tariffs for increasing oil prices, it has had a less publicized agenda of supporting higher prices through subtle foreign policy gestures.[49] Although not intended, the Reagan administration's reflagging actions in the Persian Gulf increased uncertainty in the region and briefly propelled spot prices above $20 per barrel for the first time since late 1985.

[45]"Reagan Signs Superfund; 'Back-door' Import Fee," *National Petroleum News,* December 1986, p. 52; Steve Marcy, "Debate on Import Fee Not Just Inside U.S.; GATT Also May Back," *Oil Daily,* February 9, 1987, p. 11.

[46]"Talking About Oil," *Wall Street Journal,* April 3, 1986, p. 24.

[47]Youssef Ibrahim, "OPEC Gaining in Bid to Boost World Oil Price," *Wall Street Journal,* January 14, 1987, p. 3.

[48]Art Pine, "Baker Tells Saudis U.S. Won't Sell More Arms to Iran," *Wall Street Journal,* February 3, 1987, p. 38.

[49]See Fred Barnes, "Oil Together Now," *New Republic,* February 9, 1987, pp. 12–13.

Sanctions. Executive Order trade sanctions have directly affected the U.S. oil industry in recent years. In March 1982, President Reagan first imposed sanctions on Libya, although it was effectively circumvented with crude exchanges in the international market and product imports made from Libyan feedstock. Reimposed sanctions against Libya, effective February 1, 1986, prohibited oil imports and required U.S. firms Amerada Hess, Marathon, and Conoco to cease operations in the country by June 30, 1986.[50] The pullout was accomplished despite the fact that Moammar Khadafy gained the equivalent of an uncompensated nationalization. The Libyan oil import prohibition experienced various enforcement problems, including unsuccessful Reagan administration pleas to Italy and other European countries to buttress the boycott. Like the oil equipment export ban discussed earlier, unilateral action by the United States is doomed without effective support from "substitutor" nations. Such cooperation has not been the case with oil sanctions.[51]

Standby tariff quota authority. Under several trade laws, the president has the authority to impose trade barriers on petroleum, as on other imported products. Section 232 of the Trade Expansion Act of 1962 gives the president, after a Commerce Department investigation and finding (with input from the departments of energy, state, labor, defense, and treasury, among others), wide latitude to restrict imports for national security reasons.[52] Section 201 of the Trade Act of 1974 establishes a procedure whereby a firm can petition the International Trade Commission to investigate whether imports have caused economic damage through dumping, subsidy, or other "unfair" trade practices.[53] The ITC can then make an affirmative finding to the president who has authority to impose a tariff or other means of relief, for a period not to exceed five years, on the particular import.

[50]"Reagan Orders Economic Sanctions Against Libya," *Oil & Gas Journal,* January 13, 1986, p. 38.

[51]The only oil embargo by the United States, a prohibition of aviation fuel sales to Japan in 1940 in protest of their invasion of China, was too successful—it boomeranged to haunt the United States. With 80 percent of their fuel supply cut off, Japan retaliated militarily at Pearl Harbor as a first step toward gaining access to oil fields in the Dutch East Indies. See George Ball, "The Case Against Sanctions," *New York Times Magazine,* September 12, 1982, p. 119.

[52]Public Law 87-794, 76 Stat. 872 at 877 (1962).

[53]Public Law 93-618, 88 Stat. 2011 (1974)

With congressional support lacking, this protectionist avenue has been the focus of a new drive for tariffs in the independent sector. Enserch Exploration has spearheaded an effort to petition the ITC for a ruling to force President Reagan's hand on the issue, although the Independent Petroleum Association of America has declined to join the petition to date.

Deregulation and Repeal

Current tariffs from longstanding GATT schedules and "user fees" should be abolished, and exhortation and discretionary authority to informally influence prices or formally enact tariffs or quotas should be made a thing of the past. Ineffectual sanctions, which the record shows have hurt domestic interests more than they have hurt target countries, should also be taken from the political arena and left to individual company policy. It is important for international and domestic reasons that world and domestic prices be directly linked and that oil policy and foreign policy be separated.

The benefits from "depoliticizing" oil trade are persuasive. The resources that industry, consumer, and government groups have expended on the tariff debate can be redeployed elsewhere. There are better things to do than to debate increasing tariffs, keeping tariffs the same, or reclassifying products for tariff purposes. Precedents for further "mini-tariffs," or expanding tariffs to electricity and natural gas imports, can be removed. Private- and public-sector paperwork occasioned by tariff administration can be similarly dispensed with, not to mention the fee payments themselves.

C. Policy Reform for Free Markets

Reform of the status quo along the lines recommended below does not promise "energy security," "energy independence," or "national security." These terms and goals are not easy to define, much less achieve. Neither is the following program a guarantee to "keep us out of the gas lines," as protectionists claim for their program. An absence of price and allocation controls, not a certain tariff level and "energy independence," is necessary to avoid the shortages and energy crises that have historically occurred.

The following free-market reforms offer increased supply and lower prices for consumers and lower costs, expanded entrepreneurial opportunities, higher demand, higher net income, and political stability for the industry. This desirable combination of consumer and industry benefits constitutes an attractive case for free-market reform as an alternative to national security protectionism.

1. Policy Reform for Industry and Consumer Benefit

Four important areas of policy reform for immediate consumer and industry relief concern taxation, public land leasing, refining incentives, and mandatory conservation law.

Taxation

Taxation reduction and repeal in the petroleum industry is a fertile area for reform.[54] It has the stellar attraction of simultaneously helping the industry *and* consumers. It should be foremost on both the consumer and national security agendas.

For much of its history, petroleum exploration and production has been the least taxed major industrial activity in the United States. A combination of the depletion allowance and intangible cost expensing allowed superaccelerated capital cost recovery that lowered the effective corporate tax rate of this sector below effective tax rates elsewhere. To critics, this advantage artificially stimulated petroleum resource development compared with other sectors of the economy.[55]

The situation has been reversed in the 1980s. The wellhead sector is now one of the most taxed industries in the U.S. economy.[56] Traditional deductions have been scaled back, and new levies have been enacted. For competitive parity, if not for the more substantial reason of helping consumers, the industry, and the national economy, tax relief is highly appropriate.

Windfall Profits Tax. Repeal of the Crude Oil Windfall Profit Tax Act of 1980 (WPT), which is set to be phased out beginning in 1991, has wide support in the industry, the Department of Energy, and (reversing earlier support) the Reagan administration.

---

[54]The other side of taxation reduction is less government expenditure. The free-market policies recommended in this section offer areas of substantial savings. Abolition of the energy functions of the Department of Energy would save around $6 billion per annum, and reduced Persian Gulf military activity and privatization initiatives would add billions of dollars more.

[55]See Stephen McDonald, "Taxation System and Market Distortion," in *Energy Supply and Government Policy*, ed. Robert Kalter and William Vogely (Ithaca: Cornell University Press, 1976), pp. 26–50.

[56]See Alan Auerbach, "Corporate Taxation in the United States," *Brookings Papers on Economic Activity*, 2, 1983, pp. 451–98.

This wellhead tax is complicated and burdensome. For pre-1980 (Tier 1) discoveries, major integrated companies pay a 70 percent tax on the difference between a base price (around $17 per barrel) and the market price of production. Independents pay a 50 percent tax on the same. For post-1980 (Tier 3) discoveries, a uniform 22.5 percent tax is paid on the price differential between the base price (around $28.50 per barrel) and the market price, making it less of a factor compared to Tier 1 production.

The WPT has raised over $80 billion in its seven-year existence. Since 1986, however, revenue has been virtually nonexistent because of low prices, leaving a large administrative burden for the industry and government, with nothing to show for it.

The opportunity cost of collected moneys can be measured in both cash flow and reinvestment for firms and in barrels of oil for consumers. Prospectively, the negative consequence is that workovers and development drilling on Tier 1 leases will be discouraged by the 70 percent tax takeaway above the base price. Since development drilling accounts for as much as 80 percent of new wells, service and supply firms are hurt along with involved producers.[57] Consumers, with less supply and higher-priced oil to turn to, are clearly disadvantaged as well.

While the negative effect on Tier 3 discoveries is only potential under present and anticipated prices, the depressive effect of the WPT on Tier 1 crude is significant and reason to repeal the tax ahead of schedule. The tax is also industry-specific and thus discriminatory—contradicting the philosophy behind the Tax Reform Act of 1986, which was intended to make the tax code uniform.

Superfund tax. The effect of the Comprehensive Environmental Response, Compensation, and Liability Act (Superfund) tax on domestic oil firms, as on oil importers, illustrates a case of many innocent parties making restitution for the guilty. In the original 1980 law, domestic and imported crude was taxed at $0.079 per barrel, and oil and chemical firms paid over 90 percent of the feedstock taxes that financed "orphan waste" removal.[58] The new Superfund excise tax, enacted in late 1986, retains the tax burden on the oil industry (with the oil industry's share estimated at $700

[57]"Old Oil Taxation Fictions Let WPT Undermine U.S. Energy Policy," *Oil & Gas Journal*, June 22, 1987, p. 13.
[58]Public Law 95-510, 94 Stat. 2767 (1980).

million per year) and chemical industry, despite a finding that oil and chemical firms are responsible for under 15 percent of the waste dump problem.[59] Clearly this is an unfair burden that substitutes political expediency for restitutive justice.

Corporate tax. The corporate tax reduction from 46 percent to 34 percent, enacted in the Tax Reform Tax of 1986, effective July 1, 1987, is a positive step toward increasing the profitability and competitiveness of U.S. business, oil exploration and production included. This reduction, coupled with remaining percentage depletion and intangible cost expensing benefits, places the petroleum industry in a position to regain part of its historic attractiveness to investors, with benefits to both industry and consumer. But what is also necessary are the revisions suggested below, repeal of the Windfall Profits Tax, and at least a major reduction in the wellhead Superfund tax.

A number of tax revisions can help the industry by minimizing double taxation from the corporate levy. Former deductions (full percentage depletion and intangible cost expensing in particular) can and should be restored, with no preference between majors and independents. Short of full restoration, selected revisions emphasized by the American Petroleum Institute, Independent Petroleum Association of America, and other industry groups should be enacted. They include the following:

- Repeal of the "transfer rule" to allow independents to apply favorable tax provisions to properties purchased from major companies.
- A broader definition of intangible drilling costs to include geological and geophysical expenditures for current year expensing.
- Repeal of the 50 percent net-income limitation to allow full deduction for percentage depletion.
- Removal of oil (and gas) preference items from the alternative minimum tax enacted in the Tax Reform Act of 1986.
- Special tax incentives to marginal properties that would otherwise be abandoned.

The Department of Energy has estimated that restoration of traditional tax deductions along with repeal of the WPT could increase

---

[59] *API Response* R-385, February 13, 1987.

domestic production by between 500,000 and 1,000,000 barrels per day, replacing imports by the same amount and reducing world oil prices significantly.[60] Far from "draining America first" as does a tariff, however, such incremental output represents calculated depletion in response to market signals, with proper incentives to develop the reserve base. It is proconsumer and proindustry in the short run and long run.

State taxation. State taxation of wellhead activities is another candidate for reform. With the average state severance tax standing above 12 percent, $6.5 billion was collected in 1985, followed by $5.2 billion during the depression year 1986. Texas, with the second highest severance tax in the country and 1986 collections exceeding $1.5 billion, does not have to look far to see a cause of the industry's problems and an avenue for relief. Yet reduction was not considered; instead, state politicians and Texas Railroad Commission officials called for an oil import fee to spare the deficit-ridden state budget.

Other wellhead taxes such as "user fees" to underwrite conservation agency budgets are eligible for repeal, along with many of the unnecessary or counterproductive regulations themselves. Like reform at the federal level, state tax reform offers both consumer and industry relief.

Public Land Leasing

From its beginning in 1866 to the present, petroleum leasing on federal land has been mired in controversy. The politicized environment of oil development on the public domain has alternated between rapid development and nondevelopment philosophies, each bringing controversy and unintended negative consequences.[61] Opening and closing public land to "rectify" these "imbalances" is a tradition now in its second century, with no sign of abatement. Temporary politicial majorities, after all, do not breed stability or predictability.

An argument can be made that the environmental and esthetic preferences of politically well organized groups have overwhelmed the need of politically unorganized consumers (oil industry lobby

---

[60]*Energy Security*, pp. 74–78.

[61]For a history of these problems, see chapter 7, "Petroleum Lease and Environmental Policy on Government Land," in my *Oil, Gas, and Government: The U.S. Experience* (forthcoming, Cato Institute).

groups notwithstanding) for increased domestic reserves and production. Consequently, the "national interest," or at least the right "balance" between environment and development, has been lost. The policy implication would be to expand mineral development in disputed or reserved areas. This, however, does not remove the cause of the problem but swings the pendulum in the opposite direction—a direction that politics could again reverse. After briefly examining some areas of contemporary dispute, this section will advance a more fundamental policy change than the "prodevelopment" five-year plans of the Interior Department.

On both the federal and state levels, major barriers have been placed in the way of expedited petroleum development on government lands. Much blocked acreage concerns offshore drilling, but onshore prospects are prominent too.

On the federal level, the Arctic National Wildlife Refuge (ANWR), established in 1960 to preserve the area's natural state, is the top industry prospect currently being considered for petroleum development. The Interior Department in November 1986 fueled the fire when it released a study reporting that this Alaskan domain potentially contained the third largest oil field in U.S. history, capable of supplying as much as 4 percent of national consumption in the 1990s. A find anywhere near this predicted magnitude would be a timely supplement to the nearby Prudhoe Bay field, whose production is expected to decline in the 1990s. At stake environmentally is the development of approximately 15,000 pristine acres of natural wildlife habitat to support a major drilling operation within the 19-million-acre reserve. The small size of the projected development area, the successful envionmental experience at Prudhoe Bay, and the prodevelopment national-security concerns within the Department of the Interior, all favor a decision to put the area out to lease, with exploration to follow.

Offshore California, a prolific oil belt, is a second area of dispute, with much at stake, between developers and environmentalists. Development of the Santa Maria Basin (located in the Outer Continental Shelf), one of the largest new fields in the United States, is well underway after much environmental delay, but it is not nearly at full potential. Within state jurisdiction, extending to three miles offshore, the going has been difficult and slow. The California State Lands Commission's denial to ARCO of a permit to build a $400 million development in the Santa Barbara channel (Coal Point), because of "visual impacts," is the latest controversy in this regard.[62] Expanded development of Exxon's Santa Ynez Project, requiring siting and air emission permits from Santa Barbara County, has been delayed five years. San Luis Obispo County has successfully delayed expansion of the San Miguel Project. Inflexible state royalty requirements and environmental delays by the California Coastal Commission, in addition to obstacles erected by these county governments, have also discouraged production of heavy crude concentrated in the area.[63]

Other areas of industry-environmental debate concerning oil leasing and development include offshore leasing in the Atlantic Coast, Pacific Northwest, Florida Straits, Alaska, and eastern Gulf of Mexico. Onshore, 37 million acres of land designated by the U.S. Forest Service and Bureau of Land Management as wilderness are in the fifth year of a leasing moratorium.

The present "closed" position on much promising acreage offers another ripe area for policy reform that, like tax reform, is advantageous to the industry and consumers alike. Simple opening of such lands, however, may not be the most stable and successful option. More fundamental reform would be to *remove onshore and offshore land, and thus leasing decisions, from the public sector and place them in private hands.* As a privatization strategy, new incentives could be offered to firms to successfully blend mineral development and environmental gain. The transfer could be effected by a traditional bid system, and acreage in uniquely pristine areas could be sold to qualifying environmental constituencies who may then find it in their interest to lease their land for mineral revenue, while retaining the right to supervise operations to ensure environmental quality. Development parties may also choose to sell lands to environmental groups once development drilling is complete. Alternatively, mineral-extraction firms and environmental groups could jointly own and operate areas contractually to achieve their separate ends.

Adversarial relationships in the public domain need not be adver-

[62]Bob Williams, "Environmental Delays Continue to Plague Projects Off California," *Oil & Gas Journal*, June 29, 1987, p. 16.

[63]State decisions against oil company plans have led to intervention by the Commerce Department, which oversees state coastal-zone management programs. Court decisions will decide the issue of state versus federal jurisdiction and disputes over regulatory compliance if the issues remain unresolved.

sarial in the private sector. Successful petroleum development in environmental reserves, already accomplished on National Audubon Society acreage in Louisiana and on Welder Wildlife Foundation land in Texas, offers a private sector glimpse into a solution to both an environmental and oil development problem.[64] This new approach to public land policy removes a divisive issue from the political arena to allow a true "cost-benefit" analysis to be performed in the private sector. The industry can find vital new frontiers to explore and develop to outcompete imports at the margin and benefit consumers in so doing. With expanded onshore and offshore prospects, it might be found that the U.S. industry is not such a high-cost competitor in the world market after all—just that the conditions for being lower cost were out of political reach.

Refining Incentives

One of the few contributions of the independent refiners' drive for gasoline tariffs was their emphasis on the importance of a healthy refining industry to the U.S. oil industry.[65] Crude oil does not power cars, fly planes, ignite boilers, or heat homes; refined products do. While talk of a "national security refining minimum" exaggerates this point and creates a credibility problem, it is true that artificially discouraged distillation capacity hurts the upstream and downstream domestic industry, subsidizes imports, and leaves consumers with less product at higher prices. Counterproductive, unaffordable refinery regulation and taxation, therefore, must be corrected, with environmental issues dealt with on a tort basis.

Environmental and tax burdens are at the top of the list of refining impediments. The Environmental Protection Agency's stringent lead phase-down program, often ahead of the scientific findings in the area, is an example of too much, too fast. The disproportionate tax burden placed on refiners under Superfund legislation is another example of political expediency racing ahead of property rights and equity considerations. "National security" reform should include

---

[64]See John Baden, "Oil and Ecology Do Mix," *Wall Street Journal*, February 24, 1987, p. 32. For eight examples of oil production in state and federal wildlife refuges and private environmental sanctuaries, see Alaskan Oil and Gas Association, *Alaskan Update*, Spring 1987, p. 5.

[65]The importance of refining to "national security" is emphasized in the editorial, "Refiners' Health Critical to U.S. Energy Security," *Oil & Gas Journal*, March 2, 1987, p. 13.

"pro-refiner" legislation that at the same time helps consumers through increased supply at lower prices.

Mandatory Conservation

Many oil executives have favorably contrasted their current operations and business strategies with the same operations and strategies during the boom period. Indeed, dramatic efficiency gains have been realized. But one costly and unnecessary carryover from the "energy crisis" period remains: support for energy conservation, voluntary if not mandatory, as a public-spirited gesture. This practice is a sign that the industry has still not fully recovered from the Carter era of demand management and still labors under the delusion of impending scarcity.

In other industries, firms go to great lengths to *increase* the demand for their products; it is high time that the oil industry supplements its aggressive gasoline and motor oil commercials with clear language that fossil fuels are abundant, market entrepreneurship is reliable, and increasing consumption makes for a stronger domestic oil industry. Repeal of the Fuel Use Act for natural gas, relaxed fuel efficiency standards for automobiles, partial repeal of the 55 MPH speed limit, and termination of the Residential Conservation Service Program are beginnings that should be continued.

Consumers and the industry should work to repeal the last vestiges of mandatory conservation on the state and federal level. Existing regulations or programs include minimum appliance, building, and automobile energy-efficiency standards as well as a variety of conservation programs by the Department of Energy that in Fiscal Year (FY) 1988 will cost taxpayers $86 million.[66] (This is down substantially from over $400 million averaged between FY 1981 and FY 1987.) The recently enacted National Appliance Energy Conservation Act promises to increase the cost of appliances for consumers while restricting consumer choice.[67] It also promises to shrink important P1 (residential) gas demand. The American Gas Association, as well as the Natural Gas Supply Association and the Interstate Natural Gas Association of America, should target this

[66] An overview of current DOE conservation programs is contained in Department of Energy, *Annual Report to Congress: 1986* (Washington, D.C.: Government Printing Office), chap. 2.

[67] Public Law 100-12, 101 Stat. 103 (1987). For criticism of minimum appliance standards as anticonsumer, see Doug Bandow, "Federal Appliance Standards: Inefficient at Best," *Wall Street Journal*, February 19, 1987, p. 24.

law, and similar state laws, for repeal, with the same tenacity that won repeal of the Fuel Use Act.

Mandatory conservation underestimates the role of *market prices* to "tell" consumers how to consume and "tell" producers how to produce. Mandatory conservation replaces market information with misinformation about relative scarcities and, in the process, consumes scarce resources.

2. Policy Reform for "National Security"

The above reforms, in addition to their other attributes, advance "national security" by increasing supply and enhancing the ability of the industry to respond to incentives in the world petroleum market. Other measures can enhance national security, namely, privatization of the Strategic Petroleum Reserve, legalization of crude oil exports from Alaska and California, withdrawal from the International Energy Agency, and deregulation of the natural gas and electric industries.

A particularly critical policy aspect of national security is part of the status quo—the absence of "standby" price and allocation controls. President Reagan's decision in March 1982 to veto a bill giving him such authority has been a highlight of his energy policy—and the single most consequential step taken toward creating conditions for national security for oil. Thus the final policy recommendation in this section builds upon the Reagan veto in recognizing entrepreneurial confidence in a free market as the basis for "emergency" energy policy.

The Strategic Petroleum Reserve

One of the most universally prescribed energy policies to avert an oil-related national-security threat is increased storage rates for the Strategic Petroleum Reserve. Tariff advocates see the SPR as inadequate at present levels (525 million barrels, representing over a hundred days of U.S. consumption of oil imports) but sanctify its potential contribution. Many critics of tariffs, ranging from the Department of Energy to *Natural Gas Week* editor John Jennrich, temper their opposition to a tariff with a bullish view toward the federal crude oil stockpile. Academicians, both for and against tariffs, have been equally supportive.[68] Yet the SPR, when viewed

[68]"Every analysis of energy security problems has pointed to the need for a substantial oil reserve." Harry Broadman and William Hogan, *Oil Tariff Policy in an Uncertain Market* (Cambridge: Harvard University, Energy & Environmental Policy Center, 1986), p. A-21. James Griffin and Henry Steele add: "Almost all studies

in terms of opportunity cost instead of a "good" or "bad" in itself, is open to complete review.[69] It has had numerous administrative problems and has been held hostage to political factors. "Optimal" use of the reserve requires "optimal" foresight, which government does not have (and may not be able to implement if it did have). It has been and continues to be a very expensive "insurance premium" whose future use is problematical. With its average cost to date of $38 per barrel, double above-ground market levels, and five to six times above reservoir market prices, the storage project represents a "black elephant."

The SPR was born out of an exaggerated view of resource finiteness and import dependence, not unlike the Synthetic Fuels Corporation program, whose failure was less subtle. The SPR is simply a case of too much insurance at too high a premium, with uncertain redemption value. In its present form, moreover, the SPR can only discourage private stocks, the first line of defense against any oil import interruptions.

Rather than accelerating or even maintaining SPR fill rates as a national security strategy, Congress would do better to recognize the world energy situation, the taxpayer burden, and the superiority of private entrepreneurship over bureaucratic decision-making. To ensure its use in a true (market-determined) emergency, the SPR should be privatized; in that way, a political asset would be turned into an entrepreneurial one better able to mitigate supply and price instability. The proceeds from a sale would reduce, although not nearly eliminate, the associated financial loss to taxpayers.[70]

Legalization of Oil Exports

Modern oil export regulation began in 1973 under the Export Administration Act, which complemented comprehensive petro-

---

recommend a reserve greater than 750 million barrels and most recommend a reserve greater than 1 billion barrels." Griffin and Steele, *Energy Economics and Policy* (New York: Academic Press, 1986), p. 235.

[69]This review supplements earlier criticism of the SPR found on pp. 106–7, 160–62.

[70]The same privatization argument that applies to the SPR also applies to the federal government's second largest crude oil asset, the Elk Hills Naval Petroleum Reserve (#1) near Bakersfield, California. Elk Hills, the nation's seventh largest oil field, has been proposed for sale by the Reagan administration. The government's 78 percent share (Chevron owns the other 22 percent) has an estimated worth between $3 and $5 billion. The Teapot Dome Naval Petroleum Reserve (#3) in Wyoming has also been proposed for privatization.

leum regulation elsewhere. When an end to the energy crisis and price and allocation controls, export regulation remained as a special-interest fixture. By banning exports of Alaskan North Slope and California oil, this supply was "domesticated" to require shipment on U.S.-flag tankers (rather than cheaper foreign-flag vessels) pursuant to Section 27 of the Merchant Marine Act (Jones Act).

The ban on the exportation of crude oil from Alaska and California is now in its second decade. One cost of the domestic shipping subsidy is the transportation premium incurred from greater distances traveled within the United States (from Alaska to the Gulf Coast in particular) and the inflated cost of U.S.-flag vessels. But there is another cost of the tanker subsidy: an oil glut on the West Coast that has artificially depressed prices and discouraged wellhead activity west of the Rockies (PAD District 5). This second cost is directly linked to "national security." With exports free to travel to Japan, Singapore, Malaysia, and other Pacific Rim countries instead of being forced upon California, higher prices would emerge to spur oil exploration and production. The California Oil Producers Association's attempt to obtain a 50,000 barrel per day exemption from the Commerce Department would alleviate this pressure, but full decontrol is needed. One recent study has estimated that access to export markets could improve wellhead netbacks by $4 to $5 per barrel for new Alaskan and California production.[71]

With expanded offshore exploration and production in PAD District 5 from improved pricing incentives, declining crude output elsewhere in the country could be countervailed to improve the ratio of imports to U.S. consumption. And with the impending completion of the 300,000 barrel per day All American Pipeline linking the major offshore and onshore California oil field with West Texas and Gulf Coast refineries, the national security role of PAD District 5 production will be greater than ever before.

Withdrawal from the International Energy Agency

The International Energy Agency (IEA), formed in November 1974 within the Organization for Economic Cooperation and Development (OECD) as a consumer-nation counterweight to OPEC, is a foreign policy misadventure from the energy crisis era that has

---

[71]Samuel Van Vactor, et al., "Report on Alaskan Benefits and Costs of Exporting Alaskan North Slope Crude Oil" (Fairbanks: University of Alaska, May 1987).

the potential to hurt domestic consumers in a future crisis. Under the major plank of the IEA guidelines, the United States would be obligated to share its oil supplies if any of the other 21 member-nations lost more than 7 percent of their supply. The IEA Secretariat would determine the transfer price, the countries that would supply oil, and the countries that would receive oil.

Before turning to the potential consequences of the IEA, the flawed rationale of the plan should be emphasized. The goal of oil sharing is to neutralize an embargo against a member country. But as explained in previous chapters, an embargo is *naturally* neutralized by market forces that redirect supply to where it is in most demand. A pervasive international spot market and a sophisticated trading network will do the IEA's work free of politics and government distortion.

The real national-security threat of the IEA sharing plan is that the United States would dispense oil and never receive it in an "emergency." In the event the United States did receive oil, *who* would receive the oil, *how much* would be received, and other basic allocation questions would be a political football. In this regard, IEA oil could be as unproductive as state set-aside oil was during the 1970s energy crisis.

Several other criticisms of the sharing plan should be mentioned. Foreign countries that are much smaller consumers of oil than the United States would not have the capacity to significantly supplement a U.S. shortfall. The United States, whose oil access is relatively greater than potential recipient countries, is much more likely to be a supplier than a beneficiary. The plan also creates the wrong incentives by subsidizing inefficiency and penalizing efficiency and precaution. The *entrepreneurial* first line of defense in a supply emergency is potentially incompatible with the findings and directives of an international oil czar. This legacy from the energy-crisis era, a foreign aid program waiting to happen at the expense of U.S. oil consumers and taxpayers, should no longer have U.S. involvement.

Natural Gas Deregulation

Appendix 4A explained the essential role of natural gas in the nation's energy future. It is an effective substitute for oil in boiler fuel applications and a potential substitute for home heating oil and motor fuel. Natural gas passes the environmental test compared to other fuels and is abundantly located not only in the United States but in Canada and Mexico. Gas-fired combined cycle, in particular, is a competitive force against coal, hydro power, and nuclear plants for new electric generation capacity.

While the natural gas revolution in recent years has resulted in unprecedented service to consumers, regulation still plagues the industry, preventing the full contribution of the "ideal fuel." De facto wellhead deregulation by the FERC with Order 451 is an inferior substitute for legislative deregulation, although better than nothing at all. This quasi-decontrol program will increase prices for many wells otherwise threatened with premature abandonment, and to this extent it will advance the national security ideal of increased supply and scarcity pricing.

At the transmission level, regulation is even more pervasive. Common carriage requirements, a new phase of interstate transmission regulation under the Natural Gas Act, have proven disruptive to producers and end-users, discouraging reserve development and thus the full potential of gas to supplement, and in some cases supplant, petroleum.[72] Repeal of the Natural Gas Act, removing public utility regulation from interstate gas transmission companies, will significantly reduce costs and increase incentives for new, timely investments in the area. An improved infrastructure for gas, and improved incentives for producers (including reestablishment of long-term contracts free of regulatory uncertainty), is a positive contribution to national security.[73]

Power Market Deregulation

The power market is one of the most regulated sectors of the U.S. economy. Electricity sold in interstate commerce, or sold from facilities engaged in the same, is regulated under the Federal Power Act (FPA) with "just and reasonable" rate regulation and facility certification (much like interstate natural gas transmission). In addition to the FPA, utilities since 1978 have been required to purchase all

[72]Order 436, 50 *Federal Register* 42208, October 18, 1985. Order 500 (Docket No. RM87-34-000, August 7, 1987) has superseded Order 436 with the central characteristic of mandatory contract carriage remaining intact.

[73]Deregulation of interstate natural gas transportation should be joined by interstate oil pipeline deregulation. The latter, neglected in energy policy debates, has been far less stringent than its counterpart. Traditionally "lighthanded" federal regulation of oil pipelines, however, has recently been reorganized toward heavyhanded public utility regulation, with regulated rates based on trended original cost. Such regulation is a threat to an efficient inland oil transportation industry and should be removed by repeal of the Hepburn Amendment to the Interstate Commerce Act.

electricity offered from "qualifying facilities," at the utilities' "avoided cost," pursuant to the Public Utility Regulatory Policies Act (PURPA).[74] A case can be made that neither law is compatible with the national security ideals of efficient energy consumption and capacity.

Incentives for efficient utilization of existing capacity and efficient new capacity to meet load growth are paramount for a healthy electric market, a big slice of the energy pie. This not only requires repeal of the FPA for franchised electric utilities (with concomitant termination of territorial monopolies at the state level) to escape the distortions of public utility regulation. It requires deregulation of independent power producers (IPPs), as recently advocated by the FERC's Office of Economic Policy.[75] IPPs, without franchise protection under state regulation and without guaranteed markets under PURPA, have nonetheless been subject to rate and return regulation based on depreciated cost and burdensome reporting requirements via the Uniform System of Accounts. Consequently, new electric capacity from IPPs, the very incremental additions needed for the low load growth projected for many markets, has been discouraged. Capacity increments from new coal and nuclear plants, in contrast, are far too large, expensive, and lengthy to be undertaken for the large majority of power markets. (See appendix 4A.) Mandated purchases from PURPA qualifying facilities (QFs), on the other hand, are artificially expensive compared to other alternatives.

Electric utility deregulation also requires repeal of PURPA. The requirement that utilities pay "avoided cost" rates for electricity to QFs forces the utility to forgo cheaper electricity purchases from other utilities. Voluntary interutility transactions of "economy energy" are very inexpensive, since they reflect surplus output produced at very low incremental cost from baseload facilities that in many cases must be run continuously. The differential between PURPA must-buy power and interruptable (dispatchable) economy energy is not small. One major utility, Pacific Gas & Electric, has estimated that the extra cost of QF power to its rate payers could reach $850 million by the early 1990s.[76]

[74]Public Law 280, 41 Stat. 1063 (1920); Public Law 333, 49 Stat. 803 (1935); Public Law 95-617, 92 Stat. 3117 (1978).

[75]Office of Economic Policy, "Regulating Independent Power Producers" (Washington, D.C.: Federal Energy Regulatory Commission, October 13, 1987).

[76]George Melloan, "Californians Will Pay Dearly for PURPA Power," *Wall Street Journal*, March 31, 1987, p. 37.

Other distortions could be eliminated by repeal of PURPA. Wasteful investment decisions to attain QF status could be ended. Decisions to add baseload capacity to the electric grid could be returned to the marketplace. Consumption of natural gas, the predominant QF energy, could be replaced by output from surplus coal, nuclear, and hydro power facilities with lower variable costs. Because natural gas is the leading national security fuel compared to the other three—since it is the most capable of substituting for oil on a present and prospective basis—incentives should be removed for its artificial consumption (reserve depletion). With efficient combined cycle plants poised to take up the slack when interutility power purchases become insufficient, gas has a bright future, without the artificial crutch of PURPA.

Emergency Energy Policy

Essential to a national security policy agenda is reliance on free-market processes in any future crisis situation. The free market is clearly preferable for normal times; it is even more advisable in abnormal times. Benjamin Zycher, after summarizing the government's ill-fated planning effort in the 1970s, made this point forcefully:

> The overriding goal of government energy policy must be to facilitate and defend the operation of market forces. This is true particularly for emergency policy because only the market can adjust smoothly in the face of price shocks and other important exogenous phenomena. Regulatory policy cannot do it and causes substantial damage when it tries.[77]

Market forces, propelled by profit-seeking entrepreneurial adjustments, have the ability to *prepare* for abrupt changes in the world oil market and temper the "aftershocks." The mistakes of 1970s energy policy and earlier wartime petroleum planning experiences, namely, forsaking the market for government planning, should not be repeated.

Entrepreneurial confidence is the key market "insurance" against a sudden energy crisis, whether measured in terms of price changes

---

[77]Benjamin Zycher, "Emergency Management," in *Free Market Energy*, ed. S. Fred Singer (New York: Universe Books, 1984), p. 96.

or supply availability.[78] If entrepreneurs are concerned about punitive taxation or regulation, they will not perform their speculative/ hedging functions, and the crisis will not be blunted. Therefore, it is imperative that "standby" regulation before the fact and "emergency" regulation after the fact not occur. Such entrepreneurial confidence can be fostered by eradicating the mentality and institutions breeding energy planning. Decisive steps in this direction would be to abolish the Department of Energy, other federal agencies active in petroleum matters, and Carter-era state petroleum agencies.

3. Toward a New Industry Mentality

The tariff debate has witnessed many prominent and revered industry leaders advocating what many thought impossible just a decade ago—government price planning. These individuals can be criticized for having a part, along with other interventionist special-interest groups across the economy, in "killing the goose that laid the golden egg." *Natural Gas Week* editor John Jennrich, for one, has pointedly called tariff and government price-floor proponents "philosophical failures in the free-market system."[79]

A plea for the industry to forsake talk of an impending national-security crisis and the need for emergency government intervention can be made on self-interested grounds. Philosophical purity is not required. Trying to scare up interest for legislative reform on this basis is not only "crying wolf" but undermining confidence in the future ability of the petroleum industry to meet demand in a reliable, efficient manner. Such talk raises uncertainty and encourages incremental markets to think twice about "insecure" oil (and gas). Such talk encourages the substitution of coal-fired boilers for oil- or gas-fired boilers, despite the relative efficiency and lower capital costs of the latter. To use another example, individual consumers may pay higher up-front prices for energy-efficient appliances and high-mileage motor vehicles, in order to be less susceptible to scarce supply and higher prices.

Reducing demand by rhetoric is counterproductive to an industry

---

[78]An "atmosphere of entrepreneurial confidence" as an alternative to petroleum price and allocation regulation has been emphasized by Sheldon Richman in "Where Angels Fear to Tread: The United States and the Persian Gulf Conflict," *Cato Policy Analysis* (September 9, 1987): 13.

[79]John Jennrich, "Know Thyself—and Kill the Competition," *Natural Gas Week*, December 8, 1986, p. 2.

whose current predicament is more attributable to falling demand than to increased supply. It also plays into the hands of environmentalists who are hawking demand-side management as an alternative to increased drilling on public land.[80] *Increasing* demand should be a high priority, and to this end the curtain should be closed on industry-sponsored conservation campaigns. Demand reduction as a load-management strategy by utilities to manage peaking problems short of costly new capacity is one thing; "public service" exhortations to conserve energy for its own sake is quite another. It is time to exhort consumers to use more gasoline, fuel oil, and other petroleum products—in short, to take that Sunday drive and to leave the lights on. The industry's future will be brighter, and consumers will enjoy increased consumption.

A critical review of recent industry pronouncements must include the lament over "the lack of a comprehensive national energy plan." The very concept of any national plan sanctifies government involvement , in contradiction of the central theme of the market—spontaneous order. There should be no central plan, no energy czar, no Department of Energy, no "targets" to achieve through tax or regulatory policy. The "plan" should be no plan, consisting of maximum discretion for market forces and a minimum of regulation, subsidization, and taxation.

D. Scarcity, Uncertainty, and the Limits of Knowledge: A Concluding Comment

"The outstanding fact of history," Ludwig von Mises has stated, "is that it is a succession of events that nobody anticipated before they occurred."[81] Certainly the events of the 1970s, and no less the events of the 1980s, were unforeseen by layman and expert alike. For this reason it cannot be guaranteed that another oil "shock" will not occur in the 1990s, to give credence to this part of the protectionist argument. But the major point of this book is that such a possibility is not a decisive consideration for a protectionist response. Throughout this century, the government has tried and failed to deal with worst-case events. It should be the market's job to antic-

---

[80]See, for example, Gaylord Nelson, "Turn to Conservation Instead of ANWR to Achieve Real U.S. Energy Security," *Oil Daily*, July 15, 1987, p. 4.

[81]Ludwig von Mises, *Theory and History* (New Rochelle: Arlington House, 1969), p. 378.

ipate and mitigate the "worst case" of America's energy future, just as the market should reign in better times.

"Energy security" and even an approach toward petroleum self-sufficiency are not free goods but prohibitively expensive. These ends require tremendous sacrifices by consumers and the economy in general. They are, in short, unaffordable. If superabundance instead of scarcity existed, on the other hand, hard choices between mutually exclusive alternatives could be replaced with the "best of all worlds." The United States could have home-supplied oil with perfect security, with timely availability, and at minimum prices. But this is nirvana, not the reality that the social scientist must describe, debate, and recommend policy for.

In the conclusion of his Nobel Memorial Lecture in Economics, F. A. Hayek spoke of the "knowledge problem." While generic, his remarks are directly applicable to the national security argument for oil protectionism:

> If man is not to do more harm than good in his efforts to improve the social order, he will have to learn that in this, as in all other fields where essential complexity of an organized kind prevails, he cannot acquire the full knowledge which would make mastery of the events possible. He will therefore have to use what knowledge he can achieve, not to shape the results as the craftsman shapes his handiwork, but rather to cultivate a growth by providing the appropriate environment, in the manner in which the gardener does this for his plants.[82]

Banking on the experts' calculations of oil-import premiums, import peril points, national security thresholds, optimal tariffs, and other constructivist notions will not assure the nation's energy future. Rather, theoretical contemplation and historical understanding of the 125-year experience of market and government in the U.S. petroleum industry point to simply "cultivating" the free-market environment and allowing the statistics to fall where they may. This is Adam Smith's "invisible hand" and Hayek's "spontaneous order," which may not be satisfactory for those who feel that their knowledge and expectations must prevail over market realities. But unfortunately for such grand designs, the decentralized market is "smarter" than oil czars, planning committees, and

---

[82]F. A. Hayek, "The Pretence of Knowledge," *New Studies in Philosophy, Politics, Economics, and the History of Ideas* (Chicago: University of Chicago Press, 1978), p. 34.

bureaucracies. The only affordable means of "energy security" available to the United States is full reign for entrepreneurial alertness to profit opportunities, particularly those associated with potential or real dislocations in the world oil market. This requires fundamental reform of the status quo, but in the direction of less, rather than more, government involvement in the energy industry.

Appendix A
AVERAGE U.S. WELLHEAD PRICES: NOMINAL AND INFLATION-ADJUSTED
(dollars per barrel)

Year	Nominal Price	CPI (1986 = 100)	Inflation/Adjusted Price	Percent Change
1900	1.19	8	15.63	—
1901	0.96	8	12.61	−19
1902	0.80	8	10.10	−20
1903	0.94	8	11.43	13
1904	0.86	8	10.46	−9
1905	0.62	8	7.54	−28
1906	0.73	8	8.88	18
1907	0.72	9	8.44	−5
1908	0.72	8	8.76	4
1909	0.70	8	8.51	−3
1910	0.61	9	7.15	−16
1911	0.61	9	7.15	0
1912	0.74	9	8.38	17
1913	0.95	9	10.50	25
1914	0.81	9	8.84	−16
1915	0.64	9	6.91	−22
1916	1.10	10	11.05	60
1917	1.56	12	13.34	21
1918	1.98	14	14.42	8
1919	2.01	16	12.74	−12
1920	3.07	18	16.80	32
1921	1.73	16	10.60	−37
1922	1.61	15	10.53	−1
1923	1.34	16	8.61	−18
1924	1.43	16	9.17	7
1925	1.68	16	10.51	15
1926	1.88	16	11.65	11
1927	1.30	16	8.21	−30
1928	1.17	16	7.49	−9
1929	1.27	16	8.13	9
1930	1.19	15	7.82	−4
1931	0.65	14	4.68	−40
1932	0.87	12	6.99	49
1933	0.67	12	5.67	−19
1934	1.00	12	8.19	44

Appendix A (continued)

Year	Nominal Price	CPI (1986 = 100)	Inflation/Adjusted Price	Percent Change
1935	0.97	13	7.75	−5
1936	1.09	13	8.63	11
1937	1.18	13	9.01	4
1938	1.13	13	8.79	−2
1939	1.02	13	8.05	−8
1940	1.02	13	7.98	−1
1941	1.14	13	8.49	6
1942	1.19	15	8.01	−6
1943	1.20	16	7.61	−5
1944	1.21	16	7.54	−1
1945	1.22	16	7.43	−1
1946	1.41	18	7.92	6
1947	1.93	20	9.47	20
1948	2.60	22	11.84	25
1949	2.54	22	11.68	−1
1950	2.51	22	11.43	−2
1951	2.53	24	10.68	−7
1952	2.53	24	10.45	−2
1953	2.68	24	10.99	5
1954	2.78	25	11.34	3
1955	2.77	24	11.34	0
1956	2.79	25	11.26	−1
1957	3.09	26	12.04	7
1958	3.01	26	11.41	−5
1959	2.90	27	10.91	−4
1960	2.88	27	10.66	−2
1961	2.89	27	10.59	−1
1962	2.90	28	10.51	−1
1963	2.89	28	10.35	−2
1964	2.88	28	10.18	−2
1965	2.86	29	9.94	−2
1966	2.88	30	9.73	−2
1967	2.92	30	9.59	−1
1968	2.94	32	9.27	−3
1969	3.09	33	9.24	0
1970	3.18	35	8.98	−3
1971	3.39	37	9.18	2
1972	3.39	38	8.88	−3

Appendix A (continued)

Year	Nominal Price	CPI (1986 = 100)	Inflation/Adjusted Price	Percent Change
1973	3.89	41	9.60	−8
1974	6.74	45	14.99	56
1975	7.56	49	15.40	3
1976	8.14	52	15.68	2
1977	8.57	55	15.51	−1
1978	8.96	60	15.06	−3
1979	12.51	66	18.90	25
1980	21.59	75	28.73	52
1981	31.77	83	38.30	33
1982	28.52	88	32.40	−15
1983	26.19	91	28.82	−11
1984	25.88	95	27.32	−5
1985	24.08	98	24.54	−10
1986	12.66	100	12.66	−48
Average Price:	4.08		11.55	

SOURCES: American Petroleum Institute; Bureau of Labor Statistics

Appendix B
OIL IMPORT/EXPORT STATISTICS: 1918–86
(thousand barrels per day)

Year	Total Imports[a]	Total Exports[b]	Net Imports[c]	Total Consumption	Net Imports as Percentage of Consumption
1918	107	188	(81)	—	—
1919	148	175	(27)	1,026	− 0.03
1920	297	218	79	1,245	0.05
1921	353	197	156	1,254	0.12
1922	373	204	169	1,455	0.12
1923	273	280	(7)	1,787	0.00
1924	258	321	(63)	1,878	− 0.03
1925	214	312	(98)	1,992	− 0.05
1926	223	363	(140)	2,139	− 0.07
1927	197	390	(193)	2,201	− 0.09
1928	250	423	(173)	2,350	− 0.07
1929	298	447	(149)	2,577	− 0.06
1930	289	429	(140)	2,539	− 0.06
1931	236	341	(105)	2,473	− 0.04
1932	204	282	(78)	2,282	− 0.03
1933	124	292	(168)	2,379	− 0.07
1934	138	314	(176)	2,520	− 0.07
1935	144	353	(209)	2,694	− 0.08
1936	156	361	(205)	2,985	− 0.07
1937	157	474	(317)	3,203	− 0.10
1938	149	531	(382)	3,114	− 0.12
1939	162	520	(358)	3,371	− 0.11
1940	229	356	(127)	3,625	− 0.04
1941	266	298	(32)	4,071	− 0.01
1942	99	320	(221)	3,972	− 0.06
1943	174	411	(237)	4,168	− 0.06
1944	252	567	(315)	4,566	− 0.07
1945	311	501	(190)	4,857	− 0.04
1946	377	420	(43)	4,912	− 0.01
1947	437	451	(14)	5,487	0.00
1948	514	367	147	5,798	0.03
1949	645	327	318	5,809	0.05
1950	850	305	545	6,556	0.08
1951	844	422	422	7,065	0.06
1952	952	432	520	7,290	0.07

Appendix B (continued)

Year	Total Imports[a]	Total Exports[b]	Net Imports[c]	Total Consumption	Net Imports as Percentage of Consumption
1953	1,034	402	632	7,608	0.08
1954	1,052	355	697	7,764	0.09
1955	1,248	368	880	8,464	0.10
1956	1,436	430	1,006	8,783	0.11
1957	1,574	568	1,006	8,827	0.11
1958	1,700	276	1,424	9,118	0.16
1959	1,780	211	1,569	9,526	0.16
1960	1,815	202	1,613	9,798	0.16
1961	1,917	174	1,743	9,976	0.17
1962	2,082	168	1,914	10,400	0.18
1963	2,130	208	1,922	10,743	0.18
1964	2,259	202	2,057	11,023	0.19
1965	2,468	187	2,281	11,513	0.20
1966	2,573	198	2,375	12,085	0.20
1967	2,537	307	2,230	12,560	0.18
1968	2,840	231	2,609	13,393	0.19
1969	3,166	233	2,933	14,137	0.21
1970	3,419	259	3,160	14,697	0.22
1971	3,926	224	3,702	15,213	0.24
1972	4,754	223	4,531	16,367	0.28
1973	6,256	231	6,025	17,308	0.35
1974	6,112	221	5,891	16,652	0.35
1975	6,056	209	5,847	16,322	0.36
1976	7,313	223	7,090	17,461	0.41
1977	8,708	243	8,465	18,431	0.46
1978	8,364	362	8,002	18,847	0.42
1979	8,456	471	7,985	18,516	0.43
1980	6,909	545	6,364	17,056	0.37
1981	5,995	595	5,400	16,058	0.34
1982	5,113	815	4,298	15,296	0.28
1983	5,051	739	4,312	15,231	0.28
1984	5,437	722	4,715	15,726	0.30
1985	5,067	781	4,286	15,726	0.27
1986	6,061	772	5,289	16,281	0.32

SOURCE: Bureau of Mines, Mineral Industry Surveys; American Petroleum Institute, *Basic Petroleum Databook*

[a]*Sum of crude and product imports*
[b]*Sum of crude and product exports*
[c]*Total imports minus total exports*

Appendix C
U.S. Refinery Closings: 1981–85

Name	PAD District	Location	Primary Capacity (B/D)	Downstream Capacity (B/D)	Years in Operation
1981					
Amoco Oil	II	Wood River, Ill.	104,000	127,000	25
Conoco, Inc.	II	Wrenshall, Minn.	23,500	25,700	5
Dow Chemical	II	Bay City, Mich.	20,000	0	25
Energy Development	II	Crossville, Ill.	1,000	0	22
Glenrock Refinery	IV	Glenrock, Wyo.	6,000	0	5
Gulf Oil	II	Toledo, Ohio	50,300	61,800	25
Gulf Oil	III	Venice, La.	28,700	46,300	13
Indiana Refining	II	Princeton, Ind.	5,000	0	23
Manatee Energy	I	Port Manatee, Fla.	28,400	0	2
Mobil Oil	I	Buffalo, N.Y.	43,000	67,000	25
Quad Refining	V	Bakersfield, Calif.	7,000	0	2
Southern Union Refining	III	Monument, N.M.	5,400	0	25
Southland Oil	III	Yazoo City, Miss.	5,500	3,080	25
Southwestern Refining	IV	La Barge, Wyo.	1,040	0	7
Texaco	II	Lockport, Ill.	72,000	136,000	25
Texas Refining	III	Midland, Tex.	2,500	0	1
Texas Standard Refining	III	Houston, Tex.	1,800	0	1
Wireback Oil	II	Plymouth, Ill.	1,800	1,800	25
Total 1981 closings:	18		Total Capacity 406,940	468,680	
			Average Capacity 22,608	26,038	

Appendix C (continued)

Name	PAD District	Location	Primary Capacity (B/D)	Downstream Capacity (B/D)	Years in Operation
1982					
Adobe Refining	III	La Blanca, Tex.	5,200	0	25
Amoco Oil	II	Sugar Creek, Mo.	104,000	185,500	25
Amoco Oil	I	Baltimore, Md.	15,000	0	25
ATC Petroleum	I	Newington, N.H.	13,400	0	7
ATC Petroleum	I	Wilmington, N.C.	11,900	0	8
Bayou State	III	Hosston, La.	3,000	0	25
Bronco Refining	III	Houston, Tex.	2,250	0	1
C&H Refinery	IV	Lusk, Wyo.	180	0	25
Carbonit Refining	III	Hearne, Tex.	11,000	0	6
Clinton Manges	III	Palestine, Tex.	6,000	0	25
Copano Refining	III	Ingleside, Tex.	11,100	0	4
CRA, Inc.	II	Scottsbluff, Neb.	5,600	3,650	25
Dillman Oil	II	Oblong, Ill.	1,200	0	4
Dow Chemical	III	Freeport, Tex.	190,000	143,000	1
Eagle Refining	III	Jacksboro, Tex.	1,800	0	1
Energy Cooperative	II	East Chicago, Ind.	126,000	190,000	25
E-Z Serv Refining	II	Shallow Water, Kans.	9,500	0	25
Glacier Park	IV	Osage, Wyo.	10,000	0	4
Grant Industries	III	Farmington, N.M.	13,500	5,000	7
Husky Oil	IV	Cody, Wyo.	11,500	17,800	25
Industrial Fuel	II	Hammond, Ind.	7,600	0	25
Lake Charles Refining	III	Lake Charles, La.	28,000	0	2
Listo Refining	III	Donna, Tex.	3,500	0	4
Longview Refining	III	Longview, Tex.	14,000	14,000	25
Mid-America	II	Chanute, Kans.	3,000	1,800	25
Natchez Refining	III	Natchez, Miss.	16,000	0	2
Northland Oil	II	Dickinson, N.Dak.	5,000	0	7
Phillips Petroleum	II	Kansas City, Kans.	80,000	156,700	25
Placid Oil	III	Mont Belvieu, Tex.	8,500	0	2
Quitman Refining	III	Quitman, Tex.	6,600	0	4

Appendix C (continued)

Name	PAD District	Location	Primary Capacity (B/D)	Downstream Capacity (B/D)	Years in Operation
Rio Grande Crude	III	Brownsville, Tex.	9,500	0	3
Rio Grande Recovery	III	Brownsville, Tex.	1,000	0	2
Road Oil Sales	V	Bakersfield, Calif.	6,000	0	9
Sabre Oil & Refining	V	Bakersfield, Calif.	10,000	0	10
Sage Creek Refining	IV	Cowley, Wyo.	1,000	0	17
Schulze Processing	III	Tallulah, La.	1,760	0	4
Seminole Refining	I	St. Marks, Fla.	15,000	10,000	25
Sentry Refining	III	Corpus Christi, Tex.	25,000	0	4
Shepard Oil	III	Jennings, La.	10,000	0	4
Sooner Refining	III	Darrow, La.	8,000	32,200	2
T&S Refining	III	Jennings, La.	10,500	0	2
Texaco, Inc.	IV	Casper, Wyo.	21,000	35,500	25
Texas American	II	West Branch, Mich.	11,500	3,200	25
Tipperary Refining	III	Ingleside, Tex.	7,320	0	4
United Independent	V	Tacoma, Wash.	730	0	7
Wickett Refining	III	Wickett, Tex.	8,000	0	25
Total 1982 closings: 46		Total Capacity	870,640	798,350	
		Average Capacity	18,927	17,355	
1983					
Arizona Fuels Corp.	V	Fredonia, Ariz.	6,000	0	11
Bro Refining	III	Friendswood, Tex.	12,500	0	4
Champlin Petroleum	II	Enid, Okla.	53,800	58,500	25
Demenno-Kerdoon	V	Compton, Calif.	10,000	2,000	6
ELK Refining (Pennzoil)	I	Falling Rock, W.Va.	5,600	2,000	25
Erickson Refining	III	Pt. Neches, La.	30,000	0	4
Evangeline Refining	III	Jennings, La.	4,500	0	25

Appendix C (continued)

Name	PAD District	Location	Primary Capacity (B/D)	Downstream Capacity (B/D)	Years in Operation
GHR Energy	III	Good Hope, La.	300,000	433,000	15
Hudson Refining	II	Cushing, Okla.	19,000	12,150	6
Independent Refining	III	Winnie, Tex.	50,000	63,000	23
Mallard Resources	III	Gueydan, La.	7,400	0	4
Marion Corp.	III	Theodore, Ala.	25,000	14,500	15
McTan Refining	III	St. James, La.	19,300	0	6
Mobil Oil	II	Augusta, Kans.	50,000	83,900	25
Okmulgee Refining	II	Okmulgee, Okla.	25,000	13,200	25
Petraco-Valley Oil Refining	III	Brownsville, Tex.	12,300	0	5
Pioneer Refining	III	Nixon, Tex.	15,000	15,900	9
Quaker State	I	Emlenton, Pa.	0	2,980	25
Shore, Inc.	III	Kilgore, Tex.	550	0	3
Silver Eagle Oil	IV	La Barge, Wyo.	1,500	0	9
Thriftway Oil	III	Graham, Tex	1,184	0	25
Total 1983 closings:	21		Total Capacity 648,634	701,130	
			Average Capacity 30,887	33,387	
1984					
Ashland Oil	II	Louisville, Ky.	25,200	29,000	36
Ashland Oil	I	Buffalo, N.Y.	64,000	106,500	36
Ashland Oil	II	Findlay, Ohio	20,400	8,000	36
Caribou-Four Corners	IV	Farmington, N.M.	2,200	2,400	19
Caribou-Four Corners	IV	Woods Cross, Utah	8,400	8,200	21
Celeron Oil & Gas	III	Mermentau, La.	11,000	0	6
Dorchester Refining	III	Mt. Pleasant, Tex.	26,500	38,800	6
ECO Petroleum	V	Long Beach, Calif.	0	7,000	8
Eddy Refining	III	Houston, Tex.	3,250	0	36
Hill Petroleum	III	Knots Springs, Tex.	57,400	62,000	7
Marlex Oil & Refining	V	Los Angeles, Calif.	21,100	0	7
Mid-Gulf Energy	III	Ingleside, Tex.	39,400	20,000	3
Oklahoma Refining	II	Thomas, Okla.	11,600	0	4
Oklahoma Refining	II	Cyril, Okla.	12,750	23,100	36
Port Petroleum	III	Stonewall, La.	3,200	0	5

Appendix C (continued)

Name	PAD District	Location	Primary Capacity (B/D)	Downstream Capacity (B/D)	Years in Operation
Powerline Oil	V	Santa Fe, Calif.	44,120	100,100	34
Quintana Petroleum	III	Corpus Christi, Tex.	33,000	54,000	30
South Hampton Refining	III	Silsbee, Tex.	18,100	28,000	24
Southern Union Refining	III	Lovington, N.M.	36,100	18,500	8
Tesoro Petroleum	III	Carrizo Springs, Tex.	26,100	3,500	27
Tonkawa Refining	II	Arnett, Okla.	12,000	6,000	16
Tosco Corp.	V	Bakersfield, Calif.	38,800	80,000	33
Tosco Corp.	II	Duncan, Okla.	47,000	85,000	4
U.S.A. Petroleum	V	Ventura, Calif.	24,000	7,000	7
Warrior Asphalt	III	Holt, Ala.	5,500	2,000	30
Total 1984 closings: 25		Total Capacity	591,120	689,100	
		Average Capacity	23,645	27,564	
1985					
Allied Materials	II	Stroud, Okla.	7,600	2,500	37
BT Energy	II	Louisville, Ky.	3,000	0	3
Coastal Petroleum	V	Bakersfield, Calif.	10,000	0	6
Damson Gas Processing	III	White Deer, Tex.	0	1,000	12
Flint Chemical	III	San Antonio, Tex.	1,500	0	23
Gary Refining	IV	Fruita, Colo.	15,200	18,100	19
Golden Eagle Refining	V	Carson, Calif.	16,170	0	37
International Processors	III	St. Rose, La.	28,356	14,000	6
Texaco Refining & Marketing	III	Lawrenceville, Ill.	79,000	134,000	37
Texaco Refining & Marketing	III	Amarillo, Tex.	20,000	24,400	37
Vicksburg Refining	III	Vicksburg, Miss.	6,000	0	7
Total 1985 closings: 11		Total Capacity	186,826	194,000	
		Average Capacity	16,984	17,636	

SOURCE: Energy Information Administration, U.S. Department of Energy

Appendix D
U.S. REFINING CAPACITY CHANGES IN 1986

Name	PAD District	Location	Primary Capacity (B/D)	Downstream Capacity (B/D)
New or Reactivated:				
City Gas & Transmission	I	Wilmington, N.C.	10,000	0
Augusta Refinery	II	Augusta, Kans.	0	23,000
Hill Petroleum	III	St. Rose, La.	32,000	20,000
Louisiana Oil & Refining	III	Egan, La.	8,400	0
Warrior Asphalt	III	Holt, Ala.	5,000	0
Petro Star (New)	V	North Pole, Alaska	6,700	0
Powerline Oil	V	Santa Fe Springs, Calif.	33,400	84,910
Western Oil & Refining	V	Long Beach, Calif.	19,200	0
Total Capacity:			114,700	127,910
Deactivated:				
Chevron USA	I	Baltimore, Md.	14,200	14,300
Chevron USA	II	Cincinnati, Ohio	43,700	40,200
Gladieux Refinery	II	Fort Wayne, Ind.	19,000	0
Petromax Refining	III	Houston, Tex.	2,000	0
Chevron USA	V	Bakersfield, Calif.	26,000	6,000
Total Deactivated Capacity:			104,900	60,500
Net Capacity Additions:			9,800	67,410

SOURCE: Energy Information Administration, U.S. Department of Energy

Index

About the Author

Robert L. Bradley, Jr., is currently a senior marketing analyst with an interstate gas transmission company in Houston. He is program director of the Institute for Humane Studies of Texas and an adjunct scholar of the Cato Institute. Bradley is author of the forthcoming *Oil, Gas, and Government: The U.S. Experience,* the most comprehensive analysis of U.S. oil and gas regulation ever published. He has testified before Congress and lectured in the United States and Europe on the economics and politics of petroleum regulation.